"Exiting a Racist Worldview (Revised):

A Journey Through Foucault, Said, Marx to Liberation, The Revolution that Failed"

Daurius Figueira

Table of Contents

Introduction to Second Expanded Edition

In this revised version (2023) of "Exiting a Racist Worldview" chapters 16 to 19 were omitted in order to present new analysis which flows with the quest for a liberationary discourse for non-white peoples of the world, afflicted with hallucinatory whiteness who live under the hegemony of the white world order of power driven by the discourse of white supremacy. This is necessary to align the focus of this text with the works published since 2004 which deconstructed the oeuvre of Michel Foucault, Frantz Fanon, Derek Walcott and that of the discourse of white supremacy in the history of the Caribbean. The groundwork laid in 2004 has now been expanded and further critiqued in the works listed above on Foucault, Fanon, Walcott and white supremacy in the Caribbean. This evolution of my research and writings then demanded the addition of new analysis to the revised edition of "Exiting a Racist Worldview" which adds to an expansion of knowledge on the path of liberation adopted by non-white persons in the Caribbean and the USA. To this end a deconstruction of the discourse of Toussaint L'Ouverture of the Haitian Revolution, a deconstruction of the discourse of African liberation in Amerikkka of George Jackson and the reality of skin bleaching and the collapse of Black nationalism in the Caribbean have been added to this edition. This section titled: "The Revolution That Failed" focuses on a deconstruction of the discourses that drove these three actions of non-white peoples in response to their existential condition under the hegemony of the white world order of power. What is exposed in these studies is the inability of non-white persons to attain liberation at the level of the idea where they do not command a discourse with its instruments of power which cannot erase hallucinatory whiteness thereby impacting the spectrum of trauma that impacts each and every one of us. Liberation is only possible with the process of engaging with and falsifying the discourse of white supremacy by silencing its instruments and order of power at the level of the idea in our minds. The liberated mind/ self will then guide action which liberates us objectively from the white world order of power.

Introduction to first edition

The texts that comprise this book were written at specific periods in my life commencing the decade of the 1990's to the present, i.e. – January 2004. The process commenced in 1997 with my focus on the attempted coup d'état of 27th July, 1990 by the Jamaat al Muslimeen in Trinidad. In order to understand the discourse that constituted the action of 27th July, 1990 fundamental self- critical questions were asked concerning my perceptions of my academic exercise, where did I locate myself at the level of the idea and most of all what contribution would this academic exercise make to my journey seeking liberation at the level of the idea?

This was not simply research exercised for the sake of earning a post-graduate degree from the University of the West Indies at St. Augustine Campus in Trinidad. The exercise must be of useful importance, it must impart insight and add to my knowledge base in the never-ending quest for liberation embarked upon in 1969.

Text 1 written in the 1990's was written after text 2 and is the surgical cutting edge that text 2 lacks. Text 2 is my journey through a series of North Atlantic thinkers of the social sciences that were utilised in the hope of understanding the events of 27th July, 1990. The inability of the discourses of these individuals indicated the potency of alternate worldviews and discourses and the need to now journey through worldviews and discourses in the quest for understanding. Both texts 2 and 1 present western theorists of social realities stripped naked and bare to reveal the core of their worldview which renders them manifestly inadequate to understand alternate ways of viewing the world. It is then a journey through epistemologies and ontologies of the Enlightenment, which commences with the European who insisted that his discourse was premised on rejection of the Enlightenment, but the core of his discourse was in fact Enlightenment in origin.

That thinker, Michel Foucault, in fact beckons towards a discursive breach, a rupture that enables one seeking liberation to exit the racist discourse of the North Atlantic which he was unable to utilise because he refused to shed all that was essentially him, the white European male homosexual. He rejected the Enlightenment but alas he refused to embrace an alternate non- white worldview. He died then a white European male in discursive denial, hence his refusal to embrace the concept of liberation, settling in fact for the nihilism of socially constituted desire. The texts presented then circulate around the nucleus of the discourse of Michel Foucault and the discursive rupture as the exit point from racist North Atlantic discourse.

The book also presents sections on Caribbean social theorizing to indicate the paucity of understanding and the absence of the potential for liberation, which underpins the use of North Atlantic discourse as an instrument of understanding. This understanding completes the depiction of the reality that in my attempt to understand the action of 27th July, 1990 by the Jamaat al Muslimeen; clearly the need was then to understand the discourse that articulated the worldview of the Jamaat al Muslimeen from 1984 to July 1990. To attain this desired understanding would necessitate my journey through the most salient and potent alternate worldview engaged with the discourse of the North Atlantic, i.e. – Islamic Discourse, an experience that would heighten in sensitivity with the events of 11th September 2001 in New York.

This book is then a depiction of a journey of liberation that was attained at the level of the idea. Geographically, I still live in the Belly of the Beast under the hegemony of the North Atlantic, but at the level of the idea I have liberated myself from the worldview of the North Atlantic. I see the matrix for what it truly is, and I do not desire the matrix, all I desire now is physical release.

A Statement of Intent

The work that this statement introduces deals with my readings of the works of Michel Foucault and the two major discoveries in the texts of Foucault which fostered and enabled me to finally walk away from the white racist colonial worldview which entraps the periphery up to today.

The treatment of Foucault is in no way a review of his work, for it focuses on the specific instances of his text that beckoned, that pointed to the existence, the possibility of a discursive rupture that enabled me to transcend, to walk away from this white racist worldview that had assaulted my sensibilities since my first waking moments of consciousness.

In addition, the method of presentation of the text focuses firstly on my statements on the works of Foucault, i.e. – the texts that conjured up the discursive rupture. Following these statements, the specific instances of Foucault's text are presented in support of the statements made. This method is deliberately adopted for I am neither speaking nor writing from within the worldview in which Foucault located himself.

Since all I am doing is mapping an escape route for fellow people of the periphery who are still entrapped within the white racist worldview, my task is to present the signposts along the route towards the exit point. I am therefore presenting a route map, which culminates at a given discursive rupture, which enables, offers, beckons liberation from a worldview that negates, denies, and denigrates our humanity.

Liberation is attainable because there exist alternate worldviews on the next side of the rupture, which negate the very ontological structures of our racist prison. Liberation is being summoned, expressed via language, the language of the racist colonizer. That language must then reflect the fact that we, the people of the periphery, have liberated that very language from the colonizer.

The work that follows is therefore but another attempt by a person of the periphery to utilize English for our specific, unique interests to re-make ourselves in the image and likeness of our alternate worldviews.

At this juncture the words of Salman Rushdie are most relevant when he states as follows: "Outside the whale there is a genuine need for political fiction, for books that draw new and better maps of reality and make new languages with which we can understand the world." (Rushdie 1991 Pg. 100). "One of the changes has to do with attitudes towards the use of English... And I hope all of us share the view that we can't simply use the language in the way the British did; that it needs remaking for our own purposes. Those of us who do use English do so in spite of our ambiguity towards it, or perhaps because of that, perhaps because we can find in that linguistic struggle a reflection of other struggles taking place in the real world, struggle between the cultures within ourselves and the influences at work upon societies. To conquer English may be to complete the process of making ourselves free." (Rushdie 1991 Pg. 100).

To conquer English is a must, and one way to accomplish this is to unravel the ontology that drives the white man's languages. But much more than the understanding of origins and motivations is needed, for the people of the periphery who utilize the languages of the colonizer must now through written use radically re-engineer these languages.

What follows is but my attempt at re-engineering the English I write in a limited way. The jargon of the white racist social science that appears in this work has all been re-engineered, hopefully to the extent that persons who locate themselves in the white racist worldview upon reading this work should be appalled at my ignorance of the theorists who coined the jargon.

If I elicit comments that reflect the racist perceptions of the reader, then I can safely assume there was some modicum of success to my task of re-engineering.

At best re-engineering should necessitate the presentation of a glossary on my part to aid my readers through the discursive minefield of language. The glossary is in itself a compromise to the hegemonic worldview, for it could never enable a reader from the hegemonic racist worldview to grasp, to feel the pain of the text. For language is much more than a mechanism of signs and symbols. This text is generated for us of the periphery, in our image and likeness, and towards our liberation.

Those of the racist worldview who traverse the pages of this work would find umbrage, with every single word written in the text. For in this text, we of the periphery are central to the text and linkages via written language are sought with members of the periphery, no one else. We, the silenced of the planet must now become vociferous; this work is then simply my contribution to the cacophony of voices that must come from the periphery. The dissonance of voices from the periphery is but one tool available to use to de-hegemonize the white racist worldview.

Finally, in closing this statement of intent I present my glossary or better yet my vocabulary of the re-engineering of English.

[1] WORLDVIEW: that structure of perceptive matrices, sieves, filters through which the world is grasped, viewed, perceived. It is the structures of perception that in fact create a specific world, which can only be seen in that given specific way by the persons who share a common worldview.

Persons coming from different worldviews can then view the same object and see entirely different realities, thereby for each person their truth is unique to their worldview and there is therefore in that given situation no commonality of understanding on what is 'truth'. Truth then becomes relative to each person's worldview.

The basis of any worldview is the ontology/ the metaphysic that drives the worldview. The ontology defines the nature of the human being and the nature of the non-human beings the worldview encounters. By this definition the position of the human in the schemata of things encountered, experienced is defined.

A dualist worldview is driven by an exclusionary ontology that only sees, generates categories of existence and experience that are mutually exclusive and antagonistic to each other. Such as good /evil, truth/ lies, black/ white, male/ female, human/ animal.

A dualist worldview postulates that the human is the centrally posited, the dominant life force enjoying suzerainty over all other forms of life on the planet. The dualist worldview fosters the march of an ontology that relentlessly divides and sub-divides all reality into mutually exclusive antagonistic dual categories which ultimately gave birth to the white man's intolerance, his relentless racism seen in his never-ending thirst for genocide.

The non-dualist worldview does not view the world in dualities but in unlimited diversity. Life / existence, perceptions are common to all non-human beings that share the planet with humankind. Humankind is not central to, nor holds suzerainty over the planet, for humankind's presence on the planet is tenuously held at best.

The worldview constitutes diversity, tolerance and most of all humankind that recognize their obligation to all forms of life and consciousness on the planet, including the planet itself.

The reality created by the matrices of perception of the non-dualist worldview constantly seeks consensus, for it is only through consensus that specific truths necessary to survival can be affirmed. Conflict retards the creation and re-generation of consensus, therefore periods of conflict /warfare, even when necessary, must be expeditiously carried out for the task at hand, the re-affirmation of consensus, is the basis for survival for the worldview.

This is the primary reason why the white man's colonial genocide decimated the non-dualist worldview for without the space within which to re-affirm consensus, we of the periphery withered and died.

The non-dualist worldview created a concept of time and history uniquely its own for it enabled the survival of the worldview. Time for us is not linear and history is not the linear march of 'progress', whatever 'progress' is. It was impossible for us to build and re-affirm consensus, both with our ancestors past and humankind present, extrapolated on a concept of linear time. For us our past, present and future must be accessible to us at all times, we must be able to transcend the passage of time to forge bonds across the prime event of all time: death.

We accomplished this by creating a circular de-compartmentalized concept of time in which we saw the past, present and future as being accessible to us no matter where we were placed in the circularity of past, present and future. One cannot express via language, much less the white man's language, the pain of spatial dislocation unleashed upon us with the coming of the white man's linear time, which insists that the past is past and the future still to come.

To lock us up into the boxes of linear time was to sever our links with the consensus of the past and future. This was simply to deny our being, to cast us adrift from our worldview. The reaction to this was to simply wither away and die either physically or perceptually, or both. Regardless of the nature of and the characteristics of the worldview, it has to be replicated; it has to constitute individuals who embody the matrices of perception of the given specific worldview.

With reference to humankind the replication of the worldview, the constituting of individuals is done at the level of, via and through language. For language gives meaning and relevance to the worldview at the level of the human. The replication and constituting of humans who share common perceptive structures is the domain of discourse.

Discourse that serves the worldview is then wrapped up with, focuses solely on power/ knowledge. For it is the discursive structures of power/ knowledge that replicate the worldview, constitute the individual who views the world through the matrices of perceptions of the specific worldview and ultimately polices the space dominated by the specific worldview it is part of. Worldviews contend within given spaces for dominance, for hegemony. Within the space de-lineated by human consciousness worldviews contend for the rule of their specific matrices of perceiving the world.

Discourse being the constituting agent of worldviews; discourses then become locked in battle for dominance within any number of given spaces along the continuum of human existence. A hegemonic discourse is then the active constituting agent of a given worldview that at a specific moment is enjoying dominance in its suzerainty over the constituting of individuals. The worldview is then hegemonic in its relation to contending worldviews, which it has displaced or is yet to become hegemonic.

My position does not conceive of human existence without matrices of perception, therefore all human action is the by-product of a specific worldview, which is articulated via language. Worldviews are the basic building blocks of human existence as they can transcend the realm of language; therefore, it is a misnomer to speak of the extra-discursive within these worldviews for discourse does not enjoy primacy. Worldviews that are based on the primacy of language must contemplate the existence of the extra-discursive and its relationship to discourse.

The debate is of little or no relevance to those of us who situate ourselves within a non-dualist worldview in which discourse is but a tool of the worldview at the level of articulation via language.

The underlying perception of the work that follows is then the periphery, a specific given extent of geographic space, in which a battle has raged between worldviews for hegemony since that fateful day in 1492 when the white man set foot on Guanahani. The white man's worldview has enjoyed an albeit constantly challenged hegemony since 1492 not because of some inherently superior essence/s of his worldview.

The reason lies simply in the fact that he came in 1492 armed with superior technologies of death, the by-product of a worldview that could have sustained warfare and conflict for significant periods of linear time of its existence. His is a worldview that glorifies, that revels in, that regenerates itself in total warfare. He came to the Western Hemisphere in 1492 properly outfitted to wage the wars so vital to his enterprise of hegemony. Herein lies the possibility of discursive rupture, of discursive breach, for the white man's worldview has held hegemonic ascendancy solely by dint of its technological prowess.

The white worldview has failed to silence the alternate worldviews, which constantly challenge its hegemonic privilege to constitute individuals in the image and likeness of the worldview. The discursive ruptures and breaches at the level of the individual in the periphery are attested to by the white man's descriptions of us as marginal and ambivalent. Our marginality and ambivalence are a result of the failure to constitute us individuals firmly rooted in the white man's worldview. As used by the white man, our marginality and ambivalence are but two more racist terms to add to the long list used to describe us of the periphery.

From my perceptive matrices our marginality and ambivalence are but a reflection of the reality of mutually antagonistic worldviews constantly in competition with each other for the power/ knowledge to constitute individuals within specific worldviews. The outcome of this struggle for hegemony is individuals who commute between different and varied modes of perception during every second of their existence as humans.

We of the periphery living in this minefield of worldviews seek wholeness and perceptive continuity by creating a strategy of pragmatism so necessary for our survival physically and perceptually; i.e. - whatever works at a specific instance we utilize regardless of its origin from the amalgams of worldviews.

This condition of worldview pragmatism is but the end result of discursive rupture, for rupture is created in the structure of hegemonic discourse whenever humans, the object of knowledge / power, answer the call of a competing non-hegemonic discourse, no matter how fleeting the response was. Whenever we in the periphery utilize matrices of perception entirely alien to the hegemonic white worldview that then is the essence of discursive rupture.

With specific reference to Foucault that is why there is no hope of liberation within his worldview; because there is no discursive rupture for

Foucault as he cannot imagine an alternate worldview since he accepted implicitly the white racist worldview for it defined his race, his cosmology, his very concept of himself.

Foucault's matrices of perceptions simply could not visualize an existence for him as a white man devoid of his white racist worldview. His entire exercise then reeked of being nihilist for he denied the possibility of liberation even though he passionately sought it, for this has been the elusive holy grail the white man has always sought and is yet to be found, save and except by those who have made the pilgrimage to alternate worldviews. It was during the search for liberation in his texts that Foucault would expose the metaphysic of his worldview and by extension point to the rupture. A rupture I would perceive only because of my marginality and ambivalence as a person of the periphery.

Foucault's Texts as a Point of Exit

Michel Foucault would in various texts reveal the ontological structures of the European worldview and the fact that these structures were integral parts of his worldview and its matrices of perception. Foucault's work would then systematically reveal the workings of the European worldview, but the said works never sought to transcend the worldview that informed his works. Foucault recognized the dualities of the white worldview and his works were in themselves edifices of thought processes built on dualist perceptions. One instance of this in his work is as follows: "When a judgment cannot be framed in terms of good and evil, it is stated in terms of normal and abnormal. And when it is necessary to justify this last distinction, it is done in terms of what is good or bad for the individual. These are expressions that signal the fundamental duality of Western consciousness." (Foucault 1986 Pg. 230).

From the quotation above it is manifestly clear that Foucault recognizes, accepts this "fundamental duality of Western consciousness." Foucault in maintaining his dualist worldview posits that language was in fact the by-product of man's attempt to cheat the finality of death. The mechanism of perception is again dualist and is but another example of Foucault's insight within the confines of his worldview. But that is what it is, just insights within his worldview for he is unable to transcend his worldview.

Foucault states: "It is quite likely that the approach of death- its sovereign gesture, its prominence within human memory hollows out in the present and in existence the void toward which and from which we speak." (Foucault 1986 Pg. 53).

The imagery of the quotation above is purely dualist in conceptualization. The mutually exclusive dualities are: man/ death, and language is simply man's attempt to address the salience of death.

Foucault's perceptions are ultimately the product of his worldview for another writer who situates himself in a non-dualist alternate worldview would have formulated the scenario in an entirely and radically different way.

We the members of a specific non-dualist worldview would state that in humankind's eternal quest to cheat death, language was a gift of intent that enabled humankind to transmit the knowledge of power to initiates so vital in their quest for power. Language was simply then a limited tool that can actually retard the initiates' quest for power, and for this reason it must be transcended by the primacy of sensory experiences.

The dualist stance of Foucault is therefore worldviews apart from the non-dualist position presented above, but Foucault's value is his presentation of the dualist worldview cogently. In his antagonism with the prevailing discourse of the day, he reveals for our viewing structures hitherto hidden from the gaze of those of us in the periphery so driven to understand the white man's worldview.

Foucault continues on the theme of the dualities of language and death: "Perhaps there exists in speech an essential affinity between death, endless striving, and the self-representation of language. Perhaps the figure in the mirror to infinity erected against the black wall of death is fundamental for any language from the moment it determines to leave a trace of its passage." (Foucault 1986 Pg. 55).

In the passage quoted above Foucault is now venturing that the white man's endless quest to transcend the finality of death can only create solutions within the ambits, the boundaries of his worldview.

The dualist perception of reality must then throw up a "mirror to infinity erected against the black wall of death" but there is a figure in the mirror, a mirror reflection of the white man. This mirror reflection, this representation of self is expressed via language, which by extension must be the "self representation of language."

What then is the end result of this representation of the mirror image for Foucault? He states as follows: "that forms one of the most decisive ontological events of language, its mirrored reflection upon death and the construction, from this reflection, of a virtual space where speech discovers the endless resourcefulness of its own image and where it can represent itself as already existing behind itself already active beyond itself, to infinity." (Foucault 1986 Pg. 55).

Foucault therefore insists that the white man's ontology is driven by language which insists it has transcended death. Language has transcended death for it is the self- representation of the mirror image thrown up when the white man is juxtaposed against the black wall of death. By being the self- representation of the mirror image language can now assert its transcendence of death for language in the white man's worldview can represent itself "to infinity."

Language asserting and enforcing its primacy in the white man's dualist worldview insists that the absence of language is death, silence. More so the assertion of primacy for language enables the formulation of the structures of discourse and the extra discursive.

Foucault continues: "writing in Western culture, automatically dictates that we place ourselves in the virtual space of self- representation and re-duplication, since writing refers not to a thing but to speech, a work of language only advances more deeply into intangible density of the mirror, calls forth the double of this already doubled writing, discovers in this way a possible and impossible infinity, ceaselessly strives after speech, maintains beyond the death which condemns it, and frees a murmuring stream." (Foucault 1986 Pg. 56).

Foucault in the passage above supplies a fundamental insight for the people of the periphery in search of understanding the white man's worldview. He insists that written language in the white man's worldview is but self-representation and re-duplication of a dance of doubles. This is so because in the white man's worldview written language refers not to the objects signified, but to speech.

Since speech is already the self-representation of the mirror image thrown up to transcend death and language insists it has transcended death, then written language can only be the double of the already doubled.

What Foucault is methodically teaching us is that the dualities of the white man's worldview are articulated via language that engages in a circular dance of dualities and doubles. These dualities and doubles all reverberate in the enclosed space that language expresses in its transcendence of death.

The outcome of this is a worldview that is yet to come to grips with death, for language has cheated man of his final triumph over death. More so, it is a worldview in which language by virtue of its self-representation and re-duplication continuously throws up a dance of dualities and doubles entirely divorced from the representation of things, objects in reality.

For Foucault language in the white man's worldview is in fact the motive force of a perceptually closed system, a perceptual black hole.

The summation of the idea is as follows: "The mirror to infinity, to which every language gives birth once it erects itself vertically against death was not displayed without an evasion; the work placed the infinite outside of itself - a real and majestic infinity in which it became a virtual and circular mirror, completed in a beautifully closed form." (Foucault 1986 Pg. 60).

Foucault did not evade the conclusion he was pointing to in previous quotations. The conclusion is in itself of salient importance to the mental workers of the periphery. He teaches that in the white man's worldview, language is in itself a "virtual circular mirror", a "beautifully closed form."

That language for Foucault is then a dance of dualities, of doubles because of a specific ontological event: the transcendence of death. What in effect he is teaching us is the basis for the resilience of the white man's worldview. The puzzling reality that racism continues to be ontologically salient irrespective of the material realities of the race must now be viewed through Foucault's construct.

The dance of self-representation and re-duplication traps the white man in a perceptual black hole in which no external light penetrates. All incoming data has to be re- constituted via the structures of self-representation and re-duplication, for it is only through this dance of doubles data can be perceived, seen, much less assimilated.

The white man has therefore to constantly seek hegemony; to constantly constitute individuals within his worldview for it is a matter of survival for his worldview. For his worldview is perceptually hobbled, it is perceptually intolerant, to the extent of being myopic. The separation between written language and the object signified is but one example of this perceptual myopia. The white man's worldview can then only see, can only perceive what it has constituted, it therefore in its quest for survival must constitute everything in its image and likeness, which is essentially a process articulated upon violence.

I would now present Foucault's dualist continuum of the will to knowledge/ truth/ power/ knowledge and discipline/ punish. These are the final pieces of the puzzle uncovered by myself, which culminated in the opening of the portal that allowed my exit from the white man's worldview.

The construct of will to knowledge/ will to truth Foucault expresses as follows: "In appearance, or rather according to the mask it bears, historical consciousness is neutral, devoid of passions and committed solely to truth. But if it examines itself and if, more generally, it interrogates the various forms of scientific consciousness in its history, it finds that all these forms and transformations are aspects of the will to knowledge; instinct, passion, the inquisitor's devotion, cruel subtlety and malice...The historical analysis of this rancorous will to knowledge reveals that all knowledge rests upon injustice (that there is no right, not even in the act of knowing, to truth or a foundation for truth) and that the instinct for knowledge is malicious (something murderous, opposed to the happiness of mankind.) Even in the greatly expanded form it assumes today, the will to knowledge does not achieve a Universal truth; man is not given an exact and serene mastery of nature. On the contrary, it ceaselessly multiplies the risks, creates dangers in every area; it breaks down illusory defenses, it dissolves the unity of the subject; it releases those elements of itself that are devoted to its subversion and destruction. Knowledge does not slowly detach itself from its empirical roots, the initial needs from which it arose, to become pure speculation subject only to the demands of reason; its development is not tied to the constitution and affirmation of a free subject; rather it creates a progressive enslavement to its instinctive violence. Where religion once demanded the sacrifice of bodies, knowledge now calls for experimentation on ourselves, calls us to the sacrifice of the subject of knowledge." (Sheridan 1980 Pgs. 119-120). What Foucault is in fact saying in the text quoted above is that the will to knowledge is but another structure of the white man's worldview. He insists that historical consciousness its "forms and transformations" are aspects of this will to knowledge.

The will to knowledge consistently strives after universal truth, but is yet unable to attain this for "man is not given an exact and serene mastery of nature". Methodology of the will to knowledge is violence and injustice for in its striving for universal truth it must ceaselessly and relentlessly attack the unity of the subject. This methodology of the will to knowledge is circular for it constantly justifies and replenishes its attacks upon the subject by releasing elements of itself, which subvert its drive for knowledge.

The will to knowledge is therefore not blessed with autonomy from its enterprise for it must constantly justify the desirability of its enterprise by itself creating hindrances to the success of the enterprise.

For Foucault, the will to knowledge was then but another instance of the circular dance of dualities and doubles that is the white man's worldview. Moreover, his language in this passage definitely indicates the re-formulation of the Nietzschean metaphysic. But it is a re-formulation that retains the focus of the metaphysic, for as his statements on language, he posits the will to knowledge as another ontological construct of the white man's worldview.

By implication, Foucault insists that the will to knowledge drives historical consciousness. In addition, the will to knowledge constantly seeks a universal truth, that is yet unattainable, because man has not transcended death / nature. This will to knowledge driven by this fixation with a universal truth ensures the continuity, the self-propagation of its enterprise by subverting its very enterprise.

To my mind, the conclusion is inescapable; Foucault was via his works, articulating on a linear continuum his conceptualizations on the metaphysic of the white man's worldview. His position on language, written language forms a linear continuum with each segment flowing into the other, thereby forming a coherent conceptual whole.

The fixation of the will to knowledge with the search for the elusive universal truth is linked to language, the mirror- image, death and the dance of doubles, self- representation and re- duplication.

The will to knowledge, in its drive for truth, must relentlessly assault the unity of the subject because language clothes the subject in layers of self-representation and re- duplication which must be peeled away to uncover, to reveal this elusive truth.

The methodology of the will to knowledge has then to be violent to force entry into and to ultimately deconstruct the subject. That the will to knowledge must always subvert the integrity of its enterprise is the result of again the nature of language within the worldview.

The language of self- representation and re-duplication ensures that the will to knowledge must subvert its enterprise, for the will to knowledge can never grasp the holy grail sought: truth. The enterprise must then be subverted to avert the risk of accepting as truth the products of self-representation and re-duplication. The will to knowledge must always overturn its enterprise to retain its integrity, thereby ensuring but another dance of circular dualities.

Finally, the culmination of my argument is the very use of language Foucault adopted in articulating these concepts. The construct of the will to knowledge is presented as a motive force active across the limits of linear time and history. In both instances, the concepts of language to infinity and the will to knowledge are presented without any reference to a materialist grounding in linear time/ history. Both concepts transcend linear time in their presentation and must therefore be expressions of ontology, a metaphysic enclosed by Foucault's worldview. Their materiality lies in their transcendence of linear history, which makes them part of Foucault's articulation of the white man's worldview.

At this juncture I would now delve into the constructs, which Foucault presented in his text from the late 1970's, that in fact indicated his furthest extrapolation of concepts inherited from Nietzsche. I would commence this textual journey with the presentation of a passage taken from an interview Foucault gave in 1970.

Foucault speaks: "In short, humanism is everything in Western civilization that restricts the "desire for power", it prohibits the desire for power and excludes the possibility of power being seized. The theory of the subject (in the double sense of the word) is at the heart of humanism and this is why our culture has tenaciously rejected anything that could weaken its hold upon us." (Foucault 1986 Pgs. 220-221). The signposts in this passage are: (a) humanism and its relation to power, (b) that power can in fact be seized, (c) that the "heart of humanism" is the "theory of the subject" in "the double sense of the word".

The first question I have is what exactly is humanism, is it an artifice, a device, ideology, incarceration used by persons in power to remain in power?

Foucault further insists that the fact that power can be seized necessitates the existence on operation of the structures of humanism, which ensure power remains in the hands of the powerful.

Humanism in Western civilization therefore transcends the linear history of the white man for as it is used by Foucault it has no specificity or materiality grounded in specific material conditions of time. He speaks and conjures visions of a panoramic linear view of the white man's history in which specific locomotives, motive forces, essences are discerned, identified, and withdrawn from the linear flow of the white man's history.

In turn, at this point in Foucault's history he is definitely postulating a theory of possible liberation, a praxis of liberation that attacks these essences as humanism and language at specific intersections.

Foucault's praxis for liberation is as follow: "But it can be attacked in two ways, either by a "de-subjectification" of the will to power (that is through political struggle in the context of class warfare) or by the destruction of the subject as pseudo sovereign (that is through an attack on "culture"); the suppression of taboos and the limitations and divisions imposed upon the sexes, the setting up of communes; the loosening of inhibitions with regard to drugs; the breaking of all prohibitions that form and guide, the development of a normal individual." (Foucault 1986 Pg. 222). "Revolutionary action, on the contrary, is defined as the simultaneous agitation of consciousness and institutions, this implies that we attack the relationships of power through the notions and institutions that function as their instruments, armature, and armor." (Foucault 1986 Pg. 228). The two passages quoted are presented for the reader to read and refer to when we enter the discussion of the concepts of Foucault presented in 1975 in "Discipline and Punish."

"Discipline and Punish" was for the writer the seminal text of Foucault's patrimony to humanity. My search for the path to liberation ended with "Discipline and Punish" for in experiencing Foucault's text I found the signposts that pointed the exit out of the white man's worldview. In "Discipline and Punish" Foucault presents his position on the question of power and social control. He methodically unseats previously articulated concepts of power and social control and in doing so leaves his revolutionary praxis of the early 1970's in tatters.

This is of little relevance to my enterprise for my pilgrimage through Foucault was a journey seeking exits out of a worldview, which refused to even recognize my humanity.

Foucault defines the work "Discipline and Punish" accordingly: "This book is a correlative history of the modern soul and of a new power to judge; a genealogy of the present scientific- legal complex from which the power to punish derives its bases, justifications and rules, from which it extends its effects and by which it masks its exorbitant singularity." (Foucault 1979 Pg. 23). At first reading, one says yes, at long last Foucault is now grounding his concepts in specific material conditions. But, look closely at the text and you would discover that the locomotive essences that transcend linear time are the linchpins of the passage under consideration. Look closely and you want to know what is this "modern soul," what is this "exorbitant singularity" that the new power masks?

Both these concepts/ constructs we hold in memory as the journey through the text continues. Foucault states: "in what way a specific mode of subjection was able to give birth to man as an object of knowledge for a discourse with a specific status." (Foucault 1979 Pg. 24). In a specific "mode of subjection" man was produced, constituted as "an object of knowledge." We can immediately respond with chants of Foucault's embrace of materialism at long last!

Readers in the tradition of Marx rejoice for Foucault has finally seen the light. But alas, he insists that this specific mode of subjection gives birth to man as objects of knowledge for a specific discourse. Man is therefore no longer the autonomous subject, for humankind is now the product of the copulation of the dualities of a specific discourse and a specific mode of subjection.

Are these "objects of knowledge" the products of a discourse and a mode of subjection capable of initiating action towards liberation, much less attaining it? A question of pressing importance to the writer for I have yet to accept the inevitability of human suffering.

Foucault continues: "That is to say there may be a knowledge of the body that is not exactly the science of its functioning, and a mastery of its forces that is more than the ability to conquer them; this knowledge and this mastery constitute what might be called the political technology of the body." (Foucault 1979 Pg. 27). The 'political technology of the body' embraces all the knowledges necessary to conquer and subjugate the body but much more than that. What are these fields of knowledges that are in excess of what is needed to conquer and subjugate the body? Are these the fields of knowledges necessary towards the replication of a worldview that transcends linear time and material conditions? I must ask these questions for it is obvious that Foucault, via his text, is playing word/ mind games with the materialists of the white man's worldview.

The quotations that follow introduce into the debate Foucault's thoughts on power. He states: "In short this power is exercised rather than possessed; it is not the "privilege", acquired, or preserved, of the dominant class, but the overall effect of its strategic positions- an effect that is manifested and sometimes extended by the position of those who are dominated." (Foucault 1979 Pg. 27). The passage quoted above and those to follow that deal with power effectively show that Foucault's concept of power walks away from the materialist view of existence. Power is then an effect that is alluded to, signified by the existence of the powerless. It then has in effect no materiality, for it has to be manifested by the powerless- an effect.

Power can then only be exercised for it can never be possessed, acquired or become a privilege of any given social grouping. Power in its non-materiality can only invest the powerful through their spatial proximity to itself. There can only be then a geography of the spaces that are strategically placed to power. The concept of power is then grounded in a specific metaphysic.

Foucault continues: "Furthermore, this power is not exercised simply as an obligation or a prohibition on those "who do not have it"; it invests them, is transmitted by them and through them, it exerts pressures upon them, just as they themselves, in their struggles against it; resist the grip it has on them." (Foucault 1979 Pg. 27). The powerless not only attest to the existence of this immaterial locomotive by their powerlessness, for power cannot be power without its effect, the powerless. It is the powerless that embrace and resist power on a continuous basis of submission/ resistance, ebb and flow that gives power its materiality through the effect. Yet another instance of Foucault's metaphysic.

Foucault continues: "We should admit rather that power produces knowledge and is not simply by encouraging it because it serves power or by applying it because it is useful); that power and knowledge directly imply one another; that there is no power relation without the correlative constitution of a field of knowledge that does not presuppose and constitute at the same time power relations." (Foucault 1979 Pg. 27).

Foucault moves from the position "that power produces knowledge" to assert, "power and knowledge directly imply one another" which in effect is a statement, which transcends a materialist grounding. He moves from the position of circular causality – power produces knowledge, knowledge produces power, by extension power is knowledge, knowledge is power; to the position, which dismisses this nexus, to one in which power and knowledge are entities, which imply each other. There is therefore no crude causal inter-relationship; it is simply one of the interdependence of unique and distinct "essences" of a metaphysic. It is only at the level of the effect of each essence do we have the interplay of causalities, and by extension it is the material existence of the effect that attests to the existence of both essences.

The effect of power is power relations, whilst the effect of knowledge is a field of knowledge. Without the interplay and mutual dependence of both effects there can be neither power relations nor fields of knowledge. That is why power and knowledge imply each other, the essences being always one step divorced from the material conditions.

The conclusion is then inescapable, Foucault's essences and their effects are simply the framework of a metaphysic clearly woven within his text that dealt with specific effects – madness, the clinic, parricide, prisons and sexuality.

Finally, I will present passages, which deal with Foucault's concept of the modern soul, which is but another effect of power. "I would be wrong to say that the soul is an illusion or an ideological effect. On the contrary it exists, it has a reality, it is produced permanently around, on, within the body by the functioning of a power that is exercised on those punished." (Foucault 1979 Pg. 29). "The man described for us, whom we are invited to free, is already in himself the effect of subjection much more profound than himself. A "soul" inhabits him and brings him to existence which is itself a factor in the mastery that power exercises over the body, the soul is the effect and instrument of a political autonomy; the soul is the prison of the body." (Foucault 1979 Pg. 30). Foucault of the passages quoted above presents what is perhaps the most potent construct of "Discipline and Punish", i.e. – the modern soul. The modern soul is but another effect of power, but of a specific power "exercised on those punished." Again, this specific power is only witnessed, gazed upon, given materiality in its effect – the punished.

But this soul is more than effect, it is also instrument, for through its possession of the body and the immediate space, which cocoons the body it imprisons the body, it renders it docile and punishable. But the instrumentality of the soul upon the body is an effect of power, for power gives birth to the soul as an effect upon the body one stage divorced from the effect. The effect and the instrumentality of effect brings the docile body into existence, thereby the soul is the material force that breeds existence into man the punishable, the powerless.

The modern soul, and by extension all souls in the history of the white man's worldview, are the effects of specific power through time. Power and knowledge, which imply each other, would then in their transcendence of time always seek to imprison the body within the effects of power/ knowledge for that is how docile bodies are constituted.

The effect always ensures that the "essences" are always one step divorced from materiality, whether it is the modern soul, language, and the powerless.

This is by way of presentation Foucault's metaphysic that I discerned from his text. Alas, it is a nihilistic metaphysic for in his works the structure of effects and essences is expressed in terms of resiliency over the capabilities of the constituted. One is always left to question whether any structure of effects and essences so empowered to constitute man as objects of knowledge would have enabled the constituted object to liberate themselves from the hegemony of power/ knowledge, language, humanism.

One infers from the text that the only struggle possible is with the effects of power/ knowledge. The effects mutate, re-duplicate and re-represent themselves in response to resistance from the powerless. This struggle and resistance by the powerless in effect ensures the continuity of the essences, for in and by these challenges to their effects power and knowledge flow, has continuity and effectively re-constitute their transcendence over and across time.

The struggle of the powerless within the worldview is then an effect of the action of the essences. Foucault ultimately indicates the circular dance of futility founded on dualities that is the white man's worldview. The lesson in this for myself was that the liberation I sought could only be found in an alternate worldview structured along entirely different and diametrically opposed lines of constitution.

The path to liberation does not exist within the white man's worldview; the only choice was to cease looking within his worldview, cease debating within his worldview. Liberation was now dependent on my exiting a worldview and my entry into an alternate worldview. The task at hand was to find such an alternate worldview.

Summary

By way of summation, I will now present the legacy left by the works of Foucault to mental workers of the periphery as myself. In his corpus of work, he articulated the white man's metaphysic that drives his worldview. By adopting the position of the effect and the essence divorced one step from the effect Foucault taught us of the periphery to differentiate between the effect of power and knowledge and power and knowledge itself.

Before Foucault, the theories of liberation concentrated at the level of the effect giving these effects of motive forces determinist materiality in the realm of human action. He aggressively rejected this stance and by grasping the metaphysical focus of Nietzsche he would separate essence and the effect of essence acting upon human subjects.

What then are these essences of Foucault upon which we must focus our gaze in order for us of the periphery to unravel the white man's worldview? These are:

(a) Language that dances the circular dance of self-representation and re-duplication.

(b) Humanism that restricts the access to power through the creation of the human subject.

(c) Power/ knowledge that constitute man as objects of knowledge.

The effects of these instances listed above are central to any enterprise of understanding of the white man's worldview. These are:

(a) the dualities of Western consciousness.

(b) The transcendence of language over linear time.

(c) The representation of speech by written language rather than the signification of objects.

(d) The constituting of the subject an effect of humanism, which masks the effect of man as object of knowledge, the effect of power/ knowledge.

(e) The effects of power/ knowledge such as:

(i) the modern soul, the prison of the body.

(ii) The scientifico-legal complex, the effect and instrument of power, which is itself also an effect of power.

(iii) The political technology of the body, which is more than the sum of the mastery of the forces of the body and the knowledge of the science of the functioning of the body. The political technology of the body is then greater than the sum of the knowledges that constitute a docile body, for it is an effect of an essence, one step divorced from the process or determination in the last instance.

(iv) The micro-physics of power is another effect of power that polices the space created between the effects that constitute the docile body and the body itself. The modern soul is located in the realm of the micro-physics of power, but transcends this specific space as it transcends the material body of the object of knowledge.

Given any undertaking which sets out to deconstruct the white man's worldview, the essences and their effects listed above are the tools that must be applied to pry open the said worldview. You seek out the effects and their essences and methodically map the action of the effects upon the human subject. With the mapping of the effects, you work back in circularity to identify the essences one step divorced from the process.

Given the overarching focus of the project which drives this work, which is primarily the Islamic worldview in a non-hegemonic position within the white man's worldview, the mapping of the white man's worldview through the matrices formulated by Foucault is for another work in the future. This task was engaged in with the works on Foucault's discourse which followed the publication of this work in 2004. The content of these later works reflects Foucault's emphasis on the study of power and power relations following the publication of "Discipline and Punish."

What then are the failings of Foucault's patrimony to the writer? In the first instance, Foucault formulated no praxis of liberation from the dictatorship of his metaphysic. To achieve liberation necessitated the creation of an alternate worldview that was in its essences and the effects of these essences diametrically opposed to the existing worldview.

Foucault never tackled this issue for he devoted himself until his death to continued articulations of effects of the essences of the white man's worldview. The silence of Foucault after the mid 1970's on the praxis of liberation was deafening and merits no speculation on my part as to the reasons why. What is cruelly obvious is that the only way/ path to liberation in Foucault's worldview is the adoption of an alternate worldview, which in the effects of its essences is diametrically opposed to the white man's worldview.

Foucault would never publicly admit to having made that move to transcend the discursive rupture created by his mental labour. He faced death as all humans do by themselves, and at that instant where death grips the body, consciousness, sensory experience his language failed him miserably. For the language to infinity flees when faced with death itself rather than the mirror image. This was for myself the salient reality felt in the pit of my consciousness. For he gave me no answers on the reality and inevitability of death and the means possible to defeat, even cheat death. I needed to experience an alternate worldview that faced death head on, embraced it and rolled with it until disengagement. This alternate worldview I would have to seek after exiting the white man's worldview for Foucault taught by his example. To continue to locate myself within the white man's worldview meant that I would never be able to perceptually "see" the alternate worldview, even if it came up and bit me on the ass.

To search for my holy grail, I would have first to walk away from the worldview that created, "sees" the grail. The act of escape meant that the search was no longer for the grail, for it was perceptually constituted by a worldview that I shed as a snake changes its skin.

The debates within the exited worldview no longer matter; they no longer excite and entice me. I no longer need to remonstrate on the racism of the white man's worldview, his denial of my humanity. These are now given, accepted facts of a worldview now alien to me for I no longer need to search for, to demand space, respect and justice within the spaces of his worldview. Now, when I remonstrate on the racism of his worldview it is spoken from spaces external to his worldview and my language is a sharp sword flailing away at the fortifications of his worldview.

In closing I would now present two passages from the writings of Salman Rushdie, which are of relevance to this section of my work. Rushdie speaks: "If you want to tell the untold stories, if you want to give voice to the voiceless, you've got to find a Language, which goes for film as well as prose, for documentary as well as autobiography. Use the wrong language, and you're dumb and blind." (Rushdie 1991 Pg. 115). "The effect of mass migrations has been the creation of radically new types of human being; people who root themselves in ideas rather than places, in memories as much as in material things; people who have been obliged to define themselves - because they are so defined by others - by their otherness; people in whose deepest selves strange fusions occur, unprecedented unions between what they were and where they find themselves. The migrant suspects reality; having experienced several ways of being, he understands their illusory nature. To see things plainly, you have to cross a frontier." (Rushdie 1991 Pgs. 124-125).

I am then a migrant having crossed the frontier between worldviews carrying the weight of the worldview of the past, ever seeking liberation, healing, my humanity previously denied to me.

Edward W. Said as a Point of Exit

Edward W. Said's seminal work "Orientalism" does not address the issue of the Islamic worldview as an alternate worldview to that of the white man's. In fact, Said states quite plainly on the emphasis of his work as follows: "My contention is that without examining Orientalism as a discourse one cannot possibly understand the enormously systematic discipline which culture was able to manage and even produce the Orient politically, sociologically, militarily, ideologically, scientifically, and imaginatively during the post- Enlightenment period." (Said 1979 Pg. 3). With reference to the passage quoted above it is clear that Said's position is that this thing he calls "Orientalism" is a "discourse", a "systematic discipline", the effect of "culture". The obvious question follows from whence came the terminology, the worldview that gave it life? Said states as follows on this: "I have found it useful here to employ Michel Foucault's notion of a discourse, as described by him in the "Archaeology of Knowledge" and in "Discipline and Punish", to identify Orientalism." (Said 1979 Pg. 3).

In keeping with Said's reading of Foucault's texts he was able to state as follows: "The relationship between Occident and Orient is a relationship of power, of domination of varying degrees of a complex hegemony." (Said 1979 Pg. 5). My specific response to Said's statements quoted above is to seek in his work instances of the exiting of worldviews. Instances of the use of Foucault's analytical tools to rip open discursive ruptures, thereby laying bare the entrances to alternate worldviews.

I have already written on my journey of discovery through Foucault's text and its empowering of my desire to find exits from the white man's worldview. Said's promise lies in the focus of his work on racism or in his words "Orientalism" as a discourse, this power relationship between "Occident and Orient." The question that would be answered in my presentation on Said is: does he flatter to deceive?

Said defines, articulates his thesis that drives "Orientalism" as follows: "My thesis is that the essential aspects of modern Orientalist theory and praxis from which present day Orientalism derives, can be understood, not as a sudden access of objective knowledge about the Orient, but as a set of structures inherited from the past, secularized, redisposed, and re- formed, which in turn were naturalized, modernized and laicized substitutes for (or versions of) Christian supernaturalism. In the form of new texts and ideas, the East was accommodated to these structures." (Said 1979). Scrutiny of the passage quoted above leaves but one conclusion of relevance to be made. That is Said is insisting that the structures that drive Orientalism, the effect, transcend a materialist conception of time and history.

Said speaks of "laicized substitutes" or versions of "Christian supernaturalism" as being this metaphysical essence one step/ level divorced from the reality of the effect. Said is now positing a metaphysical essence that drives Orientalism, which is one of its effects, in keeping with the worldview of Foucault's work. This then is the exit that Said points to, the discursive rupture that he creates within Foucault's worldview.

Said's statement is in fact pointing to a discursive rupture in the white man's worldview for he is insisting that this thing he calls "Orientalism" is an effect of an essence that transcends the white man's concepts of linear time, history and historicist materialism.

As with Foucault Said locates, identifies this locomotive, this essence and simply moves on to devote the energies of the work to description and articulations of the "effect" of the locomotive. In Said's case he names the effect he has identified: "Orientalism".

He says: "I shall be calling Orientalism a way of coming to terms with the Orient that is based on the Orient's special place in European Western experience." (Said 1979 Pg. 1). "The Orient is an integral part of European material civilization and culture. Orientalism expresses and represents that part culturally and even ideologically as a mode of discourse with supporting institutions, vocabulary, scholarship, imagery, doctrines, even colonial bureaucracies and colonial styles." (Said 1979 Pg. 2). From the passages quoted above it is obvious that Said commences with a dualist construct; Orient/ Occident. For Said the dualist embrace, danse macabre of Orient/ Occident transcends European history and in effect invalidates historical materialists of whatever persuasion. He insists that "Orientalism" the effect, in fact creates the Orient via a mode of discourse that "expresses" and "represents" a reality entwined in, with the Other. The effect, Orientalism, then produces this thing called the Orient in the image and likeness of the Occident.

Said, via his danse of dualities inherited from Foucault, is then insisting that this reality called the Orient is a manufactured materiality. We who are trapped in the Orient are constituted individuals, the objects of knowledge thrown up by power/ knowledge.

Said then insists on the following positions: "One ought never to assume that the structure of Orientalism is nothing more than a structure of lies or of myths which, were the truth about them to be told, would simply blow away." (Said 1979 Pg. 6). For Said to focus on Orientalism other than as an "effect" a mode of discourse would then be a fundamental strategic blunder for those of us trapped in the constituted reality of the Orient. But there are implications behind accepting and adopting Said's specific perceptive portal on Orientalism.

Said insists that Orientalism transcends European colonialism and has an existence that antedates European colonialism. Said states his position as follows: "To say simply that Orientalism was a rationalization of colonial rule is to ignore the extent to which colonial rule was justified in advance by Orientalism, rather than after the fact." (Said 1979). How then does Said support the statement quoted above which strikes at the heart of historicist interpretations of colonialism since 1492? Said states as follows: "The periods of immense advance in the institutions and content of Orientalism coincides exactly with the period of un- paralleled European expansion." (Said 1979). Said by conceding that there was a blossoming of the content and institutional structures of Orientalism directly related to European colonial expansion end runs any suggestion of causality. European colonial expansion stimulated, gave the shot of adrenalin to Orientalism rather than being its creator. In fact, Said insists that

Orientalism by antedating Europe's colonial expansion justified the event when it did occur.

The question arises, out of Foucault's worldview, then of how could Orientalism be an "effect" a mode of discourse without the appropriation/ constituting of objects of knowledge? In other words, Foucault's worldview takes as given that there must be actual bodies to discipline and punish, to imprison within the "soul" thereby creating the discursive spaces controlled, monitored and constituted by the micro- physics of power.

If Said is to dance with Foucault, he then has to find these bodies being constituted, disciplined and punished before and after the end of the un-paralleled European enterprise of conquest and colonialism. Said purports to resolve his antinomy by positing two positions. The first one I would present via quotations from Said's work is as follows: "The point is that in each of these cases the Oriental is contained and represented by dominating frameworks." (Said 1979). "in short, Orientalism is better grasped as a set of constraints upon and limitations of thought then it is simply as a positive doctrine." (Said 1979). Orientalism must be viewed as a dualist discursive structure, an effect, which contains the constituted Oriental to the constituting Occidental. Further Said insists that we must first conceive of this discursive structure at the level of its actions upon thought. Said is therefore dancing his dualist danse macabre, for he is creating a dualist enterprise imbued with transcendence over time and linear history. For he is insisting that at the level of ideas the Occident, could have, it was possible and in fact they did, create representations of non- Occidental peoples and their realities for the consumption of the Occidental. Therefore, by extension all what Said labels as Occidental is in itself an effect of an instrument, which in the last instance is an effect. Orientalism is then the effect of a specific discursive structure, which in itself is an effect of a transcendental European metaphysical essence. Said's metaphysical essence he calls "Christian supernaturalism."

The Occident is then constituted, just as is the Orient a constituted object of knowledge, a by-product of power/ knowledge. At the level of representations, for Said it was then possible for the Occident to create the structures of Orientalism at the level of thought, without the need to control space in the Orient, to constitute Oriental objects of knowledge. But the discursive structures laid down at the level of representation, of thought would call into existence, would enable the conquest of space, the constituting of Oriental objects of knowledge when the European colonial enterprise was launched.

Said states as follows on this issue: "Moreover, the Orient studied was a textual universe by and large, the impact of the Orient was made through books and manuscripts." (Said 1979). "Even the rapport between Orientalist and Orient was textual." (Said 1979). By way of textual climax, Said puts the icing on his multi-layered marble cake of ideas as follows: "Our initial description of Orientalism as a learned field now acquires a new concreteness. A field is often an enclosed space. The idea of representation is a theatrical one; the Orient is the stage on which the whole East is confined. On this stage will appear figures whose role it is to represent the larger whole from which they emanate. The Orient then seems to be, not an unlimited extension beyond the familiar European world, but rather as a closed field, a theatrical stage affixed to Europe. An Orientalist is but the particular specialist in knowledge for which Europe at large is responsible, in the way that an audience is historically and culturally responsible for (and responsive to) dramas technically put together by the dramatist." (Said 1979). The discursive structures of Orientalism active at the level of representation replicated in and on, as well as replicating fields of Orientalist knowledge in the texts existed in a realm divorced from, even independent of, the discursive need to constitute space and human subjects in the Orient.

Representation was in effect matrices of perception affixed to the eyes of the Occidental whenever he/ she viewed things Oriental. Representation did in fact constitute a subject of knowledge and a field of knowledge, which would entrap the Occidental, and by extension the constituted Oriental. This constituting would occur and be replicated repeatedly without causal linkages to historical realities.

The second position Said adopts in resolution of the specific antinomies thrown up by Foucault's worldview is to posit that the initial need, the locomotive pushing Europe to constitute, create Orientalism was the clash of worldviews, of Christian supernaturalism and Islam in Europe's Middle Ages.

Said posits that the aggressive expansionism of Islam into the heartland of Europe in the Middle Ages was to be an event of such traumatic proportions that Europe was forced to respond via the same survival mode thrown up by the European worldview. Said states: "But it was in the Near Orient, the lands of the Arab Near East, where Islam was supposed to define cultural and racial characteristics, that the British and French encountered each other and "The Orient" with the greatest intensity, familiarity and complexity." (Said 1979). "Consider how the Orient, and in particular the Near Orient, became known in the West as its great complimentary opposite since antiquity." (Said 1979). Said now presents the nexus between the Near Orient, the Arab Near East and Islam. That "great complimentary opposite" which exists today in all its potency, that transcendental "Other" constituted since antiquity in the psyche of Europe. Said continues: "Yet where Islam was concerned, European fear, if not always respect, was in order." (Said 1979). "Not for nothing did Islam come to symbolize terror, devastation, the demonic hordes of hated barbarians. For Europe, Islam was a lasting trauma." (Said 1979). Said is therefore insisting that the visions of Islam's armies forcibly overpowering European civilization constituted the creation of the discursive structures of Orientalism as a mode of survival in response to Islam's incursions.

But what of the ideational structures of this discourse of Orientalism, specifically, since Said is primarily dealing at the level of representation? What of racism? Said in speaking of the nexus between Islam and Orientalism as a survival response states: "and in time European civilization incorporated that peril and its lore, its great events, figures, virtues and vices, as something woven into the fabric of life." (Said 1979). "The point is that what remained current about Islam was some necessarily diminished version of those great dangerous forces for Europe." (Said 1979).

Orientalism by constituting a field of representations in which to contain the fear, the paranoia over the "barbaric hordes of Islam" enabled the European to incorporate this fear, this paranoia into his/ her worldview. Thereby enabling the race, the worldview to be constantly on the alert, ever keeping vigil towards the "Arab Near East" for the wave of "barbaric hordes." But more so, it enabled the European to ever seek solutions both at the level of representation and materially/ physically to the always immanent problem.

For Said's worldview it is therefore no coincidence of history that the Spanish undertook their enterprise of "New World" conquest with the defeat of the Islamic incursion into the Iberian Peninsula. Or that routes to the riches of the East were being sought that evaded Islamic hegemony over the traditional routes, both land and sea. Said by way of summation states: "Islam became an image - the word's Daniel's but it seems to me to have remarkable implications for Orientalism in general - whose function was not so much to represent Islam in itself as to represent it for the medieval Christian." (Said 1979). At this juncture I now return to the question of Said's position on European racism and the worldview that drives European racism. He hints at the constituting of racism as a survival strategy in Europe's struggle with Islam. But he finally grapples with racism when he deals with this thing he terms "modern Orientalism." The underpinning statement of his treatment of "modern Orientalism" is as follows: "We must remember the extent to which a major part of the spiritual and intellectual project of the late eighteenth century was a reconstituted theology - natural supernaturalism." (Said 1979). Said insists that the Christian supernaturalism of the middle ages has been transformed by the late eighteenth century to natural supernaturalism. The metaphysical "essence" remains unchanged, as the "effects" of the essence are re-formulated at the level of the idea.

Said therefore terms it a project in re-constituted theology or the self-representation of the mirror image to infinity in Foucault's work. To quote Said on what is this modern Orientalism: "The four elements I have described - expansion, historical confrontation, sympathy, classification-are the currents in eighteenth century thought on whose presence the specific intellectual and institutional structures of modern Orientalism depend." (Said 1979). "In other words, modern Orientalism derives from secularizing elements in eighteenth century European culture." (Said 1979). "But if these interconnected elements represent a secularizing tendency, this is not to say that the old religious patterns of human history and destiny and the "existential paradigms" were simply removed. Far from it, they were reconstituted, redeployed, redistributed in the secular frameworks just enumerated." (Said 1979). The conclusion is manifestly apparent and has been stated and repeated elsewhere in my text. The passages quoted are leading us into Said's position on European racism and its relationship with Orientalism.

With this quotation that follows we step one step closer to Said's position on European racism. Said's text continues: "it also retained, as an undislodged current in its discourse, a reconstituted religious impulse, a naturalized supernaturalism. What I shall try to show is that this impulse in Orientalism resided in the Orientalist's conception of himself, of the Orient, And of his discipline." (Said 1979). What then is the Orientalist's conception of himself, his worldview and the issue of racism? Said states: "Yet in the end, being a white man, for Kipling and for those whose perceptions and rhetoric he influenced, was a self - confirming business. Being a white man was therefore an idea and a reality. Being a white man, in short, was a very concrete manner of being - in - the world, a way of taking hold of reality, language, and thought. It made a specific style possible." (Said 1979). Said is then simply stating in the passage quoted above that being a white man located a European in a specific racist worldview. Said continues: "Kipling himself could not merely have happened, the same is true of his white man. Such ideas and their authors emerge out of complex historical and cultural circumstances, at least two of which have much in common with the history of Orientalism in the nineteenth century." (Said 1979). The inescapable conclusion on the genesis of the white man's racism for Said is stated in the text as follows: ""Semitic", therefore was transtemporal, trans individual category, purporting to predict every discrete act of "Semitic" behavior on the basis of some pre-existing

"Semitic" essence, and aiming as well to interpret all aspects of human life and activity in terms of some common "Semitic" element." (Said 1979). We the people of the periphery have simply to replace "Semitic" with every other racist label, which denies our humanity, and repeatedly re-read the passage quoted above from Said's work. At the end of the exercise in deconstruction we grasp the threads of the tapestry that Said's text is weaving. The conclusion is inescapable, for he is insisting that the white man's racism is founded on ontological categories of representation. These racist categories represent us to them and in turn constitute us for their convenience, thereby ensuring the sanctity of their worldview. For without affirmation, a worldview buckles under the weight of its irrelevance to its human end users.

Said continues: "The point to be emphasized is that this truth about the distinctive differences between races, civilizations, and languages (was/ or pretended to be) radical and eradicable. It went to the bottom of things, it asserted that there was no escape from origins and the types these origins enabled; it set the real boundaries between human beings, on which races, nations, and civilizations were constructed." (Said 1979). The basis of the process of differentiation between the various dualities was then the creation of ontological categories. Ontological categories ensured the mutual exclusivity of the dualities constituted as elements of a dualist dance to infinity ever based on violent contradictions. The Orient, niggers, coolies, Islam are all the representations thrown up by specific mutually exclusive dualist ontological categories. Racism that emanates from the white man's worldview is therefore ontologically constituted racism.

I am a person of the periphery seeking liberation, which can never be found within the ambit of the white man's worldview. For the white man's worldview ontologically replicates his racism, for it is organically vital to the survival of his worldview. To remain within the white man's paradigm and seek liberation from his paradigm is a misnomer in terms. I simply cannot grasp liberation within a worldview that must constantly constitute me as an inferior sub-human species in order to re-affirm its hegemony.

By Summation.

Said, walking within Foucault's worldview inevitably replicates the antinomies and agnostic of Foucault's worldview. The first of these is his refusal to grasp the discursive ruptures he himself creates within his text. Said refuses to depart the white man's worldview and in doing so he has to make some sensational acrobatic tricks to preserve the integrity of his enterprise.

The first textual instance of acrobatic skills is as follows: "The Arab world today is an intellectual, political, and cultural satellite of the United States. This is not in itself to be lamented; the specific form of the satellite relationship, however is." (Said 1979). In my 'self', my personage as a person of the periphery this is the most brutal cut of all visited upon us by Said. In this statement he refuses to recognize, to believe in our ability to offer up, to challenge the white man's hegemonic worldview with alternate worldviews of the periphery. Said calmly and matter of factly states that satellite hood is the periphery's lot in life. In this manner he affirms the white man's metaphysic that drives his worldview and his own ambivalence as a black skinned, blue eyed boy; which is but another "type", a "thing" constituted by the white man's racist discourse of power/ knowledge.

The fatalistic self- immolation of the passage quoted above forms a dualist double with the passage quoted as follows: "the real issue is whether indeed there can be true representation of anything, because they are representations, are embedded first in language and then in the culture, institutions, and political Ambience of the representor." (Said 1979). "If the latter alternative is the correct one (as I believe it is), then we must be prepared to accept the fact that a representation is eo ipso implicated, intertwined, embedded, interwoven with a great many other things besides the "truth" which is itself a representation." (Said 1979). "What this must lead us to methodologically is to view representation (or misrepresentations - the distinction is at best a matter of degree) as inhabiting a common field of play defined for them, not by some inherent subject matter alone, but by some common history, tradition, universe of discourse." (Said 1979). As you read and re-read the passage quoted above the inescapable conclusions are: firstly, Said is in fact apologizing for the white man's genocide towards us. The very metaphysic that drives the white man's discursive structures, his ontology of racism and the consequent "effects" of the metaphysic are absolved of blame, of being culpable, for truth is relative.

Representations always serve their discursive master and given the fact that we of the periphery share the same discursive structures and spaces with the white man, blame must then be assigned at the level of language and discourse. In a very circular dualist danse macabre Said is in effect placing the blame for the white man's genocide against us at the doorstep of language and discourse. He can do this for he carries with him Foucault's burden, his agnostic, and his antinomy, which he never resolved in his works. This agnostic is the question of the transcendence, the omnipotence of discourse in a worldview in which language is afforded primacy and centrality in the ontology of being.

Said's position on representation/ misrepresentation, truth/ untruth comes straight out of Foucault's agnostic, for Said can only constitute an apologetic for the white man's genocide given his acceptance of Foucault's position of the transcendence/ omnipotence of discourse. Said is therefore saying in effect that the devil made the white man do it, the devil that is discourse.

Secondly, Said's embrace of Foucault's worldview has clearly resulted in Said becoming infected with Foucault's terminal illness, which was metaphysic nihilism. Foucault imprisoned himself in a worldview that was in fact a prison, for he never strove to discover an alternate metaphysic in which to ground himself. Said walked into the same pitfall which forced his blatantly nihilist passages previously quoted in my text. Above all Said's "Orientalism" offers no liberation, no alternate worldview driven by a metaphysic that is diametrically opposed to the white man's worldview. It is sadly apparent that he could not attempt this enterprise in "Orientalism" for he perceptually saw no viable alternative worldviews from the periphery worthy of his enterprise. So, writing from a fatalistically nihilist discourse with its worldview/ perspective Said insists to the people of the periphery if rape is inevitable lie back and enjoy.

Ultimately, I can understand Foucault's refusal to abandon his worldview for he was in the final instance the quintessential white man. But, Said is non-white, Palestinian Arab, the quintessential white man's other, and his textual position can then only be explained as yet another example of non-white immolation. For no matter what Said does, says or how much he affirms the white man's worldview can never affirm his non-white humanity. The best the said worldview offers Said is honorary white status, a freak in a white academic sideshow.

In conclusion, Said's work Orientalism is then the product of the application of Foucault's worldview towards the conceptualization of Ontological Racism as constituted by the white man's metaphysic. The Foucault/ Said continuum enabled me to finally transcend what has always been a perceptive obstacle for those of the periphery who once situated ourselves in the discourse of historicism, specifically historical materialism.

The resilience of racism from the middle ages to the "postmodern condition" in the white man's linear history has always caused serious perceptual problems. For the simple reason that racism transcended modes of production, superstructures, social formations; in fact, racism refused to be contained within the limits set for it by historicist conceptualizations. Foucault and Said simply and clinically dismiss the historicist problematic and points to the discursive structure, "effect", representation and metaphysic. But this creates the nihilist persuasion, which can only be transcended by a flight from the white man's worldview.

This flight to a worldview that dismisses the notion of the primacy and centrality of language enables me now to reflect upon the role of discourse in such a worldview. This alternate worldview enables me to juxtapose both worldviews and in so doing focus on the different ways specific worldviews replicate themselves at the level of the human subject. In turn, Said's position on Islam and the genesis of the white man's Orientalism indicates the basis of my position that the Islamic worldview continues to be locked in a struggle for hegemony with the white man's worldview.

The focus of my enterprise of research is then to locate the Jamaat al Muslimeen within the Islamic worldview. By situating their position within the Islamic worldview one can then trace, map and textualise the strands of the worldview that influenced the action of July 27th, 1990. I am then showing the flow of perceptions, the matrices of perceptions that enabled the Jamaat Al Muslimeen to respond to specific realities perceived by themselves via the mechanism of the coup d'état.

It is therefore incumbent upon me to map the perceptive signposts that sent specific signals to the Jamaat Al Muslimeen. To then map the schemata of alternatives offered by the Islamic worldview given the worldview conditioned perceptions of the reality. And finally, to map the mechanism of choice which accepted the military alternative.

The linchpin of this exercise is an understanding of the Islamic worldview and the specific streams of discourse, which flowed into the Jamaat Al Muslimeen. In this enterprise I am alone in my endeavor, as Said has taken me so far but not far enough for reasons stated before.

The text that follows upon this is the product of my attempt to come to grips with realities/ experiences external of me within the Islamic worldview. I have in effect no academic signposts with which, like Hansel and Gretel of the famous fable, to mark my pilgrimage. There are innumerable academic questions to be answered, with the most pressing of these in my mind dealing with the specificities of alternate non- white worldviews of the periphery, for it is lunacy to simply transpose Foucault's constructs upon alternate worldviews.

What is necessary, vital to the enterprise of the alternate worldviews of the periphery is for the mental workers of the periphery to now immerse themselves in the alternate worldviews. By doing this immersion of our fractured selves we can then undertake the task of articulating the metaphysic of these worldviews. My enterprise contained in this text is hopefully my contribution to the task of giving voice to our alternate worldviews, but more so, it is intended to be my opening knock in a life's work at the wicket.

A Frenzied Prancing with Foucault

On the afternoon of July 27th, 1990 members of the Jamaat al Muslimeen, by their actions, ushered in a new era in the postcolonial history of the people of Trinidad and Tobago. As a people we crossed the Rubicon that fateful Friday afternoon and the aftershocks of the event continue to reverberate through the body politic of the nation.

The decision to undertake the task of research on a specific aspect of the events of July 27th, 1990 and thereafter, bounded by the restraints of formal institutionalized academia and to express the catharsis of that said journey within the textual and otherwise limits of the dualist Western worldview speaks volumes about the intensity of the pain that calls out for discursive or non-discursive expression.

With mental pictures of the television broadcasts made by Imam Yasin Abu Bakr on that fateful Friday afternoon the link was made with imagined images of the nineteenth century French parricide Pierre Riviere. One saw two individuals who by their actions reached out and ripped a hole, made a rupture in the fabric of the ruling discourses of the day. And in and with the rupture created, a twilight world of a ruling discourse in ebb, seeking to regroup itself to reclaim its rightful hegemony, one saw two persons, worldviews apart seizing the opportunity to state their discursive worldview.

The worldview of the powerless when finally articulated imparts panic of the frenzied variety on the consciousness of the ruling elites. The frenzied panic continues unabated in our society whilst the worldview of Pierre Riviere was absorbed, turned against itself and relegated as a footnote of history. The difference being the inability of the ruling discourses of the day in Trinidad and Tobago to absorb and turn against itself the worldview of the Jamaat al Muslimeen.

In my attempts to grapple with the coup d'état of July 27th, 1990 and the Jamaat al Muslimeen I was locked in a frenzied 'prancing' with M.

Foucault. I looked towards the works of Michel Foucault to provide the insights to create a theoretical framework or matrices through which the Jamaat al Muslimeen would be sifted leaving behind the power/ knowledge structures which are the basis of the ruling discourse and the challenging discourse of the Jamaat al Muslimeen.

The methodological basis or inspiration for the work I found in "I Pierre Riviere, having slaughtered my mother, my sister, and my brother", Edited by Michel Foucault.

In the foreword to the work M. Foucault in speaking of the way in which the work to follow was conceptualized states: "But we were still faced with the question of publication. I think that what committed as to this work, despite all our differences of interests and approaches was that it was a 'dossier' that is to say, a case, an affair, an event that provided the intersection of discourses that differed in origin, form, organization, and function". (Foucault 1982 Pg. x). "But in their totality and their variety they form neither a composite work nor an exemplary text, but rather a strange contest, a confrontation, a power relation, a battle among discourses and through discourses". (Foucault 1982 Pg. x). "I think the reason we decided to publish these documents was to draw a map, so to speak of those combats, to reconstruct these confrontations and battles, to rediscover the interaction of discourses as weapons of attack and defense in the relations of power and knowledge". (Foucault 1982 Pg. xi). After prolonged frenzied grappling with Foucault towards creating a theoretical framework through which the coup d'état of 1990 would be exposed to the 'gaze' or a panopticon of the mind, the enterprise of research was determined and finalized. In keeping with the worldview of Foucault I was called upon to go out and first map the discourse of the Jamaat al Muslimeen with specific emphasis on its origin, form, organization and function.

Secondly, with this done I would then map the intersection of discourses towards uncovering: "the interaction of those discourses as weapons of attack and defense in the relations of power and knowledge." (Foucault 1982 Pg. xi). The task of the researcher was conceptualized as being biased in favour of the silenced discourses of the weak and powerless, therefore the discourse of the Jamaat al Muslimeen became the entire focus of the research effort. The discourse was to be recorded during the final days of the ebb tide of the ruling discourse as it steeled itself to reassert its hegemony with urgent, desperate longings for the unchallenged integrity of its totality.

The product of the exercise was not only providing catharsis, but it was to extol the relevance of Foucault's intellectual enterprise to the study and understanding of social events in a peripheral dependent third world nation. The act of recording an ascendant discourse of the powerless, no matter how short its ascendancy measured in linear time, was the defining accomplishment and its relevance to the world of formalized dualist academia was of secondary importance, even bordering on irrelevance.

Since the heady days of post-coup d'état 1990 much water has flowed under the bridge and the structure of this chapter and the one to follow would reflect and mirror the mental journey of the researcher. The fundamentalist enterprise conceived of no need to engage in a debate with Western social theorists over either the Islamic discourse in which the Jamaat al Muslimeen situated itself or the relevance of Foucault's thought.

But the researcher was not spared the rude awakening by the texts experienced that the Islamic discourse has been locked in various levels of contradictions with various Western discourses for its entire existence to date. The textual experiences of the researcher not only confirmed the deep-seated incompatibility between the Islamic and Western worldviews, but the fact that this hostility between worldviews has spanned the course of European history since its initial contact with Islam.

That the unabated contradiction or collision of the discourses has left its mark on the development of linear, dualist Western social theory is for the researcher now a given. And following upon this arises the need to come to grips with the strands of theory which have through their human articulators contributed to the development of the Western discourse on or about Islam. Simply, because these human articulators have not only influenced how the West views or experiences the Islamic discourse, they have also impacted upon how persons situated within the Islamic discourse view or experience themselves and the West.

The mechanism through which this intersection of discourses was realized on an existential basis was colonialism and its sterile mutant, the postcolonial condition. The artifice of colonialism created myriads of discursive intersections where the mutually antagonistic worldviews met and engaged in a never-ending war of attrition played out with, on and through the human subjects of discourse.

In colonized geographic areas where Islam was once in discursive ascendancy, amongst those discursively powerless, debate arose which focused on the inherent weaknesses of the Islamic discourse, which facilitated its colonial dependency. To rectify these perceived weaknesses various solutions were formulated with one common genesis, their adverse reaction to and refusal to accept the ascendancy of Western discourse.

And with one common methodology; exposition of the perceived nature of Western discourses; critiques of the said discourse showing its contradiction to and with Islamic discourse and the framework for change leading to an Islamic resurgence were formulated.

The upshot of it all for the researcher is that whether the researcher wanted to recognize it or not, the Islamic discourse has been from its inception locked in contradiction with various Western discourses. Islamic discourse by dint of the structure of its various schools of thought mirrors the dialectical relationship that has and still impacts on the perceptual developments of both discourses. Islamic discourse offers signposts of this dialectical contention or discursive intersections stretching from Plato to the post-modern theorists of the decade of the 90's in the twentieth century.

In the act of turning away from the task of mapping the linear thought of Western social theory of relevance to the researcher, in this mapping exercise of the Islamic discourse the researcher could have then only mapped a sterile, closed worldview which was incapable of proactive excursions and doomed to reactive involuntary responses to the pin pricks of colonialism and neo-colonialism.

To have mapped such a phenomenon not worthy of the representation of discourse a la Foucault would have been to confirm the worldview of the Western discourse. Perhaps then the Western discourse in itself and for itself refuses to map the impact which Islamic discourse has and continues to have upon its development, and likewise the impact it has had and continues to have on the development of the Islamic discourse. A mapping exercise that defeats the enterprise biased in favour of the voiceless, the silenced, had then to be rejected with due haste and diligence.

The researcher for the sake of the ontological integrity of the enterprise now had to stand before the mirror and accept the need to experience the intellectual strands of the Western discourse in order to grasp and grapple with the sticky strands of the web of Islamic discourse. For the researcher situated in the periphery, the realization of having to journey to two disparate centers of two contradictory worldviews in order to grasp either one, it was and is an experience akin to schizophrenic multiple personalities. All locked in a battle for hegemony, all vocalizing language constructs which evoke images of brutal incompatibility, and immanent fragility but all personalities are not mutually exclusive, sovereign, omnipotent nor omniscient for they are doomed to share a single physical entity; the body or the Earth in its geographic expression.

Franz Fanon's Black Mirage

As the researcher stood before the mirror image, pondering the psychic brutality of once again making a pilgrimage to the shrines of the hegemonic European assembly line of discursive production in order to lay bare the structures of a silenced discourse, the reverie flashed new insights into Fanon's position on the nature of the existence he termed the 'black mirage.'

Franz Fanon expresses the reality in one instance as follows: "Then with his eyes on Africa, the West Indian was to hail it. He discovered himself to be a transplanted son of slaves; he felt the vibration of Africa in the very depth of his body and aspired only to one thing; to plunge into the great 'black hole' It thus seems that the West Indian, after the great white error, is now living in the great black mirage" (Fanon 1969 Pg. 27).

The pilgrimage via the written texts produced perceptual shifts in the mind of the researcher, who finally accepted the existence of sensory experiences the expression of which lay outside the realm of the spoken word and written language. The rejection of the primacy or the centrality of language in the creation of the person enabled the researcher to reach past the dualist worldview and experience a state of existence, which allows one the luxury of leaping past the state Fanon termed the 'great black mirage'. There was now a pilgrimage but no pilgrim; the journey was focused on the task of visiting the shrines of both discourses in conflict without the burden of striving to work within the confines of either or both discourses. The pilgrim was now devoid of the baggage that belonged to both discourses, by holding allegiance to none the pilgrim is not forced to evade and to immerse in language, constructs which attack the very foundations of their specific worldview/ discourse. To liberate the pilgrim, the pilgrim has to embrace the mirage and by doing so disperse it for its corporeality is hinged on a specific discursive worldview.

The journey back to the future with Foucault as the beacon or the homing device starts with the prominent European theorists of the era of the capitalist mode of production. The reason for this time frame which limits the move back to the future lies in the fact that it is with the appearance of European expansionism based on the capitalist mode of production that the violent discursive intersections occurred. For the simple fact that European colonialism was now set upon its strategy of integrating geographical areas defined as under the control of the Islamic discourse into Europe's colonial empires. European colonialism was no longer attempting to circumvent geographic entities under the hegemony of the Islamic discourse as in the era of Columbus, Vasco Da Gama, Pizarro and Cortez. European colonialism bred by the new kid on the block, industrial capitalism, was now virulent, technologically superior and in possession of a worldview that saw the world, its resources and its non-European peoples as objects to be appropriated and utilized solely for the benefit of the European race. For the first time in the history of the human race a mode of production developed which not only enabled a race to view itself as the centre of the universe of race types on our planet, but it enabled that race to conquer and hold entrapped the non-European races which fell under its dominance.

The capitalist mode of production therefore enabled the creation of laboratories of dominance from which sprang streams of racist discourse, the basis of which was the creation of the 'other' differentiated on ascriptive criterion. The entire edifice of scholarship created and left to posterity by Franz Fanon would not have been possible without recognition of the nexus between European colonial racism and the capitalist mode of production.

Fanon in recognition of this expressed the nexus as follows: "Here we have proof that questions of race are but a superstructure a mantle, an obscure ideological emanation concealing an economic reality." (Fanon 1969 Pg. 18). "Racism has not managed to harden. It has had to renew itself, to adapt itself, to change its appearance. It has had to undergo the fate of the cultural whole that informed it." (Fanon 1969 Pg. 32). "The perfecting of the means of production inevitably brings about the camouflage of the techniques by which man is exploited, hence the forms of racism." (Fanon 1969 Pg. 35).

In addition, Fanon was to devote himself to the study of the contradictions that grew out of the intersections of the Islamic and European discourses in colonial Algeria. Out of this experience Fanon would posit that the struggle towards decolonization must not and cannot only focus itself on the physical removal of the colonizer. The pre-colonial cultural forms must be de-colonized, re-awakened for the physical expression of colonial domination was expressed/ represented at the level of the cultural patterns of the colonized.

It is best at this juncture to let Fanon speak: "Historic observation reveals, on the contrary, that the aim sought is rather a continued agony than a total disappearance of the pre-existing culture. This culture once living and open to the future becomes closed, fixed in the colonial status, caught in the yoke of oppression both present and mummified, it testifies against its members. It defines them in fact without appeal. The cultural mummification leads to a mummification of individual thinking." (Fanon 1969 Pg. 34). Fanon so cogently and with empathy put his psychic finger in the wound of the colonized. But even more so he articulated, via European discourses, the means through which persons entrapped within the realm of Western discourse can experience the pain of the colonized persons of the Islamic discourse.

For the researcher it was through the insights offered by Fanon, the ability to identify with and feel the pain of the Palestinian Intifada as they match boys with stones against men with assault weapons. Fanon never spared us the emotion of his pain and convictions and in one extract he quantified the mental imagery of an existence never experienced by the researcher. He is speaking to the French colonizer from the worldview of the colonized of the Islamic discourse. He states: "This man whom you thingify by calling him systematically Mohammed, whom you reconstruct or rather whom you dissolve, on the basis of an idea an idea you know to be repulsive [you know perfectly well you rob him of something for which not so long ago you were ready to give up everything, even your life] well, don't you have the impression that you are emptying him of his substance?" (Fanon 1969 Pg. 14).

The trip back to the future therefore had to make a stop at the shrine of Fanon for to by-pass Fanon and recommence the researcher's journey at the most prominent European critic of capitalism would be to run the risk of embracing dominant discursive worldviews uncritically to the detriment of an enterprise situated in the periphery. Fanon warns us, the people of the periphery, to beware of failing to see, to perceive racism and its nexus with the capitalist mode of production, but more so he insists that racism is itself part of the superstructural moment that is culture.

Perhaps he was talking from the perceptive modalities of the Frankfurt or critical school of Western Marxism. This would certainly explain his focus on culture as a realm of action necessary towards the de-colonization of colonial peoples. More so it would also explain his incessant stress on the centrality of the human being to the entire exercise of liberation for he believed in liberation as an attainable and accessible goal more so in the colonial world.

He never therefore fell into the trap; others have fallen into, of de-coupling the nexus between racism/ cultural moments and the capitalist mode of production. To de-couple the nexus forces one to create a metaphysic of racism in which one seeks to create an ontological nexus for racism and the 'essence' of the race views, world views, discourses of any specific race. By creating an ontological racism one seeks no link between the discourse of racism and the material relations of any given society. The proponents of ontological racism are compelled to rewrite history to justify their metaphysical construct seeking to find instances of a racism which has persisted through/ across/ with linear time, regardless of the material relations/ mode of production.

In some instances, the same holds true for the exercise towards creating an ontological patriarchy. The enterprise of creating an ontological racism from the standpoint of the periphery is but again another example of another project spawned by the 'great black mirage' or in keeping with Fanon the 'great Arab mirage.' For in fact what is being forwarded is ontological racism in reverse, whereby the constructs of the colonizer are simply reworked or 'blackened'/ 'Arabized' to be released upon the colonizer/ ex-colonizer.

The circularity of the constructs is evident and the basis for the entire enterprise is the hegemony language enjoys on all sides of the discursive intersection. Instances within the Islamic discourse indicate that the tendency towards ontological racism in reverse is certainly fed by a fanatical rejection of Marx's ontology of being. The reader should note that the researcher grappled with Marx's ontology rather than Marxist ontology.

My concern is with Marx the theorist as he wrestled with this newborn revolutionary mode of production capitalism, and the ontology that nursed and nurtured his discursive worldview. The researcher cares little about the Althusserian debate over the early and later Marx, the Hegelian sojourn and the epistemological break that followed. Arising out of the need to do research, Marx the complex human being was discovered and appreciated.

To take a theorist out of a construct of linear time, rejecting the belief in linear progression enables the researcher to view the theorist for what he or she was or is, finite human beings with all the accompanying shortfalls, compromises and delusions.

Marx re-searched throws up an ontology that is deceptively simple in its erection, but devastating in its discursive impact on both the European and Islamic discourses. Whilst in the process of articulating Marx's ontology and juxtaposing it to that of the Islamic discourse it becomes readily apparent the reasons for the blatant, at times hysterical condemnation by adherents of the Islamic discourse. In fact, it is this aversion to 'Marx's atheism' that has fed the discursive growth of ontological racism in reverse.

But it is not only the ontology of Marx that has to be articulated because of its relevance to the Islamic discourse since European capitalist expansionism. The burning question of Marx and his position on European colonialism must also be addressed for both debates continue to reverberate within the Islamic discourse and other discourses of the periphery continually raising various questions on the relevance, applicability and desirability of Marx's worldview.

It is a debate, which continues to question the very relevance and desirability of the patrimony left to the peoples of the periphery by thinkers as Franz Fanon, Amilcar Cabral, C.L.R. James and Dr. Eric Williams. It is therefore of singular importance to once again re-address the debate through a worldview of the periphery, which is the basis of this body of research.

Marx's ontology/Epistemology/worldview.

The first premise is the existence of living human individuals differentiated from animals by the fact that man/ woman produces his/ her means of subsistence and indirectly produce their actual material life. A definite mode of life is the mode of production of any given historical epoch.

The nature of individuals is as a result of the material conditions determining their production as individuals. Therefore, consciousness can never be anything else than conscious existence, the existence of men is their actual life process. Production consists of material and mental production. The products of mental production of men are sublimates of their material life process. The products of both material and mental production are both empirically verifiable and bound to material premises. Consciousness is therefore from the very beginning a social product and remains so as long as men exist. Life is not determined by consciousness, but consciousness by life.

Language is practical consciousness, and it arises from the need, the necessity of the intercourse with other men. The mental and material division/ separation of labour creates the ability of consciousness to flatter itself that it is something other than the consciousness of existing practice. Consciousness can therefore emancipate itself from the material world and to proceed to the formation of 'pure' theory, theology, philosophy, ethics. But all forms and products of consciousness can be dissolved by the practical overthrow of the actual social relations, which gave rise to this idealistic humbug.

The sensuous world is not a thing given direct from eternity thereby unchanging, but is a dynamic product of industry and the state of society. The sensuous world is therefore the total living sensuous activity of the individuals composing it. Sensuous human activity is an objective activity and sensuousness is practical human sensuous activity.

The human essence is simply the ensemble of the social relations of a given mode of production. All social life is essentially practical and linked to human practice and its comprehension. Thinking that is isolated from practice is therefore a purely scholastic question. Material productivity being the basis of social relations results in social relations consisting of principles, ideas and categories. Principles, ideas and categories are historical and transitory products of social relations. The ideal arises from the material world reflected by the human mind and this reflection translated into forms of thought.

The existence of the division of labour based on the dichotomy/ schism between mental and material production confirms the existence of contradiction in any division of labour so configured. The existence of contradiction within the division of labour is a quite material, empirically verifiable act. The division of labour so configured explains the formation of ideas from material practice and not from or through the idea itself. This contradiction is nascent to a division of labour configured into mental and material production, thus it posits revolution as the driving force of history. Liberation is therefore an historical/ physical act, not a mental act and the genesis of liberation is situated in specific historical conditions. Circumstances make men first as much as men make circumstances. The conception of history is then materialist, and by extension historical materialism.

The ideas of the ruling class are in every epoch the ruling ideas. The class, which is the ruling material force, is its ruling intellectual force. A ruling class rules as thinkers, producers of ideas, thereby regulating the production and distribution of the ideas of their age. The ruling ideas are the ideal expression of dominant material relationships. The dominant material interests are grasped as ideas.

Marx speaks: "Philosophy and the study of the actual world have the same relation to one another as masturbation and sexual love." (Marx/ Engels 1974 Pg. 103). "The philosophers have only interpreted the world, in various ways, the point is to change it." (Marx/ Engels 1974 Pg. 123). Marx's worldview presented above has been reduced to its bare bones, its building blocks. It has been reduced to and presented in such a state to enable the researcher the luxury of seeking to uncover the worldview/ discursive basis, which informed the texts that were penned by Marx.

The potent strike force of Marx's worldview is his unceasing and unapologetic insistence on the need for and drive for achieving change in the world through human action grounded in the material relations of life. Practice is the be all and end all of all human mental and material production, and it must be defined by the concept of the inevitability of change in human social relations.

With specific reference to mental production, Marx poured scorn on the mental exercise of turning reflections on the material relations of existence to ideals in an attempt to break ideas away from the material base from which they sprang. Man, therefore, attempts to move mental production to its own specificity denying the inevitability of change in the material relations and consequently in the edifice of ideas. By so doing the products of mental production are estranged from the course of revolution, which is the locomotive of history.

Marx pours scorn on the mental exercises in futility of the philosophers, especially the idealists, who for him are the most despicable of the movement to deny the inevitability of change. Marx located this will to change in the very dynamics of any division of labour, wherein mental and material production appear as separate entities with the mental workers continually striving to create their own specificity, their own raison d'etre, thereby giving rise to the issue of thought, consciousness, the idea and the ideal. Within this division of labour, even though mental workers may view their enterprise as the representation of their specific actions, the developments within the structures of material production ensures the paramountcy of revolution.

In Marx's worldview, the central problematic was the liberation of man from the ravages of the mode of production he summed up as capitalism. He defined his entire corpus of mental production, his relevance as a thinker by his practice. His practice was relevant and correct because it accepted the primacy of material relations in the existence of man.

The mental process of conversion from the entrapped world of mental workers producing by and for them was apocalyptic in experience, in fact it was for Marx his discursive rupture. Marx relentlessly refused to accept capitalism as the climax of European civilization, and in this position he became the maverick for he placed on the political agenda of bourgeois capitalism the issue of a further stage of development in which the bourgeoisie would not and could not be in ascendancy.

Marx was the first to effectively do this because he framed his position in the positivistic language of the ruling discourses of the day. He trumpeted his position on the inevitability of revolution by using the trumpet of the bourgeoisie, i.e. – materialist, positivistic science. His was a revolution that was empirically verifiable, because you can verify the developments within the material relations of production; his was therefore the method of political economy.

The practice of Marx was based on his being a guerrilla in the war of the discourses. He played himself within the co-ordinates of bourgeois discourse, attacking it utilizing frames of reference, which were of that discourse, turning it against itself. When not playing mind games with the ruling discourses of the day he occupied himself with two other activities, which were inevitable given his worldview, i.e. – creating the means of an alternate discourse and the creation of the material means to achieve revolution.

When viewed in its totality Marx's lifelong achievement, his gift to posterity to the peoples of the world is the discursive rupture he affected through his work as a mental worker. Marx dared challenge the discursive hegemony of the European bourgeois class fed by a vision, which dared to look past and reject the position that capitalism was the climax of European civilization.

In this he was not unique, for Fourier, Saint-Simon had also held similar positions; the difference with Marx being the concept of the centrality and inevitability of revolution carried on the backs of a class now silenced, the proletariat, but chosen to become hegemonic because of developments in the mode of production.

Marx was insisting to the bourgeoisie that in their drive to maximize profits and entrap the world in trading systems the seeds of their destruction were sown. Marx believed in his constructs, which made up his worldview, thereby he talked the talk and walked the walk. He transcended the world of mental work by linking it to practice founded on the material relations of production.

The basis of the praxis of Marx was therefore not only the constant cut and thrust of guerrilla warfare within the ruling discourses of the day, but involved the task of creating an alternative discourse for the silenced. The basis of this alternative discourse of Marx was a worldview, which rejected the hegemony of the bourgeois class and its entire edifice of ideas or bourgeois consciousness. The value of any product of the twofold division of labour under bourgeois capitalism was measured against the yardstick of the proletarian revolution.

Marx, by turning his back on the German idealist philosophers and immersing himself in the materiality of proletarian revolution, was the example of the mechanics of the discursive shift via rupture and this in fact became his biggest bugbear in the world of political agitation amongst and with the working class of Europe; for he was unwilling to accept as equals persons in the working class movement who had not undergone the intensity of catharsis necessary in his worldview to effect the change from one discursive field to the next.

By his discursive shift Marx was able to create a language of the proletarian revolution, consequently a language of an alternative discourse of the silenced. The language framed the vision of the proletarian revolution and reverberations of the mind created patterns of the spoken and written language of the discourse. From Engels to Mao Tse-Tung, through Amilcar

Cabral to Frederic Jameson and Jurgen Habermas today, the language of the discourse founded by Marx lives on.

The researcher sits and experiences via television conversations with members of the People's Liberation Army of the People's Republic of China in 1994 and the language of the proletarian revolution dominates the experience. The legacy of Marx lives wherever the words are spoken, written, attacked, debated over, rejected or accepted for his enterprise was successful within the confines of his worldview.

Marx's worldview was predicated on praxis, praxis toward a fundamental discursive shift and to attain that shift there must be rupture. Rupture at the level of the twofold division of labour, to articulate this rupture language was the primary tool, hence the need to create a language to proselytize, to analyze, to confront, and to motivate in both levels of the division of labour, hence the language of the proletarian revolution.

Given a worldview hinged on praxis, it was not surprising to locate the legacy of Marx's praxis within the sphere of working class political expression. One aspect of that legacy is Marx's relentless attacks upon what he considered to be the challenges of inadequate worldviews within the working class movements. His was always one of relentless attack without compromise as he apparently strove for the hegemony of his worldview; his attacks on Stirner and Lasalle readily come to mind.

For him there was no other worldview, which recognized the historic destiny of the proletariat, and consequently the centrality of revolution, therefore conflicting worldviews within the working class movements had to be purged. The legacy of his political praxis was the creation of broad based working class movements throughout Europe, flanked by a corpus of mental workers striving to commit class suicide by serving the interests of the working class through mental production primarily.

Marx successfully replicated his own ambivalent class position vis a vis the proletariat through his worldview/ discourse and this replication continued throughout the history of the working class and his worldview.

Engels, Lenin, Luxemburg, Trotsky, Mao, Fanon, James, Castro, Che, Giap, Ho Chi Minh, Cabral, Althusser, Marcuse, Adorno, Habermas and Jameson all carry the mark of Marx, i.e. – their ambivalence via their petty bourgeois class origin vis a vis the proletarian revolution.

Marx therefore created and inspired an enterprise of mental workers in the interest of a class they don't share the same class origins with. He was able to do this through the creation of an alternate discourse held together and articulated via the language of the proletarian revolution. Herein lies the relevance of Marx and his worldview to the researcher, for it allows the luxury of understanding discourse and its operation through the medium of juxtaposed discourses in conflict or at their discursive intersections. Marx was to create from within the bowels of the ruling bourgeois discourses of the day the most potent discursive rupture to have emerged out of capitalism. Thereby, altering forever the development of bourgeois discourses since the 19th century of European history and experience.

Of specific relevance to the present body of work Marx's worldview would in time intersect with the Islamic discourse, primarily through the debate spawned by the subjugation of Dar ul Islam under the yoke of European colonialism of the capitalist epoch. The mental workers of Islamic discourse looked towards Marx's worldview for insights into capitalism and the new variety of colonialism bred by this mode of production. The movement of ideas expressed by various mental workers of the Islamic discourse range from the position of blatant rejection of Marx's worldview for various reasons, to persons who accepted the worldview and continually strove to interpret Islamic realities through the perceptions of Marx's worldview.

The fundamental question presents itself at this stage of the research demanding interpretation, which is: What is the relevance of Marx's worldview to the experiences of people of the periphery? Through the research the areas of specific relevance to this question are: (a) the position of Marx on the question of religion and its relevance to grappling with the Islamic discourse; (b) the position of Marx on the question of European colonialism during the capitalist epoch; (c) what is the relevance of Marx's worldview to the non-capitalist world of his epoch? Is it a non-entity begging for relegation to the scrap heap of bourgeois academia?

Marx's position on religion is entirely consistent with his ontological position in that religion exists at the level of practice and that is empirically verifiable. But since the driving force of religion cannot be verified, i.e. – the supreme deity, empirically then religion must be seen for what it is an 'ideal'. For Marx, religion was therefore the product of the mind of man and can only be a reflection of the material relations of man's existence. Any change in the relations of production would therefore effect change in the superstructural instance that is religion.

The primary concern of Marx was the process of midwifery that would ensure the smooth delivery of the proletarian revolution, which was conceived in the womb of industrial capitalism. The hegemony of religion in the consciousness of European man was for Marx already broken since the Renaissance and relegated to the scrap heap of European history with the French revolution, the quintessential bourgeois led social upheaval.

Marx's viewing of the non-European world was and could only have been informed by the need to discover international developments, which would have hastened the birth contractions of his brave new world. In the textual patrimony Marx left, we of the periphery were peripheral; our only importance was our unwitting contributions to the development of the fetus bourgeois capitalism were carrying.

Marx's perceptions informed the way he viewed the periphery and these perceptions were fed by revo-centrism and ethno-centrism. Marx through his writings, mainly for the New York Daily Tribune, on the non-European predominantly colonized world showed signs of a most disturbing axiom, that is/ was a fundamental construct of European ontological racism.

The co-ordinates of the axiom posit that Europe gave birth to industrial capitalism, which enabled Europe to colonize significant expanses of the world's geography. Europe stands unchallenged, for no other civilization has been able to duplicate such a feat and challenge the hegemony of

Europe. Therefore, there must be specific, intrinsic aspects of European civilization unique to the European experience, which enabled this leap in the history of man.

That Marx accepted this axiom is beyond doubt and to people of the periphery the debate over his acceptance of it or not is a non-starter and should be left by the wayside, as there are more salient issues to be debated with reference to Marx. The reality is that a range of perceptions can emerge from the co-ordinates of the axiom, from what some call ethno-centrism to blatant racism.

For the researcher of the periphery, the question remains what is the fundamental difference between ethno-centrism and Ku Klux Klan racism? We of the periphery did not create the axiom; we continue to be only people trapped within the co-ordinates of the axiom, therefore for us the exercise in shaving hairs is for the manipulators of the axiom, not its victims. We, the victims, can only focus on the effects and the impact of his writings on our visualizations of ourselves as persons, this is what we judge Marx by.

When we read the article published in 1853 titled "The British Rule in India" we can only come to one conclusion – that the man suffered from the common European ailment of ontological racism. In the article "The British Rule in India", which shows the perceptive clarity which enabled him to make some articulation of the material relations of production and the social relations thrown upon them and the consequent impact British colonialism would have had and did have on this mode of production.

The pain of the dislocation and destruction wrought by the impact of capitalism on non-capitalist India clearly bothered him, but to blame the suffering of dislocation on the backwardness of the victim is too much for us to bear as people of the periphery. Marx then gave us a lesson in victimology for we bear the guilt for the actions of predatory Europeans. WHY -—For we are not the idyllic noble savages of the worldview of Rousseau. We suffer from maladies, afflictions and shortcomings as: "barbarian egotism" "this undignified, stagnatory and vegetative life" "this passive sort of existence, evoked on the other part in contradiction, wild, aimless, unbounded forces of destruction, and rendered murder itself a religious rite IN Hindostan." "that they transformed a self-developing social state into never changing natural destiny, and thus brought about a brutalizing worship of nature" (Kamenka 1983 Pgs. 329-336). For Marx then whatever is inflicted upon us is not unique in our historical past and present, but more so it needs to be inflicted for as a people we have failed in our historic duty by denying the ever-compelling primacy of change.

But at this juncture as mental workers it is our duty to ask why and more importantly how have we as peoples of the periphery, been able to waylay the juggernaut of history, unlike the European? Why did we stall on the inevitable march to capitalism? The answer lies outside of Marx's discourse for this is one of two central questions, which let loose the mongoose amongst the chickens of his discourse.

The researcher is not burdened by the never ending, never satiated demand to save Marx's worldview from itself, for as all discourse it is man-made and suffers from the weight of its finite limits. Therefore, it should have been allowed to fall in under its own weight, opening up spaces to facilitate the creation of a stream of fresh discourses, but the most potent and damaging blow made on Marx's worldview was the mindless cult of orthodoxy created by the heirs' of Marx's worldview. By walking away from the ontology of Marx they were condemned to dance the dance of circular futility, fed by their insistence on 'essences' and a metaphysic, rather than a discourse grounded in the material relations of their societies.

Of the two questions which induce the discursive rupture within Marx's discourse it is perhaps historical irony that one question jumps out of the relation of people of the periphery to European industrial capitalism and the question of the Asiatic mode of production. The second question that triggers the rupture is: 'Mr. Marx, where is your proletarian revolution born to European industrial capitalism?'

Question one inevitably deals with the inescapability and desirability of capitalism as conceived by Marx's linear progression of change. From the outset it is the position of the researcher, that the prolonged and aimless remonstrating over why only Europe achieved capitalism is itself an enterprise created by perceptions which measure the non-European world against the yardstick that European experience is established to be. It views European history as the 'norm', model and quintessence of all historical experience and denies us, the people of the periphery, our own unique specificity. It therefore wallows in the muck of ontological racism.

The question of relevance, therefore, can only be answered by uncovering the specific dynamic of historic entities of non-European civilization towards mapping the range of options via discourse, which existed in the perceptual fields of human endeavor before the onslaught of European colonialism. It is by only doing this can we then fully understand the full effects colonial domination had on the self-regenerating mechanisms of societies of the periphery.

Marx could not accomplish this for he was only interested in addressing the central issue of his worldview, and in addition his worldview did not have the perceptual tools to 'trap' the insights to accomplish the task in the interest of the people of the periphery. His enterprise was for and in the interest of the European and specifically European proletarian interests. His discourse was created to serve those ends and no matter how you tinker with his worldview, it cannot now or ever be expected to serve the interests of people who were silenced by Marx's discourse.

The reality of this position is sadly indicated by the adherents of Marx's discourse who situate themselves within the fields of the Islamic discourse. They without fail show the effects of applying a discourse to a perceptual reality to which the discourse is ontologically irrelevant. These people of Marx's discourse are therefore locked, not in a struggle hinged on change via developments in the material relations, but a struggle between deeply antagonistic ontologies that do not have the means for resolution, except via violent means of contradiction.

Persons who are burdened with Marx's discourse in Dar ul Islam have the additional millstone of Marx's dismissal of the peoples of Dar ul Islam in racist terms. Marx never distinguished his discursive statements on the colonial peoples from that of the bourgeois theorists on colonialism and in that he shared one common feature: his race perceptions of himself, the man in the mirror. The children of Marx in Dar ul Islam are in fact the children of Sisyphus as they relentlessly struggle up the mountain of praxis, an exercise in futility for they are discursively irrelevant. Pray tell where is their proletariat, the means of liberation chosen by history? There is none because the perceptual matrices being used come from an alien discourse, so in your netherworld existence, created by a praxis of futility and a Disneyland dream world, you hold on to the last weapon offered by your borrowed discourse. You attack, denigrate and dismiss the praxis of the people you exist to serve, using the racist judgments of the colonizers discourse. Therefore, Dar ul Islam is the prisoner of an instance of capital-religion, the society is backward, primitive and stagnated, semi-feudal, neo-patriarchal and flirting with modernity. The inevitable cause for its backwardness is the domination of that instance of production – Islam, the iron grip of which must be broken. The means to that end is to release the forces of modernity.

The cliches of analysis and the solutions to the problem are not new. Colonialism destroyed the basis of the pre-colonial modes of production and pulled us screaming and kicking into the linear capitalistic epoch. Marx applauded this act, but alas where is the modernity? For the colonial enterprise did not replicate the bourgeois capitalist mode of production the world over.

The clones of Marx's discourse continue to use racist yardsticks by which to measure our actions, whilst continuing to insist on solutions which did not before make us into the economic likeness of the European god-capitalism. He could not understand the dynamic unique to each pre-European colonial society he chose to come to grips with, for that would have required the creation of a non-European centred discourse of relevance to these societies.

Marx did not care for, nor need this new enterprise so he instead created a bastard child concept, which dismissed us to the margins of his textual production and his political praxis. The concept of the Asiatic mode of production in itself confirms Marx's viewpoint of endemic stagnation and stifled creativity as being the affliction of non-European societies.

There was simply no interest in finding the dynamic of these societies, for that would destroy the view that capitalism as a mode of production was the desirable terminus/ end point for linear human progress. Non-capitalistic alternatives of economic organization could not be entertained by Marx, for it placed in jeopardy his grand enterprise: the proletarian revolution. The non-capitalist periphery must be stagnant, for it cannot be anything else, and it must be awakened to its historical destiny: the capitalist mode of production.

Let Marx speak: "England, it is true, in causing a social revolution in Hindostan, was actuated only by the vilest interests, and was stupid in her manner of enforcing them. But that is not the question. The question is, can mankind fulfill its destiny without a fundamental revolution in the social state of Asia? If not, whatever may have been the crimes of England she was the unconscious tool of history in bringing about the revolution." (Kamenka 1983 Pgs. 329-336). The conclusions are now inescapable as they jump out of the present enterprise of research of Marx and his discursive worldview. Namely, that the limitations of Marx's worldview do not enable the researcher to come to grips with the nexus between ideas and the material relations of the mode of production.

To seek insights into the continued debate over ideas and their materiality the researcher has to jettison the very perceptions of Marx's discourse, for his perceptions throw up conceptual frameworks of language which create discursive circularity, thereby limiting the ability of the user of these concepts to break out of the circularity of the discourse.

In other words, the perceptive structures of the discourse create the co-ordinates of the knowledge base of the discourse. To attempt to solve a perceptual shortfall of a discourse via utilising the very flawed knowledge producing structures of the very said flawed discourse is an exercise in futility, and a potent example of discourse at the level of consciousness and human action fighting to preserve its structural integrity in the face of the discursive rupture.

The development of 'orthodox', 'scientific' Marxism, critical theory and 'structural' Marxism are all affirmations of the human experience which teaches that ideas once framed, formulated and liberated continually aspire to create and achieve a dynamic of their own, in a bid to ensure longevity, amongst other things.

Scientific, structural and humanist Marxism have one commonality of their enterprise, which is to preserve the discourse of Marx that was of specific importance to their perceptive enterprise at that time. This allowed them to chop, discard and re-arrange the concepts of the discourse to come up with a new version of the discourse, which satisfied their perceived needs of the day towards creating a discursive knowledge of relevance to their historical epoch.

Discursive ruptures and discursive intersections forced the animators of Marx's patrimony to continually strive to create knowledges of relevance, not only in contending with bourgeois discourses, but the deepening rift between the perceptions of the class the discourse gave voice to and the framers of the discourse, but also even more so the growing call of the silenced for a discourse which gave them voice.

Women, ethnic minorities, homosexuals, children and non-discursive religion were all calling for voice, the end to silence, and there was an initial mad scramble to turn Marx's discourse into the omnibus of the silenced. A movement fundamentally doomed to failure, because the perceptual framework of Marx's discourse could not give voice to such widely disparate voices in their individual specificities and still maintain its structural integrity.

The schizophrenia of the discourse became evident as schism and fracturing threw up all forms and combinations of perceptual positions within the discourse. The parting of the ways was inevitable as the persons trapped in a discursive silence experienced the limitations of Marx's discourse simply walked away, and set about the task of creating discourse of specific relevance to their conditions. The colonized people of the periphery have also sought room on the omnibus of Marx's discourse. In a spectrum of various perceptive fields, people of the third world have wrestled with Marx's discourse from Mao Tse-Tung, to Ho Chi-Minh, to Amilcar Cabral, to Castro, to African and Arab socialism, people of the periphery have used Marx's discourse as the reference discourse from which to draw upon in their bid to build their discourses for their own specific social entities.

The discourses built upon Marx's discourse were locked in discursive contradiction with the body of bourgeois capitalist discourse from their inception. Under the steady and relentless assault from hegemonic discourse these discourses have caved in under pressure and have either ceased to command knowledge/ power or have mutated to the point of no longer being of the same species as at its inception.

Arab socialism of Nasser and the Ba'ath Party has relentlessly buckled under the pressures exerted by both the Islamic discourse and the capitalist discourse of the day. The fate of Arab socialism raises the question of the resilience of the Islamic discourse, and the need to de-construct this discourse to grapple with the concepts of a worldview which has for so long defined the resistance of Muslims the world over to the discursive hegemony of European capitalist discourse.

The Islamic discourse continues to show resilience, as it swamps, tumbles and falsifies the various experiments in social engineering, which attempted to remake Dar ul Islam in the image and likeness of capitalist Europe. In fact, the overthrow of the Shah of Iran signaled a new NAHDAH or Islamic resurgence as the Islamic discourse moved to recapture ground it abdicated only grudgingly to the alternate discourse. Algeria and its revolution, which Fanon gave his life for, is now for all intents and purposes immersed in the steel grip of the Islamic discourse. In Egypt, the capitalist discourse in alliance with the Egyptian 'secularist' discourse is fighting a last-ditch effort, and the ensuing battle would be violent for Egypt cannot be removed from the orbit of western interest without a collapse of the Arab secular order.

The discursive forces are gathering for the future mother of all battles between the discourses, and that is to be in the Muslim underbelly of the former Soviet Union. Already the capitalist western discourse has moved to eliminate a discursive intersection before it grows out of control and that is the Muslim population of Bosnia-Herzegovina. The contradictions can only be resolved via violence in whatever form, now called ethnic cleansing.

The strategy of secularization/ modernization failed miserably for they were founded on discourses built upon perceptive fields entirely alien to members of Islamic discourse. Be it Egypt, Algeria or Afghanistan, the Islamic discourse ripped the heart out of its challengers and has gone on the offensive as it sets about re-asserting a discursive hegemony based upon and fed by a vision of Dar ul Islam before the encroachment of European capitalist colonialism.

Islamic discourse has gone back to the future. Driven by the desire to grapple with this resurgent Islamic discourse the researcher discovered in the action of researching Marx that his discourse was of little value as a body of techniques of relevance to the act of grappling. His discourse trained one to grapple with an opponent who was your tag team partner, rather than your opponent in the encounter with Islamic discourse. In other words, in the intersection of Marx's discourse, bourgeois capitalist discourse and Islamic discourse, the common enemy of both Marx's discourse and bourgeois discourse is Islamic discourse.

The researcher had then to look elsewhere to seek other discourses of relevance to the enterprise at hand and this led to the re-searching of Max Weber.

Max Weber – A mental worker in flux.

The fundamental question is why research the patrimony of Weber? The initial reason was Weber's focus on instances of the capitalist structure in his quest to provide answers for capitalism's genesis in Europe. But with the daily grind of the project the researcher discovered a Weber never experienced before and that is the Weber wracked with questions over the relevance and direction of his intellectual enterprise. A Weber who began to flirt with Nietzsche, but fundamentally unwilling to peer over the precipice and then make the plunge that is a discursive rupture. As he backed away from the discursive rupture which beckoned him, he irretrievably slipped into the fatalism that the total belief in his rational god capitalism brought.

Weber's god had failed him miserably and he longed for freedom from the 'iron cage' that he himself fatalistically accepted supposedly. But his intellectual capacities drove him to seek room within the discourse and non-discursive solutions simultaneously. Alas he died a victim of his failings, his weakness in the face of the discursive rupture to make the jump, the discursive shift and be the creator of another discursive rupture in the tradition of Marx. He did not heed the call of the gift of brilliance he was burdened with, and it was left to Foucault to be the creator of another discursive shift in European discourses.

The re-search has pinpointed Weber of specific textual instances of singular importance for the enterprise at hand. There is the Weber of the texts with world religion as the central theme, which is his major works in the nexus between Protestantism and the genesis of capitalism in Europe. And then there is the Weber of the text 'Science as a Vocation '.

We deal with Weber of the texts on religion firstly. Re-search of these texts threw up a Weber that was expected, there were no surprises. Weber sets out to methodically prove to readers of the periphery that our worldviews did not preclude us to the pathway that led to bourgeois capitalism. In doing so, Weber drew on the most blatantly racist of the Orientalist works of the day in Europe and effectively worked it into his texts. The reason for this blatant acceptance of Orientalist texts can possibly be twofold: (1) Weber utilised texts, which proved his thesis and/ or (2) Weber was just not bothered with applying his famous theory of methodology in the study of peripheral societies.

Either way the final texts on religion in the periphery stand out as blatant propaganda of the racist ilk, rather than as milestones erected in the march of Weber's methodology. The question that comes to mind is whether Weber's enterprise of these texts was driven by the dictates of European ontological racism or was Weber so rigidly compartmentalized a scholar that he junked his methodology to prove his epistemology.

He shared with Marx the belief in the centrality of bourgeois European capitalism as the be all and end all of human linear progression and development. For Weber, the linchpin of capitalism was its innate rationality, hence its ability to create the inescapable 'iron cage'. The inmates of capitalism literally become prisoners of its insatiable thriving for rationality. There was therefore no debate between Marx and Weber over the desirability of attaining the stage of capitalism; and it was by this yardstick they both judged the enterprises of people of the periphery.

But Weber was to differ from Marx in the fact that Marx never compromised his methodology in coming to grips with the periphery, he simply created a new mode of production and left us in it and went his merry way. Weber in the texts "Religion and China", the "Sociology of Religion" and the "Religion of India" deliberately walked away from his methodology and engaged in the Orientalist enterprise in his bid to create a nexus between religion/ worldview and the genesis of European bourgeois capitalism. Weber was to stand Marx on his head, but did he?

Not for one instance did Weber in his texts on religion in the periphery ever consider if capitalism as a means of production was ever possible given the worldviews of the periphery. The answer is no, for before European capitalist colonialism there were on the agenda in these areas non-capitalist/ alternative models of economic organization and development.

For Weber it was blatant heresy to even conceive, much less put on his agenda, a hypothesis, which postulated non-capitalist/ alternate economies. And that is why Weber could not see, much less fix his 'gaze' upon the impact of European colonialism on economic systems of the periphery. For Weber, the attainment of capitalism was the yardstick of societal development used to measure the accomplishments of all non-capitalist societies.

How Weber constructed this yardstick of European rationality and whether it accurately reflected the subject of the exercise, Europe, is of little or no relevance to the researcher. What is of relevance to the researcher, is the fact that what Weber measured against his yardstick and pronounced us wanting was in fact a parody of the periphery generated by Orientalist discourse.

Let Weber speak: "The typical distrust of the Chinese for one another is confirmed by all observers. It stands in sharp contrast to the trust and honesty of the faithful brethren in the Puritan sects, a trust shared by outsiders as well." (Weber 1951 Pg. 232). Mr. Weber where is your vaunted scientific method for you are skating on thin ice. "Confucianism and Confucian mentality" (Weber 1951 Pg. 237) is the discourse with its worldview that constitutes the Chinese who are inferior to the Puritans of Europe. The Puritans are the living embodiment of the Protestant Ethic which spawned industrial capitalism in Europe whilst Confucianism spawned backwardness in China. Weber never articulates the methodological exercise from whence his conclusions came, for the 'mentality' came pre-cooked from the Orientalist discourse of Europe with all its racist and imperialist baggage, which Weber failed to purge.

After giving Weber the benefit of the doubt before the Orientalist agenda of his texts on non-Protestant religion became apparent with: (1) Weber's description of the 'indispensable ethical qualities of the modern capitalist entrepreneur.' In summation this white, European, capitalist was the re-incarnation of a white god on Earth. I quote: "radical concentration on god-ordained purposes the relentless and practical rationalism of the asceticist ethic; a methodical matter-of-factness in business management; a horror of illegal political, colonial booty and monopoly type of capitalism which depend on the favour of princes and men as against the sober, strict legality and the harnessed rational energy of routine enterprise." (Weber 1951 Pg. 247). With entrepreneurs as these, it is no wonder why we of the periphery are condemned to languish, the wretched of the Earth, under colonialism and then neo-colonialism. For we failed as a people to create such incarnations of the white god and must now accept that the wage for our sin is death. But in this Weber went too far as his racism behind the mask of scientific methodology forces a breach in the camouflagic continuity. His enterprise becomes exposed, but even today people of the periphery continue to be locked in a debate with and about Weber's methodology, whilst the gloved steel fist of his racism flails away at their non-white person. What is the relevance of a methodology when its creator discards it in the very texts he wrote about the periphery? A most compelling question and since I do not share, nor value Weber's discourse I leave the search for answers to the mental workers of the periphery who continue to situate themselves in Weber's discourse. (2) Weber's short analysis of Islamic discourse in the tradition of racist European Orientalism. In fact, Weber dismissed Islam as an aberration in world religions' experience with no redeeming qualities worthy of his attention. For him Islam reeked of irrationality, thereby making it unworthy for his enterprise of discovering rational religions in the periphery and comparing them to the mother of all rational religions, Protestantism, thereby understanding the ontological superiority of European civilization.

Weber therefore dismissed Islamic discourse via the blatantly racist concepts of anti-Islamic Orientalist discourses. In the publication 'Sociology of Religion', Weber gives the reasons why Islamic discourse could not be counted amongst the rational religions of the world. These are - (1) Weber states: "the religion was transformed from its pristine form into a national Arabic warrior religion and even later into a religion with very strong class emphasis." (Weber 1965 Pg. 262). Again: "The role played by wealth accruing from spoils of war and from political aggrandizement in Islam is diametrically opposed to the role played by wealth in the Puritan religion." (Weber 1965 Pg. 263). Again: "Even the ultimate elements of its economic ethic were purely feudal." (Weber 1965 Pg. 262). In summation the 'religion of a warrior class' based on a 'purely feudal' economic ethic is irrational. (2) But more so, Weber continues: "But Islam was never really a religion of salvation the ethical concept of salvation was actually alien to Islam." "An essential political character marked all the chief ordinances of Islam." (Weber 1965 Pg. 263). "There was nothing in ancient Islam like an individual quest for salvation, nor was there any mysticism." "Wealth, power and glory were all martial promises." (Weber 1965 Pg. 264). In summation, the religion was never otherworldly in its orientation because of its warrior ethic which stressed physical gratification in the here and now. The concept of Paradise stressed the continuation of physical gratification after death. (3) Weber continues: "the original Islamic conception of sin has a similar feudal orientation." "Islam displays other characteristics of a distinctively feudal spirit; the obviously unquestioned acceptance of slavery, serfdom, and polygamy; the disesteem for and subjection of women the essentially ritualistic character of religious obligations." (Weber 1965 Pg. 264). A feudal worldview pervades Islamic discourse, but even more appalling for Weber was the introduction of orgiastic and mystical religious elements into the Islamic discourse. For him the paramount hallmark of rational religion are the banishing of magic and the libido from its worldview. Rational religion replaces magic with the centrality and certainty of male activity; rational religion therefore situates man as the master creation for Weber.

A most problematic position, for if Weber had relied on his own methodology it should have dawned on him the gulf that exists between his depiction of magic as irrational and the viewpoints of the practitioners of magic. In addition, he saw the banishing of the libido from religious ceremony as marching in step with the defeat of magic in the strivings of specific religions to attain rationality.

For Weber, and this is the crux of his position on Islamic discourse, Islam was incapable of any march to rationality, unlike its two near Eastern monotheistic predecessors, because: (1) it was a religion of a national warrior class intent on maintaining its class hegemony through the acquisition of wealth via booty seized in war; (2) since it was a religion of a warrior class its worldview was essentially feudal, as was all its institutions in consequence, but Weber never defines what is 'feudal' and (3) Weber then postulated that orgiastic and magical elements entered the feudal warrior basis through Persia and India, which finalized a structure that reeked of irrationality. Islam was therefore unable to banish magic, the libido from its religious ceremonies and its feudal vision condemned Muslims to the circularity of immediate physical gratification rather than outer worldliness.

The brilliance of Weber shines through in this exposition on Islam, for in so few words he managed to use every blatant lie, half-truth and innuendo which fed the whole phalanx of Orientalist racist stereotypes used against the Muslims of the colonial and neo-colonial world. The methodology of the exposition is not unique to him; it is common to a discourse, which represented a geographic entity, a counter discourse, and an alternative worldview. In his methodology, there is no valid historical method, much less a materialist reading of the phenomena. Islamic discourse is dismissed as the product of the narrow economic needs of a class of warriors, so steeped and reeking of irrationality it could only be destined to expire under the weight of Orientalist rationality.

Islam for Weber was the merging of three disparate streams, which could only have combined to create a colossus with feet of clay. These streams were the initial ancient Islam of the Prophet (uwbp) with its only validity being a pietist worldview. Secondly, the powerful warrior class whose only interest was war and the creation of an empire to serve their narrow class interests. Thirdly, the dervish and Sufi mystics from India and Persia who introduced the libidinal and magical tendencies.

At the heart of this polyglot of irrationality was Mohammed, an individual of dubious sexual morals saddled with a huge ego problem. To answer

Weber is perhaps a tedious task because the Orientalist discourse from which he spoke does not listen, for their task has been accomplished as they represented a reality in favour of the dominance of the represener over the represented.

The Orientalist discourse took millions of the members of the Islamic discourse and turned them into the 'other' of European Orientalist/ colonial discourse. Thereby creating the discursive foundation for the massive enterprise of European capitalist colonialism. But some debate with Weber is needed, simply because the silenced must learn to create discourse which gives them voice.

From the outset Mr. Weber it is prudent to point out the following: (1) the historical interpretations upon which your enterprise was based are at best open to the constant process of re-interpretation, at worst propaganda; (2) the tendency to resort to psychologizing to support your position is totally unacceptable given a man of your methodological credentials – therefore, your talk of the 'Chinese mentality' and the libidinal drive of the Prophet Mohammed cannot withstand the scrutiny of your methodology and (3) the use of undefined terms leaves the door open to a spectrum of interpretations, but more so for racist stereotyping. A salient example is the description of the 'feudal economic ethic' of Islam and the 'feudal spirit' of Islam. What is your definition, the panoptic vision you defined into the use of 'feudal' with reference to the Islamic discourse? Without this definition from you we can only guess and utilise conjecture, which is totally inadmissible in the discipline of your methodology.

Mr. Weber by using connotative dualist exclusionary terms as 'feudal' you open the door to racist stereotypes jumping out of the text in the mind of the reader. Is feudal the other of capitalism as irrationality/ feudal vs. rationality/ capitalism as is non-white/ irrational/ feudal Islamic vs. white/ rationality/ capitalism? Alas Mr. Weber we can only surmise for you are no longer present to answer our questions, but your texts live on, contributing to the textual enterprise of Orientalism. (4) Your a-historical method utilized in your need to inject Islamic discourse with libidinal and magical irrationality is the lynch pin of your enterprise on Islamic discourse. That you could take a fringe development of the discursive intersection of two contending discourses in the Indian sub-continent during the hegemony of Islamic discourse; and extrapolate it into a 'virus' that infected the entire Islamic discourse is simply unacceptable to your methodological tenets. That the dervishes of India, in fact unique products of discursive intersections, introduced libidinal tensions into the Islamic discourse, hence contributing to its overwhelming irrationality is dubious interpretation of the historical record at best.

Even more untenable, Mr. Weber, is your position on Sufi mysticism in which you identify its source as Persia, totally historically incorrect, but more so your attempt to trivialize Sufi mysticism as the host, which introduced magic into an already irrational religion. Sufi mysticism in Islamic discourse is by far the most potent patriot missile that Islamic discourse can launch against your characterization of Islamic discourse. Why is this so? For Sufi mysticism, which pre-dated Protestantism, overwhelmingly carries within it a worldview, which Weber could only have classified as the basis of a rational religious worldview, if only he was true to his own methodology. A deconstruction of Sufi discourse followed this work.

Weber's major contribution, whether deliberately or unwittingly, was to open the door of sociology to the Orientalist discourse. By embracing the Orientalist discourse through his utilization of its worldview in the major enterprise of his career as a mental worker, Weber left an enterprise of dubious and limited value to the mental exertions of the people of the periphery. The dichotomy between his theory of methodology, and by extension the ontology and epistemology that informed his methodological position, and the Orientalist discursive enterprise with its accompanying worldview is clearly apparent in his work on the religions of the world.

Weber did himself and the academic discipline of Sociology the great disfavor by discrediting his methodology through his dance with Orientalist discourse. He not only was the host for infection by a totally unacceptable worldview, but he sacrificed his most endearing legacy to the patrimony of the world corpus of human mental production, his methodology, on the altar of racist expediency. For this the mental workers of the periphery cannot forgive him. It is a potent verdict on the veracity of the mental production of Weber that in his corpus of work, the only area of production with some semblance of finality by his hand was situated in the Orientalist discourses of the day.

By situating his work on religion, especially religions of the colonized periphery, within the Orientalist discourse Weber turned his back on the opportunity to shed light on the issue of the relationship between instances of the capitalist superstructure, such as religion, and the prevailing mode of production. An issue of central importance to Marx's discourse during Weber's epoch.

If Weber was really out to disprove/ dismantle Marx's discourse, then he missed the golden opportunity. His was the opportunity to open a discursive rupture in Marx's discourse and challenge the ruling bourgeois hegemonic academic discourses of the day through his methodology and the ontology which informed it. Weber, faced with the opportunity of rupture, of conjuncture, turned away from forcing the breach by retreating into racist Orientalist discourse. The opportunity never again arose and today Weber occupies the netherworld reserved for greatness never realized, an enigma amongst the progression of European thinkers in the field of social analysis.

In the mind of the researcher the anger that welled up inside with the recognition that the experience of Weber in the 'Critique of Stammler' to the 'Sociology of Religion' mirrors two entirely different and mutually exclusive mental works, dissipated and mutated to a mixture of pain and empathy for the Weber of 'Science as a Vocation.' Weber of the text 'Science as a Vocation' is now the thinker resigned to the fate of existence under the iron fist of capitalist rationalism.

Weber speaks: "the fate of our age, with its characteristic rationalization and intellectualization and above all the disenchantment of the world, is that the ultimate, most sublime values have withdrawn from public life, either into the transcendental realm of mystical life or into the brotherhood of immediate personal relationships between individuals." (Weber 1989 Pg. 30). "We should go to our work and do justice to the 'demands of the day' both in human and professional terms. But that is plain and simple, if everybody finds and obeys the demon which holds the threads of his life." (Weber 1989 Pg. 31). For Weber of the text, disenchantment was a uniquely European historical phenomenon, but under capitalism it became welded with rationalization and intellectualization. Was this cocktail of human experience under capitalism the basis for his flirtation with Leo Tolstoy on the issue of the meaning of death in such experiential realities? Was it Tolstoy, or Weber through Tolstoy who says? "And because death is meaningless, so too is civilized life as such, for it is that which condemns death to meaninglessness through its meaningless progressiveness." (Weber 1989 Pg. 14). The researcher can never quite know, but Weber's predicament is obvious and his solutions are not forthcoming. He can only posit 'intellectual integrity,' the passion that informs the intellectual exercise that renders it in its limited field of subjective experience worthy of human endeavor. Other than that, there is the return to the old churches with their old prophecies for the person 'who cannot take this destiny of the age like a man.'

Weber can only promise a world of passion through work, in this case mental work, for it is the only worthy experience afforded the inmates of the iron cage, for even death is rendered meaningless. He therefore created a discursive black hole in which all light was trapped and unable to escape the gravitational pull of the most powerful sun in the linear history of European civilization, i.e. – capitalism. A black hole in which even the 'ultimate, most sublime values have withdrawn from public life.'

Weber was to introduce, perhaps unwittingly, into the discourse two specific elements, which were able to contribute to the fruition of Freud's enterprise when the discourse demanded the paramountcy of the psychoanalytic worldview. Weber was to tap into the march of discursive ideas and to contribute via his concepts of rationality, disenchantment and intellectualization to the formation of the concepts of Freud's psycho analysis, central among them being neurosis. More so, his methodology was to open the door to the creation of Freud's method, which revolved around giving meaning to the actions of the patient or subject in a value free environment of observation and evaluation. Weber states accordingly: "Thus if we understand things correctly [which must be pre-supposed here] we can force the individual, or at least help him, to give account of the ultimate meaning of his own actions." (Weber 1989 Pg. 26).

And finally, Weber of the text 'Science as a Vocation' was to show his involvement with grappling with issues thrown up by his discursive worldview now finds expression in the post-modernist debate. Weber states: "It is no accident that our greatest art is intimate rather than monumental, nor is it fortuitous that today only in the smallest groups, between individuals, something pulsates in pianissimo which corresponds to the prophetic pneuma which formerly swept through great communities like fire and welded them together." (Weber 1989 Pg. 30). This is the enigma that was Weber, flashes of brilliance that indicated his ability to create a discursive rupture within the ruling discourses of the day, but in actuality an individual who chose to keep the outcomes of his mental work within the unwritten discourse of his mental faculties.

Perhaps his intellectual exertions were so important or central to his definition of self, that to liberate them would be to jeopardize his enterprise of human development to an ideal he only knew. This is but conjecture and innuendo, for Weber through the ages challenges us to share his vision and more so to accept the rationalism of capitalist production, both mental and physical.

The researcher, whilst striving to understand Weber's discourse, cannot accept Weber's iron cage. For the researcher, death can never become or be made meaningless by any mode of production for it still is the irrevocable fate of all humanity, thereby making it our most astute teacher. For alas Weber himself died, whether it was meaningless or not, rational or irrational, his life's work was finite in expanse.

Given therefore the finite expanse of the researcher's work he refuses to accept that capitalism and the discourses it brings in its retinue from Europe or Europe's bastard child, America, is the ideal for which people of the periphery must strive to grasp. The European capitalist discourse negates the existence of my person as a knowing sovereign being, and in order to grasp this reality the researcher could only find answers and re-formulated questions in the works of Michel Foucault. Michel Foucault is therefore, after Marx, the creator of the other discursive rupture in the hegemonic capitalist discourses of the day.

Dancing with Foucault.

To attempt to embrace the enterprise of Foucault as a mental worker towards creating an orthodoxy which churns out Foucault clones, à la Marxism, is an exercise in discursive futility. He neither sought nor created disciples, for to do this he would have been forced to make his personal motivators, which drove him to study widely divergent and at times eclectic themes, subservient to the needs of creating a discursive structure to proselytize and maintain orthodoxy. The various about turns and somersaults in his positions on specific issues he made within his corpus of work attests to his abhorrence of orthodoxy.

What then does Foucault's intellectual enterprise mean to the researcher and his intellectual enterprise? Of central significance and untold impact is the fact that Foucault methodically unraveled the dualist capitalist discourses of his day by focusing on the systems that constituted the subject of discourse: humans. But of even more importance, Foucault in his silence of the gesture points us to the possibility of breaching the dualist capitalist discourse. For one who found and followed the gesture of Foucault it was incumbent upon me to discover the non-dualist, non-capitalist worldview. Why? Because Foucault gave a gesture, a sign to the discursive breach he initiated, but he himself was unable or unwilling to journey through the breach and enter the non-dualist discourses of his day. To the researcher this constant reluctance to attain the threshold was a salient feature of Foucault's work of the 1980's in the final years of his life.

Foucault's life work was defined by the hegemonic discourses as he constantly moved from project to project, the basis of which was discursive engagement. This was the strategy of hegemonic discourse that kept Foucault forever occupied with mapping the limits and nature of hegemonic discourse and by doing so it entrapped him. He was then unable to give voice to the silenced for his conversations were all with hegemonic discourse, even when he was talking for and with the silenced. He was perpetually trapped in reaction never proaction, because he never spoke from discursive territory which by its worldview belongs to a space that was beyond the discursive breach. Space beyond the breach can be defined by a range of discourses, one of them being a non-dualist discourse.

It is the contention of the researcher that Foucault never sought to make the final discursive jump, as others before and after him, because it would have involved the dismantling of an entire edifice of structures of perceptions which defines the European person, self, psyche, or whatever descriptive terms not listed. The bedrock of Foucault's work is the dualist worldview as constituted in the European worldview. Foucault still carried in his enterprise the circularity of dualist perception. It pervades his work, and the very schemata he laid out for the constituting of the subject through the discursive mechanism of power and knowledge is itself dualist.

The concept of the subject, represented and constituted 'the other', must be generated by the representer. Two entities locked in a dualist relationship towards constituting the subject, i.e. – power and knowledge. Then there is discourse and what lies outside of discourse: the extra discursive. The dualist basis of perception informed Foucault's enterprise just as it did every European thinker of renown, including Foucault's mentor: Nietzsche.

As with Marx, Foucault's enterprise was to be formulated and expressed through dualities, which has ensured the circularity of debate within the European worldview since Plato and Socrates. The debate has never lost its circularity and its linearity within the European worldview, regardless of the nature of the debate, for it is ontologically premised on the reduction of all existential experiences to duality, however limited, named or constituted.

In his dualistic perception of human action and experience, Foucault was quintessentially European and like Marx was unable, but more so unwilling, to transcend their dualist perceptions that defined their being, their race, their history as a culture. Foucault's dualism was to raise the most potent rupture within his discourse and that is the mechanism and the means towards the liberation of the subject: 'the other.'

Marx postulated that the proletarian revolution would reverse the order of dominance within the duality of bourgeoisie/ proletariat and be the means to liberation. Foucault made no such prediction, for his method of mapping the hegemonic discourse could not involve an issue that is in the domain of praxis. But Foucault created no discourse of praxis in his corpus of work and by example he avoided contending within the realm of the discourse of politics like the plague.

The question then arises: how Foucault's constituted subject was to escape the silence of the powerless? For this question Foucault has no answer, and the primary reason for this is his failure to look past the dualist ontology, for the ontology is by its effect on its adherents fatalist and nihilist.

The failure of the proletarian revolution to uncover itself from the bowels of European capitalism has the adherents of Marx's discourse running around like headless chickens to this day trying to save their discourse from itself. Foucault was to avoid this circular futility in his discourse by creating a danse macabre of his own. Insight into the workings of a discourse predicated on the systems of discipline/ knowledge, punishment/ power; but no means of liberation save and except possibly at the level of individual action and perception. The questions that launch out from this construct are as follows: (a) is liberation only an ideal that must now be relegated to the scrap heap of human history? (b) is liberation only attainable at the level of the individual? (c) if so, then the individual must not be burdened with the praxis of aggregations as class, race, ethnicity, and gender.

At this juncture it is necessary that Foucault speak: "When a judgment cannot be framed in terms of good and evil, it is stated in terms of normal and abnormal. And when it is necessary to justify this last distinction, it is done in terms of what is good or bad for the individual. These are expressions that signal the fundamental duality of Western consciousness." "I think that to imagine another system is to extend our participation in the present system." (Foucault 1986 Pg. 230). "If scientific socialism emerged from the Utopias of the nineteenth century, it is possible that a real socialism will emerge, in the twentieth century, from experiences."

(Foucault 1986 Pg. 231). "I believe on the contrary, that this particular idea of the 'whole of society' derives from a utopian context. This idea arose in the Western world, within this highly individualized historical development that culminates in capitalism. To speak of the 'whole of society' apart from the only form it has taken is to transform our past into a dream." (Foucault 1986 Pg. 232). "The 'whole of society' is precisely that which should not be considered except as something to be destroyed. And then, we can only hope that it will never exist again." (Foucault 1986 Pg. 233). We have already seen where Foucault recognized the duality of Western consciousness and the workings of the perception in the corpus of the work. The researcher would now underpin his position by looking at Foucault's position on language and humanism, which reveal windows to gaze upon Foucault's ontology. A text published in 1963 titled 'Language to Infinity' creates the windows needed to affix the gaze on the building blocks of Foucault's enterprise.

It is only within a dualist ontology, based upon the centrality of language, that language in itself and for itself can become a discursive knowledge. Foucault addresses the enterprise of language in a most unique manner for he posits that out of dualities in contradiction/ juxtaposition language arose. The base dualities are man and the immanence of death and by the contradiction of these dualities the need arises to breach death to infinity. The solution to man's finity is therefore language to infinity. Foucault speaks: "it is quite likely that the approach of death-it's sovereign gesture, its prominence within human memory-hollows out in the present and in existence the void toward which and from which we speak." (Foucault 1986 Pg. 53). "Perhaps there exists in speech an essential affinity between death, endless striving, and the self-representation of language. Perhaps the figure in the mirror to infinity erected against the black wall of death is fundamental for any language from the moment it determines to leave a trace of its passage." (Foucault 1986 Pg. 55).

Language and death now locked in the danse macabre of dualities creates the medium of written language, and the nature of and specificity of written language creates an ontological event of central importance for

Western discourse. Since writing refers to speech and not the thing designated, Western culture is ensnared in a self-propagating process of circular, self-representation and re-duplication or the danse macabre of dualities. Foucault speaks: "that forms one of the most decisive ontological events of language; its mirrored reflection upon death and the construction, from this reflection, of a virtual space where speech discovers the endless resourcefulness of its own image and where, it can represent itself as already existing behind itself, already active beyond itself, to infinity." (Foucault 1986 Pg. 55). "Writing in Western culture, automatically dictates that we place ourselves in the virtual space of self-representation and re-duplication, since writing refers not to a thing but to speech, a work of language only advances more deeply into intangible density of the mirror, calls forth the double of this already doubled writing, discovers in this way a possible and impossible infinity, ceaselessly strives after speech, maintains it beyond the death which condemns it, and frees a murmuring stream." (Foucault 1986 Pg. 56). "A work of language is the body of language crossed by death in order to open this infinite space where doubles reverberate." "The mirror to infinity, to which every language gives birth once it erects itself vertically against death was not displayed without an evasion; the work placed the infinite outside of itself-a real and majestic infinity in which it became a virtual and circular mirror, completed in a beautifully closed form." (Foucault 1986 Pg. 60). The genesis of language and all that followed created the need in the history of written European languages that the creator of language, European man, would attempt to take back the object of language from itself and restore it to the rule of man as a vehicle of written expression.

Foucault saw this revolt against European language in the novels of Sade, which set out to create the novel that forces language through the imbalance of the work to create new spaces to infinity within which a new language would be constituted. But alas, the discursive breach brings no liberation for the circular dance of dualities are again replicated, the languages of naivety sind parody which are international dualities. Western written language developed, for Foucault, through the dance with death in the European man's quest to transcend death by creating a legacy to infinity.

The project in itself created its Frankenstein monster when the written work, rather than representing an object via signs, repeated the speech of its creators via written signs.

The dualist base of the project man/ finite vs. death/ infinity was now rejected in a new duality death/ language vs. written speech/ death. Written speech became the representer although represented in the mirror image of death. Western European humans continue to labour under the circular dualities of their written speech, which robs them of control over the very structure created to ensure the existence of a legacy beyond death.

It is very interesting to say the least to experience Foucault's perceptions on the centrality of language in the European intellectual debate. He uniquely posits the enterprise of written language as being born out of the immanence of death, and the dominance of dualities in European thought as the result of the way in which the problem and its solution were visualized.

Foucault's position on language and infinity in the European context is all well and good if you accept that dualist ontology is in fact the 'correct' and 'desirable' ontology to inform human action, both mental and physical. And this is by far the most insidious aspect of his enterprise as he either inspires discursive rupture without ontological breaches, therefore discursive rupture without a discursive breach or inactive nihilism, with all its attendant self-destructive fatalism à la Weber and Nietzsche, or both.

Since Marx it is only Foucault that unmasked and laid bare the discursive structures of European bourgeois capitalism. He unmasked the nexus between specific bodies of knowledge and the constituting of the subject of discourse: humans. He also potently stripped bare the nexus between the ideological and power/ knowledge systems of discourse. But he did all of this within an ontological discourse, which he understood, but accepted as vital to the enterprise at hand.

Having accepted the nature of the ontology in which he situated himself he could not have formulated the discursive breach. His brilliance, which granted him the ability to transcend the ontology of his day, meant that his legacy is devoid of hope for the powerless. For his work was a victim of its brilliance, by punching holes in the discursive structures of major edifices of capitalist societies he challenged the subjects entrapped to question, to understand, to build discourse. But they were discourses of the powerless built upon the same ontological building blocks as the discourses of the powerful. This communality inevitably allows and fosters the eventual neutralization of discourses of the powerless within capitalism, in fact the history of the powerless under the capitalist mode of production is littered with the flotsam and jetsam of discourses of resistance ruptured, breached, compromised and absorbed by the hegemonic discourse of the day.

In effect at the level of praxis, as the discourse of Marx, Foucault's discourse contributed to the resilience of the hegemonic discourse of the day, for by creating a series of ruptures in the different geographic areas of the body of ruling discourses he gave opportunity and intent to silenced voices, and in their losing battle with discourses of power/ knowledge these discourses of the silenced inevitably added to the body of knowledge and the depths of its power over the powerless.

In all its effects it is but a danse macabre based on a dualist ontology, which stresses the rule of totalities over the person. Both Marx and Foucault in their desire to find a platform for revolution should have searched the colonial and neo-colonial experiences. Given their willingness they would have found that the most intense, prolonged and all-encompassing histories of resistance to European colonialism, both in its pre capitalist and capitalist stages, were based on ontologies/ discourses which were directly in violent contradiction with the discourse, and the ontologies that informed them and European colonialism.

The Islamic discourse stands out in history as a discourse of resistance, which refuses to capitulate. Likewise, it is now apparent that the subjects of the post-modern phase of capitalism are now seeking non-dualist discourse from the native peoples of the periphery. It is a pilgrimage fraught with irony as the inheritors of the legacy and patrimony of the colonizers/ conquerors are now depending on the survivors of genocide to give meaning to their lives, to give them a whole new ontology, discourse, worldview. The search is for meaning, for the dualist ontology continues to belabor its inmates on the finality of death.

The language to infinity carries within its baggage death itself, therefore they seek from us of the periphery, of the non-dualist worldview the means to decouple death from their quest for infinity. But awaiting them in their pilgrimages to the periphery is the realization that to decouple death to infinity they must accept and move through the discursive breach that we insist upon. For many of the North the price is too steep, for they would have to commit race suicide.

Foucault by seeking out the non-dualist survivors in his own culture would have been afforded the opportunity to investigate the mechanics of change, the creation of a discourse of liberation via conflicting ontologies. These ontologies for various reasons lie deeply submerged amongst the silenced and are now surfacing because of the whirlwind of post-modernism. But Foucault lacked a discourse of the esoteric that would have enabled him to seek out and locate discourses in contradiction to the hegemonic discourses, kept deep within the experiences of closed groups to preserve the integrity of the discourse and to ensure its survival. The grappling with esoterica, rather than ethics, was called for by the hope his enterprise created. For whether he recognized or not, his work created means to understand, it created knowledge and with knowledge came the hope of liberation.

In 1971 Foucault sat and faced the questions of students many years his junior, the events of 1968 in Paris were still fresh in the memories of both Foucault and his inquisitors, but more so the enterprise of liberation was a pressing issue for the significant centers of the capitalist world system were in turmoil. The hegemonic discourses of the day were not only threatened by resurgent discourses of the powerless, but the hegemonic discourses themselves were locked in battle amongst themselves as new discourses of knowledge were being formulated and challenging the hegemonic discourses for power.

The post-modern condition recognized by Weber was now facing a discursive rupture, and by and through the contention of discourses within the discursive hegemony a discursive breach was created. The discursive contradiction created voids in the spatial matrix in which subjects were represented, thereby allowing discourses of the powerless to regenerate themselves in the attempt to fill the void. The tornado of discursive contradiction sucked up discourses of the powerless, which were non-dualist in structure, and to date the jinn has not been returned to the bottle.

Foucault was now forced by inquisitors, the youth in revolt, to answer the question of the strategy of liberation, the paramount question of the epoch. Jean-Francois, one of the inquisitors, picked up on Foucault's attack on "humanism" and phrased a question that was in effect a fast yorker swinging to leg. Jean-Francois: "What criticism do you direct against humanism, and what values, in another system for transmitting knowledge, can replace it?" Foucault answers by saying the following: (1) "Humanism is a discursive totality." (2) "Humanism invented a whole series of subjected Sovereignties" (Foucault 1986 Pg. 221). These are the soul, consciousness, and the individual and basic freedom. "In short, humanism is everything in Western civilization that restricts the "desire for power"; it prohibits the desire for power and excludes the possibility of power being seized. The theory of the subject [in the double sense of the word] is at the heart of humanism and this is why our culture has tenaciously rejected anything that could weaken its hold upon us." (Foucault 1986 Pgs. 221-222).

But what of the praxis of liberation Mr. Foucault? Foucault answers: "But it can be attacked in two ways, either by a "de-subjectification" of the will to power [that is through political struggle in the context of class warfare] or by the destruction of the subject as a pseudo sovereign [that is through an attack on "culture"; the suppression of taboos and the limitations and divisions imposed upon the sexes; the setting up of communes; the loosening of inhibitions with regard to drugs; the breaking of all the prohibitions that form and guide the development of a normal individual]" (Foucault 1986 Pg. 222). Foucault continues: "We wish to attack an institution at the point where it culminates and reveals itself in a simple and basic ideology, in the notions of good and evil, innocence and guilt." (Foucault 1986 Pg. 228). He then defines what is for him revolutionary action as follows: "Revolutionary action, on the contrary, is defined as the simultaneous agitation of consciousness and institutions, this implies that we attack the relationships of power through the notions and institutions that function as their instruments, armature, and armor. Do you think that the teaching of philosophy-and its moral code-would remain unchanged if the penal system collapsed." (Foucault 1986 Pg. 229). Foucault therefore identified two platforms of praxis: the "subjectification" of the will to power and the "destruction of the subject as a pseudo sovereign". One platform situated itself in the realm of political struggle through class contradictions whilst the second platform embraced and gave the meaning of liberation to the whole spectrum of youth culture that swept the capitalist world in the late 1960's and 1970's. The second platform focused on the individual and the technique of deconstruction through rebellion against norms, values and specific aesthetics, which were to reveal the realities that humanism removed from the gaze of the subject. Foucault continues: "It is a long struggle, it is repetitive and seemingly incoherent, but the system it opposes, as well as the power exercised through the system, supplies its unity." (Foucault 1986 Pg. 230).

Another young inquisitor by the name of Alain now delivers the question that is the slower ball, which hails the coming of the bouncer that is aimed at the head of Foucault. Alain speaks: "This is a tiresome question, but it must be faced eventually: what replaces the system?" Foucault answer's Alain: "I think that to imagine another system is to extend our participation in the present system. This is perhaps what happened in the history of the Soviet Union." (Foucault 1986 Pg. 230). "The Soviet Union returned to the standards of bourgeois society in the nineteenth century, and perhaps, more as a result of Utopian tendencies than a concern for reality." Jean Francois releases the bouncer in the question as follows: "The present movement may require a utopian model and a theoretical elaboration that goes beyond the sphere of partial and repressed experiences." Foucault answers: "Why not the opposite? Reject theory and all forms of general discourse. This need for theory is still part of the system we reject." Jean Francois releases again: "You feel that the simple fact of employing a theory still relates to the dynamic of bourgeois knowledge?" Foucault: "Maybe so. I would oppose actual experiences than the possibility of a Utopia. It is possible that the rough outlines of a society is supplied by the recent experiences with drugs, sex, communes, other forms of consciousness, and other forms of individuality." (Foucault 1986 Pg. 231). In the cut and thrust of debate, alas Foucault used the inexperience of youth to evade the yorkers aimed at his intellectual wicket. What is apparent from the debate is that Foucault had no vision of the future society created by the two-pronged attack on humanism. And when pressed on this issue he was an intellectual escape artist in the tradition of Harry Houdini. He skillfully used the Marxist worldview of Alain, and especially Jean-Francois, to their disadvantage in the cut and thrust of debate.

By letting loose the bogeyman of WHY? revisionism in the Soviet Union, the thrust of the debate switched from Foucault and his need to stand and deliver, to the young Marxists need to defend their already threadbare worldview. And this was a feature of Foucault's interpersonal style throughout his academic life. To evade the demands for a vision of the possible alternative future of society he resorted to subterfuge at the level of language. Foucault talked the talk, but repeatedly failed to walk the walk.

It is apparent from the body of quotations presented before that Foucault's methodology of revolutionary action lacked specifics and articulation. And it is the opinion of the researcher, after repeated readings of the text, that Foucault's revolutionary action model was produced to satisfy the dictates of the epoch in which he released in (1971).

By 1975 with the publication of "Discipline and Punish" in French he was to destroy and walk away from the first platform of revolutionary action, i.e. – "the desubjectification of the will of power" and by 1978 with the appearance of the "History of Sexuality" vol.1 in French, he was to redefine the second platform of revolutionary action to the point of irrelevance.

By the end of the decade of the 1970's Foucault could have found it necessary to abandon his revolutionary praxis of 1971, because the praxis was in itself in shambles. The counterculture was already compromised and absorbed by the hegemonic discourse of the day. The counterculture was reduced, relativized into an aesthetic, a new fashion fad and an inner focus on the individual expressed through pop psychology, and plain old greed. The disco culture and worldview absorbed the counterculture of the hippies and yippies, creating the formula, which bred the culture types of the yuppies and the homeboy.

The disturbing reality of Foucault was his grasp of the currents of discursive development, which at times negated the orthodoxy of his expressed thoughts at a specific given epoch in his life experiences. In his debate with the students, whilst animating the revolutionary praxis that the epoch called for, Foucault was continually hinting at the possible failure of the project.

Foucault is now dead but as he stalked the people of the time who chose to contend with him, so he stalks the readers of his text. Towards the end of the debate Foucault moves in to finish off the prey he so ruthlessly stalked during the course of debate. Foucault states: "If you wish to replace an official institution by another institution that fulfills the same function-better and differently-then you are already being reabsorbed by the dominant structure" (Foucault 1986 Pg. 232). Jean-Francois is now wilting under the body blows of Foucault; he drops his Marxist worldview for Foucault's patriot missile just took out the scud missiles of Marx's discourse. So, Jean-Francois responds by attacking with his perception that Foucault's enterprise is nihilist. Putting all his remaining energy as the boxer who is punch groggy and needs a knock-out for victory he swings at Foucault thus – Jean-Francois: "I can't believe that the movement must remain at its present stage, as this vague, unsubstantial underground ideology that refuses to endorse any form of social work or community service, any action that requires going beyond the immediate group. It's unable to assume the responsibility for the whole of society, or it may be that it is incapable of conceiving society as a whole." (Foucault 1986

Pg. 232). Jean-Francois has released the haymaker straight to the jaw of Foucault accusing Foucault's discourse of being incapable of conceptualizing the whole of society or society as a whole. Foucault responds with the most potent counterpunch of his arsenal, his repeated refusal to accept the hegemony of concepts considered central to European intellectual exercises. Society as a whole or the whole of society is one such concept as it insists on viewing society as a totality.

Foucault states that the totality is rejected by him because its origin is placed in a utopian context. More so, Foucault's position is summed up as follows: "The "Whole of Society" is precisely that which should not be considered except as something to be destroyed. And then we can only hope that it will never exist again." (Foucault 1986 Pg. 233). Why does Foucault hope that the concept would never regenerate itself after its destruction? The answer lies in its origin in the unique ontology of the Western world that "culminates in capitalism."

The debate ends and Foucault has presented a framework for revolutionary action, which he would never expand upon or articulate. What he would in fact do is to destroy the attainability of the goals of the praxis through two seminal works. Leaving the researcher with but one conclusion: that the great enterprise of Foucault was situated in creating a new philosophy of European civilization predicated upon the drawing out of "essences", which have determined the course civilization took regardless of the historical and idealist worldviews.

The present task of research has drawn out the following "essences" which make up Foucault's philosophy as it is revealed grudgingly in various texts, most times fleetingly and without articulation. These are: (a) the ontological events of language and written speech in Europe. The mirror reflection upon death by language to space by which and through which speech discovers it. For Foucault written speech in Western culture, based on its unique ontology, creates the object of written speech in self-representation and re-duplication. Written speech in the Western vein is created in an infinite space where doubles reverberate. The re-duplication of language within the infinite space throws up signs, which are ontological indications.

The next "essence" discovered is "the fundamental duality of Western consciousness." Judgments are framed in dualist terms: good/ evil, normal/ abnormal, man/ woman, adult/ child, discourse/ extra discursive, discipline/ knowledge, power/ punish. By describing duality as fundamental to western consciousness Foucault was in fact forwarding an ontological essence. Perhaps it sprang from the ontological signs of European written speech. Foucault was never involved with the task of fully expanding the significance of his passing statement on the duality of western consciousness, thus it amounts to the silent gesture pointing to a discursive breach.

Perhaps the most difficult of the "essences" to unravel is Foucault's 'humanism'. Humanism is the concept of a specific European metaphysic, was embraced by Foucault but de-centered to the level of totality of discourse. But humanism was operative for Foucault in Western civilization commencing in the Roman epoch and had a specific purpose in its restriction of "the desire for power". Foucault states that the theory of the Subject in its duality "is at the heart of humanism". Foucault in Discipline and Punish was to subsequently blow away the concept of power he used as expressed above. For power as used in the statement on humanism constitutes power as an entity which has specific locations and positions which enable it to be seized. In Discipline and Punish Foucault dismisses this representation with utter contempt, and in turn his position that humanism can be destroyed via a praxis based on the discarded representation of power.

What is left is the "essence" that is humanism in the metaphysic of European civilization. Humanism constitutes "a whole series of subjected sovereignties". These are: "(a) the soul rules the body but is subjected to God." In Discipline and Punish a new "soul" is created in the micro-physics of power over the body in a new political anatomy centred on the body. Foucault says: "the soul is the effect and instrument of a political anatomy, the soul is the prison of the body." (Foucault 1986 Pg. 30). The new god to which the soul is subjected is the ruling discourse of the day, the power/knowledge nexus. Foucault continues: (b) "Consciousness [sovereign in a context of judgement but subjected to the necessities of truth.]" (c) "The individual [a titular control of personal rights subjected to the laws of nature and society.]" (d) "Basic freedom [sovereign within but accepting the demands of an outside world and aligned with destiny.]" (Foucault 1986 Pg. 221).

The constituted subjects of the humanist ontology, envisioned through language and expressed through dualist written speech, are themselves dualities as we dance the circular dance with Foucault. In the constituted subjects of humanism we witness the linkage in the ontology to the "essence" termed the will to knowledge. Foucault says: "it finds that all these forms and transformations are aspects of the will to knowledge; instinct, passion, the inquisitor's devotion, cruel subtlety and malice. The historical analysis of this rancorous will to knowledge rests upon injustice [that there is no right, not even in the act of knowing, to truth or a foundation for truth,] and that the instinct for knowledge is malicious [something murderous, opposed to the happiness of mankind]." (Foucault 1980 Pg. 119). Foucault in the post 1968 period, specifically by 1975-78, had now re-formulated his metaphysic on the bedrock of Nietzsche. Humanism was now re-formulated to the quintessential European essence: "the will to knowledge." The subjected sovereignties of humanism were now "effects", "aspects" or "elements" of the will to knowledge, i.e. – the soul, consciousness, and the individual and basic freedom.

Foucault continues: "Even in the greatly expanded form it assumes today, the will to knowledge does not achieve a universal truth, man is not given an exact and serene mastery of nature." (Foucault 1980 Pg. 119). Given the specific nature of the will to knowledge quoted above then there is a "will to truth" the other side of the dualist project. In Discipline and Punish Foucault would consummate the dualist union at the ontological level with the formulation of the nexus of knowledge and power, the genesis of the "effects", "specificities", "elements" of the will to knowledge. The will to knowledge is now the "essence" of Foucault's metaphysics and it was to drive his perceptive machinery until his death in 1985.

What then are the lessons for the weary researcher of the periphery? By far the most potent lesson lies in the intellectual suicide one commits if the legacy of Foucault via his texts is embraced and assimilated as truth of relevance to the periphery. Foucault was primarily involved in the creation of a metaphysic of and for the European experience, and he expressed his metaphysical position through his works, which dealt with specific experiences in relation to specific discourses. In every work Foucault presents the underpinning European worldview, metaphysic as perceived by Foucault. Foucault's texts as is, read in situ, would replicate a European metaphysic, which naturally cannot replicate the cogency of any work done in the periphery based on Foucault stripped bare of his metaphysic. Mental work informed by Foucault can only create a will to truth of relevance to European experiences. We would be situated in the periphery and imprisoned in a sterile debate over metaphysical elements, which bear no relevance to the experiences situated just outside the door of the room enclosing said debate.

The researcher cannot even dance with Foucault, for in dancing we must embrace, thereby creating a field of commonly agreed upon values. Foucault has to be researched in the first instance to uncover his perceptive worldview and by extension the articulated structure of his metaphysics. With this structure identified, the researcher can complete the task of appraising the value of his concepts of analysis with the conclusions reached based on the application of these tools to the social realm.

What is now apparent is that: (a) the concepts are of limited analytical value when you separate them from their constituting metaphysic. For the metaphysic and the concepts which sprang from it defines the entire enterprise of Foucault and no mental worker creates a body of work which destroys his/ her worldview, to do that is to entertain suicide. The basic reality is that Foucault comes with baggage and to reject the baggage is to create a poor simile, a cruel parody of the original texts and its legacy. On this level of experience then one either embraces the patrimony of Foucault and dance to infinity the circular dance of dualistic futility, thereby marginalizing your enterprise as a mental worker in a peripheral society, forever dooming yourself to a netherworld existence as a satellite of Northern Atlantic academia. Or: (b) to view Foucault's texts through the perceptive windows of an alternative non-dualist worldview. To view the world through non-dualist perceptions enables the researcher the ability to view non-European worldviews without the baggage of European dualism.

The researcher is therefore first attempting to recognize the alternative non-dualist worldviews, which have been in contention with the European metaphysic since Columbus' fateful sojourn in 1492. Works of analysis have repeatedly failed to recognize the continued intersection of two non-compatible worldviews and the structures of perception and experience constituted by conflicting worldviews, especially within the spaces created by the intersections of worldviews in conflict. Mental workers carrying the perceptual baggage of the discourses of the colonizer, have failed to recognize and record the perceptual elements of the worldviews which resist the discourses of the colonizer. As a result, the corpus of work produced in the social sciences has been dismally poor in its attempts to create the links between action and causality. The reason for this is that we continue to produce works of relevance to the European worldview, and consequently the debates raging within the European intellectual discourses of the day.

The social sciences and the humanities continue to reject and refuse to recognize, what is accepted by the persons who embody these beliefs; the reality that in the Caribbean, experience is hinged on conflicting worldviews and any given person chooses solutions to specific problems of living from the worldviews that constitute his /her perceptive fields. The mental worker of the Caribbean relentlessly pulls away and fights the whispers, signs and calls emanating from our non-dualist, non-European alternate worldviews. We feel the call at the level of sensory experience – of the Orisha drums, of the vocal chants of the Orisha, the Kali Mai and the Spiritual Baptists. We deny the urge to non-language sensory experience, for to succumb would be the ultimate act of surrender to a potent, cogent, coherent alternative worldview, which questions the relevance, and veracity of our life's work.

The task at hand is therefore to learn from Foucault's enterprise, to focus with special intensity on his metaphysics of genealogy and the will to knowledge in the European reality. The position of Foucault on discipline/ punishment, power/ knowledge is of special importance in understanding the power relations of capitalist society. The fundamental importance of the power/ knowledge construct, even though the baggage it carries is extensive, cries out for mental workers of the periphery to sift the experiences of the periphery, to un-Earth the specificities of its existence in the periphery as a transplanted metaphysic in an alien environment.

The accuracy of this exercise hinges on the recognition of the alternative worldviews, which are especially active amongst the powerless and silenced of peripheral society, and its articulation through giving it voice. The focus of this work is therefore the giving of voice to one alternative worldview silenced by the hegemonic transplanted discourses of the day. This alternative silenced worldview chose to break its silence on the 27th July, 1990 and the vehicle of articulation was a coup d'état.

As the subjects of the hegemonic discourse charged with ensuring its mental and physical integrity shriveled under the voices of silence, the spoken and unspoken question was: "How did it happen?", "Why did we not know about it beforehand?" The question lies in the fact that under the hegemony of a dualist alien, imported, inherited worldview the hegemonic discourse did not "see", "perceive", or "recognize" the existence, actions nor potency of alternative Islamic discourse.

The hegemonic discourse saw recalcitrant subjects who would be re-accommodated within the determinacy of "elements" of the discourse. It failed to and continues to fail to see, much less understand, that there is an underlying worldview that also constitutes subjects which refuse to be re-constituted in the image and likeness of the hegemonic discourse, for they are incompatible and irretrievably locked in contradiction since the first century of Islamic history.

Foucault says: "knowledge.... it creates a progressive enslavement to its instinctive violence." (Foucault 1980 Pg. 120). Are Foucault's words then a prophetic utterance on the means that would be eventually chosen by the hegemonic dualist discourses of the day to resolve this deep seated and antagonistic contradiction? Clearly the ruling discourse is creating a body of knowledge, which continues to replicate the antagonistic contradictions prevalent to the colonial mode of production. Therefore at minimum, at the level of the discursive structure of the social order, independence was simply an act which involved the raising of a new flag and singing a national anthem. Regardless of changes in the formal political structure, the discursive structures continue to constitute subjects of relevance to life under the Union Jack and the underlying violence of colonial domination. And this is the fundamental reason today for racism, and the relationship of race to perceptions of political and economic power to be so prevalent in the perceptions of the people of Trinidad and Tobago. For the inherited discursive structure continues to constitute subjects on the basis of race perceptions heightening the contradictions, fed by the fact that the East Indian race grouping continues to define themselves by various, alternate, non-dualist discourses in contradiction to the racist discursive structures inherited, and yet still to be dismantled, since 31st August 1962.

One example of the workings of this European discursive hegemony is the fact that the highest order of merit granted to citizens of the Republic is the TRINITY CROSS (since changed to the Order of the Republic of Trinidad and Tobago). In a geographic entity where citizens of the Republic refuse to accept the existence of the Trinity or the hegemony of the cross, the discursive structure cannot seek nor create consensus.

Foucault teaches poignantly that his metaphysic only relentlessly seeks hegemonic knowledge/ power. In a society discursively structured as ours to consciously maintain the hegemony of a colonial European discourse is to court disaster, as Haiti beckons. Foucault then offers potent insights to the problems at hand but no solutions, for these we would have to repeatedly grope as a people to by-pass the Bosnian debacle.

After the Dance with Foucault

To complete this section of the journey it is now necessary to state the potency of the indelible mark Foucault left on the perceptive fields of the researcher. Without a doubt it was Chapter one of Part one of Discipline and Punish. For Foucault opened power relations to the gaze of constituted subjects of the hegemonic European discourses, an act of central and lasting importance for the mental workers of the periphery. This was the product of mental work that was to inform and intensify his texts, which tore upon the fabric of hegemonic discourse exposing to the people of the periphery the reality of a discursive breach.

But on the issue of discourses of power/ knowledge Foucault must speak for himself, to him goes that honor. Foucault speaks: "This book as a correlative history of the modern soul and of a new power to Judge; a genealogy of the present scientific-legal complex from which the power to punish derives its bases, justifications and rules, from which it extends its effects and by which it masks its exorbitant singularity." (Foucault 1979 Pg. 22). Strip away the metaphysics of the statement and you are left with the concept of the scientifico-legal complex and its bases, justifications, rules, effects and most of all its ability to mask its characteristics. The concept links the scientific and legal discourses into a complex, which cries out for articulation and Foucault, speaks of masks. This raises his position on ideology, which is directly linked to his concept of the nature of power. Foucault continues: ".... in what way a specific mode of subjection was able to give birth to man as an object of knowledge for a discourse with a scientific status." (Foucault 1979 Pg. 24). The statement centers on the creation of a specific end man as an object of knowledge, an effect of a specific discursive type and a specific mode of subjection. The elements of the statement raise questions for the researcher of the periphery in our work of understanding and analysing the history of colonial/ imperialist discourses in the Caribbean.

These are: (a) have we articulated the specific modes of subjection in our history as products of colonialism? (b) likewise, have we traced the genesis and operation of a specific mode of subjection linked to a scientifico-legal complex, which creates man as an object of knowledge? The sad reality is that genealogies of successive discursive structures have yet to be written, much less visualized. Foucault continues: "That is to say there may be a knowledge of the body that is not exactly the Science of its functioning, and a mastery of its forces that is more than the ability to conquer them: this knowledge and this mastery constitute what might be called the political technology of the body." He says: "What the apparatuses and institutions operate is, in a sense, a micro-physics of power, whose field of validity is situated in a sense between these great functioning and the bodies themselves with their materiality and their forces." (Foucault 1979 Pg. 26). The political technology of the body/ the microphysics of power presupposes a specific mode of discourse with a specific end or effects. The question is: has the enterprise of mental workers embodied these concepts towards uncovering the existence of such discourse in the discursive structures of the Caribbean? The answer is no.

Foucault marches on unperturbed and thus speaks: "In short this power is exercised rather than possessed; it is not the "privilege", acquired, or preserved, of the dominant class, but the overall effect of its strategic positions-an effect that is manifested and sometimes extended by the position of those who are dominated." (Foucault 1979 Pg. 26). He continues: "Furthermore, this power is not exercised simply as an obligation or a prohibition on those "who do not have it"; it invests them, is transmitted by them and through them; it exerts pressure upon them, just as they themselves, in their struggles against it, resist the grip it has on them." (Foucault 1979 Pgs. 26-27). This effect of the political technology of the body/ micro-physics of power, this thing called power is not possessed, but it is exercised upon the powerless, who in themselves replicate it, transmit it and resist it. Given our failure to recognize the discursive structure whose effect is power, then the mental workers of the Caribbean have either evaded the need to articulate power relations or continue to struggle with concepts of power, which are illusory as they do not come out of discursive rupture. By extension we, the mental workers of the Caribbean, have failed to gaze upon and give voice to the strategies of resistance to power devised by the silenced/ powerless.

Foucault now insists that: "We should admit rather that power produces knowledge [and not simply by encouraging it because it serves power or by applying it because it is useful;] that power and knowledge directly imply one another; that there is no power relation without the correlative constitution of a field of knowledge, nor any knowledge that does not presuppose and constitute at the same time power relations." (Foucault 1979 Pg. 27). To what end are the enterprises of the mental workers devoted, for Foucault insists that there is no value in neutral mental enterprise. The products of mental work are all effects of existing fields of knowledge, and by extension the task of research is simply the process of opening virgin spaces to the predatory invasion of power/ knowledge and its fields of knowledge. The hegemonic discourses constantly seek to absorb experiences, thereby replicating power relations through and upon the body.

What then is the methodology of creating a corpus of mental work by and for the powerless? On this Foucault is at best vague and sketchy. For the researcher, the methodology can only be based on discursive structures locked in contradiction to the hegemonic discourses of the day. Foucault's position on the question of the methodology of resistance reveals his discursive limits. He says: "In short, it is not the activity of the subject of knowledge that produces a corpus of knowledge, useful or resistant to power, but power/ knowledge, the processes and struggles that traverse it and of which it is made up, that determines the forms and possible domains of knowledge." Foucault continues: "One would be concerned with the "body politic" as a set of material elements and techniques that serve as weapons, relays, communication routes and supports for the power and knowledge relations that invest human bodies and subjugate them by turning them into "objects of knowledge."" (Foucault 1979 Pg. 28). How? Thus: "the history of this 'micro-physics' of the punitive would then be a genealogy or an element in a genealogy of the modern 'soul'" "It would be wrong to say that the soul is an illusion or an ideological effect. On the contrary it exists, it has a reality, it is produced permanently around, on, within the body by the functioning of a power that is exercised on those punished." (Foucault 1979 Pg. 29). "The man described for us, whom we are invited to free, is already in himself the effect of a subjection much more profound than himself. A "soul" inhabits him and brings him to existence which is itself a factor in the mastery that power exercises over the body. The soul is the effect and instrument of a political autonomy; the soul is the prison of the body." (Foucault 1979 Pg. 30). Foucault then begs the question, where is this soul that entraps the powerless and the silenced of the Caribbean, how is this soul structured and constituted and what is the nature of the effect it has upon the human namely its discursive prison, a prison of texts? Questions that define the work of a physical lifetime of any given mental worker, sadly a path waiting to be trod.

Armed with the discursive crowbars and jack hammers created by Foucault as listed above, the researcher starts on his quest to deconstruct an alternative worldview towards uncovering answers for a body of questions. The limits of Foucault's tools are readily apparent for the metaphysic that informed the creation of the tools is deeply suspicious of the praxis of liberation. The tools therefore force discursive rupture at the level of the objects of knowledge, for it wrenches open the modern soul thereby exposing it to the gaze of the very objects of knowledge it imprisons and constitutes as an effect of its action. By opening the soul, the object of knowledge has the choice to surmount the discursive breach that accompanies rupture in a dualist discursive structure.

Foucault as an effect of power/ knowledge created and forced rupture but refused to exit his discursive reality via the breach. In the periphery the exiting of the discursive reality is less problematic for we experience in every instant of our existence the intersection of discursive structures in contradiction; which led to the position of the researcher that discursive liberation can only come via exiting to another alternate discursive structure.

The creation of rupture/ breach in the dominant discourse of the day must be accompanied by the articulation and strategic positioning of the alternative discourses to beckon the persons caught in discursive rupture to embrace the alternative discourses. It is therefore for the researcher a given that to date it is only through and with the application of the discursive tools of Foucault's creation that any hope of rupture can be achieved at the level of the object of knowledge via mental work. Other than that, rupture and breach are created in multi, non-complimentary discursively structured societies of the periphery through the contradictions and discursive intersections that arise between discourses which repel each other for their effects are mutually exclusive. That is why the researcher's gaze is fixed on the Islamic discourse and the coup d'état of July 27th, 1990.

"Is there a post-modern condition?" It is with great trepidation and foreboding, sensory experience largely beyond language, that the researcher creates the text of the post-modern condition. Why? The why lies in the fact that the debate is of little relevance to my existence as an effect of the discursive intersections of radically mutually exclusive discursive structures. In a social reality thrown up by hegemonic discourse, European in origin, perpetually locked in battle with various non-dualist discourses of the periphery, modernity is a non-starter. Modernity is a European concept that carries with it tons of racist baggage in the development debate. Modernity is the racist mirror presented to people of the periphery to enable us to measure our accomplishments via a mirror image, an alien yardstick brought by colonizing forces and kept alive by the neo-colonial condition.

Modernity is itself an effect of European hegemonic power/ knowledge relations used to constitute the people of the periphery, us, as objects of knowledge. Modernity is the battering ram to bash in walls erected by us in the immediate post-colonial years with the hope of creating space; whether political, economic or discursive, to enable us to launch the project of first finding the 'self', which was fractured into a million pieces by colonialism. The space is now up for grabs, and the political jamettes of the day sing praises to and worship at the feet of the new great gigolo: modernity. The hegemonic racist discourses are now renewed and are on the offensive; they want, keep or desire prisoners; they are only satisfied with total capitulation of the objects of knowledge. Modernity in the periphery is but the new herald for a new breed of plunderer in the great European tradition of Henry Morgan, Francis Drake and Hernan Cortez.

Today they come attired in designer three-piece suits made in the sweat shops of Sri Lanka, Hong Kong, the Philippines; the Bally or Florsheim wing tip shoes made in the sweat shops of Spain, Italy or Brazil. The notebook, laptop computer, cellular telephones made in the EPZ's of South Korea or Taiwan. Fully attired in the accouterments of power they move in and put in place the means of production of a new hegemonic phase of capitalism. And the discursive agencies herald their arrival through the media, the satellite dish and now cable. Pizza Hut follows Kentucky Fried Chicken and Pepsi and now McDonald's is here. The post-modern debate is therefore of minimal relevance to us of the periphery, for we are in the stage of battling Henry Morgan and Cortez reincarnated as Stanford, Princeton, Cornel educated yuppies down to their "Fruit of the Loom" underwear.

Modernity is now falling upon us and like Chicken Little the sky has fallen on our heads. Modernity relentlessly seeks to create clones on an international scale of the experiences of the North, i.e. – the white capitalist world. It eats up our cultural expressions in the periphery hoping to spit out a steady stream of homogenized objects of knowledge, but the resilience of our non-dualist discourses is a given having survived the shock of colonial occupation and the discursive contradictions are intensifying and can only create conjunctures demanding resolution.

At the outset, the raging post-modernist debate in the North points us to the reality that there is nothing given, concrete or of unchallenged hegemony in the discourse of modernity from the North. This reality feeds a movement of resistance in the periphery, for modernity emanating from the North is not a done deal: its agenda is still up for grabs. But more importantly, the most relevant aspect of the post-modernism of the North is the fact that in the arts, fashion, literary works, architecture of the North the non-dualist discursive experiences of peripheral people are the most potent driving influences on these experiences of the people of the North.

The post-modern chic, the avant-garde now scours the periphery for inspiration, for non-dualist, non-linear expressions to couch their own drive for a post-modern sensibility. We of the periphery have now, through the post-modern discursive rupture, been given the discursive means to now strike back, to launch a counterattack upon the discursive structures involved in the persistent battering down of the walls that enclose our psychic spaces. We of the periphery know, we experience it via our moaning grounds, our vision quests, our nagual, and our encompassing non-dualist discourses that the hegemony of the white, dualist discourse is dated.

Its date with retribution is at hand for we have groaned under the weight of its hegemony for over five hundred of their linear years. We gaze upon the objects of knowledge of their hegemonic, dualist, linear discourses and we see their flight back to redemptive, subjective, experiential Christianity; seeking forgiveness of sin, healing and most of all answers to the perennial question of white civilization: Whither death? We see them abandoning their positivistic Western medicine and coming to us in droves seeking wholistic/ holistic medicine. Healing mediums previously spurned, discarded and dismissed are now sought as alternative cures from alternative medicine. We see them struggling, to grasp and immerse themselves in our worldviews, our discourses, our ontologies as their creative enterprises can no longer express what they want expressed via their languages.

But most of all, and of crucial importance we see the wages of plunder, rape and destruction of the natural environment being paid in death, destruction and dislocation amongst the human race. The capitalist mode of production is now knocking up against the upper limits of its rapacious paradigm. It would continue to do so until the victim of capitalist plunder, the Earth strikes back with environmental disaster of gargantuan proportions. The signs of the backlash are evident for those with the perceptive vision to see them. The appearance of the "Green" movement within the North is indicative that the Earth crisis is now reverberating in the minds of the North.

The subjective crisis of vision, of worldview is now deep as it deconstructs structural piles sunk deep in the psyche of the North. Structures built to withstand the pounding of discursive effects are now shifting and are becoming de-centered. The post-modern condition that afflicted Weber in his later years is now the common property of the objects of knowledge of the North.

The strategy of the counterattack of the periphery is to welcome them to share our worldview, to stalk them, to initiate them into the heights of our esoteric knowledge, so long driven underground by their hegemonic discourses. By doing this, we heighten their post-modern condition for they seek direction from us in an attempt to absorb our solutions, to save their discourses, thereby hoping to ensure the hegemony of their discourses.

We know this, we "see" this in their tonal and we must use it to our advantage for when we expose them to our non-linear, non-dualist, sensory experiential worldview in all its complexity they inevitably become withdrawn, skeptical and aloof. We neutralize their discursive worldview; even though they withdraw and refuse to "pass through" the discursive breach they leave as objects of knowledge in experiential limbo, in sensory limbo, discursive zombies. The reverberations we plant in their psyche they never are able to exorcise. Why? Because we expose them to power/ knowledge whose effects are not involved in the creation of objects of knowledge, but in the linking of the human to power and knowledge that exists in the sensory realm regardless of the discursive structures of man, the perceiver of the tonal.

For an object of knowledge, an effect of power relations, to experience this power and knowledge solely through non/ extra language channels situated in seeing, hearing, touching, tasting is the most deconstructive vehicle available to humans of the North.

We of the periphery have the means and opportunity to deconstruct the pilgrims of the North for our survival centers on heightening the discursive rupture of the North, and thereby increasing the number of pilgrims seeking our shrines. The people of the North would then eventually learn the psychic importance of pilgrimage so central in the life of a Muslim. So again, why the foreboding and reluctance being experienced in creating the text? It is so because we know, we "see" those of us of the initiates of the alternate structures of power of knowledge, that the debate of modernity and the post-modern condition is of little relevance in our quest for power.

Modernity is a debate that is destined to fizzle and run aground on the rocks of the alternate worldview in the periphery. For we are assured that as long as our alternate worldview survives and replicates itself, there can be no modernity in the periphery and by extension no post-modern condition. As in the colonial order, you would have geographic pockets and spaces of modernity and within these spaces, objects of knowledge enclosed in these garrisons of modernity suffering from the post-modern condition.

By far today in Trinidad and Tobago the best examples of these objects of knowledge are situated in the University as it struggles to become a garrison of modernity; but plagued with the spatial drift and perceptive myopia of the post-modern condition. The inmates of the Twin Towers in times of lucidity seek healing in their spiritual mothers and their Orisha-Oya, Shango- to shore up and prop up their mental veracity, so vital to their exercise in modernity. But alas it's a dance of futility, for the seeds of negation of modernity are planted whenever they are given succor in the arms of the alternate worldview.

So, the garrisons of modernity would be and are encircled by the mass of an indeterminate existence, that "thing" produced by the intersections of a hegemonic discourse and an alternate discourse locked in a battle of attrition, and interspersed with the bearers of the esoteric knowledges that continue to replicate and reproduce the alternate worldviews. To step out of the garrison in your post-modern condition, you are fair game for the guerrillas of the alternate worldviews. The battle lines became drawn since Columbus and to date there has been no capitulation on either side.

The researcher then questions his motives for delving into the post-modern debate in light of what has been stated above. Ever suspicious, he insists that the motive underlying the exercise can be self-importance. The need to display my familiarity with the creators of texts of the post-modern discourse, even though their works were of minor impact on the creation of my texts. Why then this need to display, to show your linkages to a hegemonic discourse, which you have rejected?

Because you hope to have the corpus of work accepted as a valid statement fit for inclusion into the legacy of the discursive hegemony of the North. Why? Because you hope one day to become employed as a mental worker, if not in the same garrison of modernity in the periphery, then in some propagating unit of modernity in the North. By self-confession then it is an exercise that strokes my self-importance, for it shows my inability and unwillingness to situate myself totally, to immerse myself fully in the spaces controlled by alternate worldviews firm in my conviction that these spaces allow, create and replicate both the economic and spiritual means to replicate life.

In the action of creating texts, I have now fully understood the spatial movements of the carriers of the esoteric knowledges of the periphery. The constant movement from spaces controlled by the alternate worldview to those spaces under the hegemony of the dualist discourses. You must situate yourself in the spaces that reflect your worldview for that engenders linkage, depth and replication; but you must make pilgrimages to the spaces of the great tempter to test, to forge, to assay the effects of the battle between opposing worldviews in your psyche.

To create texts in a bid to woo acceptance from the objects of knowledge constituted by discursive structures is in effect an exercise in self-importance. I must now create texts which give the perceptive fields of the alternate worldview in which I situate myself. If the text fails to impress the objects of knowledge trapped in their garrison existence, then so be it. My duty as a guerrilla of an alternate worldview would have been served by the exercise. Rather than it being an exercise in futility it would have to be seen as yet another volley in the war between contending worldviews.

For stalk we must the objects of knowledge for our very lives depend on it, nothing has changed since that fateful day Columbus stepped onto the shores of his new world. In this situation I recall the words of Jeffner Allen, words of such unique reverie that it defined my affirmation, my refusal that the product of my enterprise as a mental worker would not be located within the hegemonic discursive structures of the day. But let my sister Ms. Allen speak: "How do I enter Into a discourse from which I a feminist, am Banished?" "How do I, a feminist, locate my selves, among which? Is a philosophical self, when post-modernism has become a dominant discourse of Western philosophy in the twentieth century?" (Allen 1990 Pg. 37). The answer to these questions is as follows: "By an assertion of epistemological and ontological autonomy, I thwart major sophisms. No longer caught between modernism and post-modernity, I discover spaces in which women beget women. To beget is not to assure the continuity of theory, textual authority, tradition. To beget is to move into a proximity with life; a spiritual conception of tales so imbued with life that there is no place for discipline." (Allen 1990 Pg. 45). The I, the researcher, the researcher refuses to locate my selves, much less enter into the spaces under the control of the hegemonic discourses for the sake of debate with these discursive structures. There would be no debate, rather the cut and thrust of guerrilla warfare and in the rules of engagement and order of battle, even the task of articulation of the epistemology and even more importantly the ontology of our alternative worldview is viewed with deep suspicion.

But it is a task we accept as a necessity in order for the deeply hidden suppressed knowledges to surface and by doing so challenge the hegemonic discourses of the day. Why? The answer to this lies in various perceptions, one I chose is as follows: "As the plane lifted off the ground, I looked back as the Lima coastline vanished from view. I look around at my fellow passengers and I felt at ease. I knew that we were spiritual beings living in a material world. We had chosen to have this experience for only one reason: to remember who we really were, spiritual beings from a mythos who have chosen to experience time." (Wolf 1991 Pg. 313). Again: "Life is myth and survival -this life we are living right now. All theory is a myth. It has no more reality than any other myth; we see a truth in it. But at some point, albeit a very deep one in modern physics, the myth begins to unravel. We find logical inconsistencies. So we try to rationalize the myth, turn it into a deeper truth." (Wolf 1991 Pg. 275). The drive to "rationalize the myth" has already begun in post-modernism, seen in the works of Derrida and Lyotard as they themselves have turned their backs and walked away from the very discursive breach they wished into existence. But their journey back into the discourse their textual production ruptured is a journey of mythic rationalizations thereby creating the need, especially in Lyotard, to find the "deeper truth." A journey of circularity as the author is bewitched by language and forever cursed to wander the labyrinth born out of the determinacy and centrality of language. In this labyrinth there is no breach, no escape to an alternative worldview for the author himself is in denial. Alas, death remains the only relief and source of liberation. But as death tightens its grip upon the life of the author the fundamental question lingers "after death is there language?"

In summation, the progenitors of the post-modern worldview release volley after volley of intellectual fire power upon two "essences": their Western ontology-duality and totality; but fail to discard these linchpins which hold together the Western worldview, the foundation of which is the way they view themselves as a dominant race and culture.

Foucault, Derrida, Lyotard all saw the genesis "of texts" and discourses upon dualist, totalist ontology, attacked the ontology with ardent fervor and then slipped away seeking succor in the very ontology they purportedly incapacitated.

Jeffner Allen again was right in questioning the discursive presuppositions, which informed the post-modernist attack in the Western ontology. The researcher picked up on this thread because it resonated with the ontology of the worldview in which he is situated. In fact, the textual experiences gained from reading Jeffner Allen's article afforded the angle, which the present enterprise takes. The angle being to focus on the ontologies of the discourses in conflict to "see" windows, which allow the researcher the opportunity to focus the gaze. The act of "seeing" is of specific importance to the worldview in which the researcher is situated, and at the end of the journey of research into specific theoretical streams that flow into the hegemonic discursive western structures, it is now necessary to state concisely the ontology of the worldview of the researcher.

Nagual Don Juan Matas

The words are those of Nagual Don Juan Matas as reported by Carlos Castaneda in "Tales of Power." The Nagual says: ""That's the flaw with words," he said in an assuring tone, "they always force us to feel enlightened, but when we turn around to face the world they always fail us and we end up facing the world as we always have without enlightenment. For this reason, a sorcerer seeks to Act rather than to talk and to this effect he gets a new description of the world where talking is not that important, and where new acts have new reflections."" (Castaneda 1992 Pg. 24). In the worldview of the Nagual, there is therefore no agnostic of language. Language is subjugated to the action of sensory experience for it allows us the luxury of transcending the limits of language for we taste colors, smell sounds and touch words.

The Nagual continues: ""Think of this," he went on. "The world doesn't yield to us directly, the description of the world stands in between. So properly speaking, we are always one step removed and our experience of the world is always a recollection of the experience. We are perennially recollecting the instant that has just happened, just passed. We recollect, recollect."" (Castaneda 1992 Pg. 47). Again: "Today I have to pound the nail that Genaro put in, the fact that we are luminous beings we are perceivers. We are awareness; we are not objects; we have no solidity, we are boundless. The world of objects and solidity is a way of making our passage on Earth convenient. It is only a description that was created to help us. We or rather our reason forget that the description is only a description and thus we entrap the totality of ourselves in a vicious circle from which we rarely emerge in our lifetime." (Castaneda 1992 Pg. 97). Again: ""We are perceivers," he proceeded "the world that we perceive, though is an illusion. It was created by a description that was told to us since the moment we were born."" (Castaneda 1992 Pg. 98). Again: "The trick of the sorcerer is the same trick of the average man. Both have a description one; the average man, upholds it with his "reason" the other, the sorcerer upholds with his "will". Both descriptions have their rules and the rules are perceivable, but the advantage of the sorcerer is that "will" is more engulfing than reason." (Castaneda 1992 Pg. 98). The ontology of the worldview is summed up via language in the four quotations given. Humans are perceivers and the world is grasped through description learnt, the description created by reason strives for hegemony in its incessant drive to suppress the alternate description created by will. The reason being that humans, the perceivers they are, cannot but live under the hegemony of a single description or discourse.

In the epoch of the hegemony of reason, the description of will has been driven deeply into the esoteric knowledges. The description of will, the alternate discourse, moves to subjugate the description of reason, therefore re-defining its structure and function. To discover the totality of ourselves, humans must embrace the alternate discourse/ description of will for that description re-defines the role and centrality of language which enables the initiate to enter the world of sensory experience for and in itself.

The description of will is based on the ontology of the "totality of oneself" and herein lies the enterprise of sorcery for Don Juan Matas. Don Juan teaches that human beings are in themselves illusory in their materiality, their solidity, for we are luminous beings. The description of reason throws up the perceptive fields that create this materiality, this solidity. A change to the description of will throws up the perceptive fields that destroy this materiality, this solidity and replaces it with a world of sensory sightings and positions, which are diametrically opposed to the perceptions of reason. In the world perceived through the discourse of will all organic beings become luminous entities.

There is no linear, chronological time, and there is a multiplicity of worlds differentiated by perceptual differences, but all having one thread in common their unique forms of existence compared to the world of discursive reason. The multiplicity of worlds and existences are all open to entry, permitting inhabitation and co-habitation whilst the world of reason remains unaffected or unimpinged by their modalities.

The totality of ourselves is realized when humans grounded in the discourse of reason or the tonal make the conscious move and adopt the alternate discourse of will. The discourse of will opens the way to self-actualization because humans would then be able to perceive entirely different worlds, the world of language and the world of sensory experience. The experiences created by situating oneself in both discourses create the hegemony of will, which enables humans to balance their duality of discourses.

The pre-disposition to create dualities in the discourse of reason for Don Juan is as a result of the discourse striving to actualize itself out of its fundamental imbalance. Likewise, it is apparent for the researcher that the only totality is the self, as it was for Don Juan who insists that the "other is the self." Language thrown up by the discourse of the will has no dualist linchpin and no striving for totality. The language of will is centred on power and the source of power, the Nagual. But this lies in the realm of the people of knowledge and outside the scope of this enterprise.

Don Juan Matas, speaking for the discursive body of knowledge in which he was situated, therefore insists that description is primary and a given in the actions of humans, for humans are perceivers first of reality. Description is therefore discursive and as all discourses it always seeks hegemony, but there are two possible hegemonies – one of language and one of sensory experience, and the specific points of intersection created when either discourse is hegemonic.

The experiences of Carlos Castaneda, Don Juan's initiate, would be entirely different in his discursive transition, for he moved from the hegemony of reason to that of will, forever destined to live in the spaces of intersection between both discourses. For as long as the initiate has to relate to the discourse of reason, one has to retain instances of the description of reason. So, in reality the initiate who moves from the discursive space of reason to that of will settles into a netherworld of perceptions, which straddle both discourses; whereas, the early members of the sorcerer's legacy were situated in the discourse of will moving to the description of reason when the need arose to deal with other civilizations under the hegemony of reason.

The Spanish conquest was therefore traumatic, and in fact apocalyptic, for the sorcerers' discourse because: (a) They had to grapple through perceptual contact with a discourse of reason which was unknown to them. Their description of reason had now to struggle to accommodate and absorb the Spanish discourse of reason in order to create a new discourse of reason to enable perceptual commonalities with the Spanish and thereby communication through verbal and non-verbal language. (b) Whilst grappling with the alien discourse of reason they had to ensure their physical survival for the Spanish were intent on genocide. (c) The alien discourse of reason was only satisfied with the hegemony of European reason, the discourse of will was hunted out and destroyed wherever it was found.

The sorcerers of the conquest had therefore to renounce their worldview and adopt the minimum vestiges of the European discourse of reason necessary for survival. The trauma of losing a worldview, compressed within the limits set by an alien linear time, was to tear and fragment the tonal of the Native American exposed to the ravages of European colonialism. Added to this the relentless hunger for hegemony meant that the discourse of will had to turn itself into an esoteric knowledge as it was the only alternative open to survival.

The experiences of the journey to power and knowledge therefore vary with the historical epoch, but the common experience is the same: self-actualization. The brutalized discourses of the colonized world do in fact have discursive positions on the debates within the discourses of the North. But the opposite is the lesson of this chapter, in that mental workers in the North crash into the limits of their discourses and the answers to remove their discursive crash barriers lie in the esoteric discourses of the periphery. The question for the future mental workers of the North is: who are the peripheral, ambivalent and under-developed? Because we hold the answers to the sophisms and agnostics of your discursive prisons.

Ontological Orientalism – its relevance to the Periphery

The researcher's journey of discovery soon uncovered references to the work of Edward W. Said "Orientalism" which all heaped praises upon as one of seminal uniqueness in the debate between the Orient, and specifically Islam, and the West. The experiencing of Said's text "Orientalism" was to reveal various streams of thought of vital importance to the researcher's journey of discovery. From the outset it must be pointed out that Said, geographically situated in North America, himself part of the Palestinian diaspora, takes on the Western discourse of Orientalism as a person of the periphery, but not as a Muslim of the periphery. Said therefore writes as a Palestinian Arab of the diaspora and this is seen in the worldview of the text, for Said writes as a secular Arab entrapped in the intense debate over modernity, Islam and liberation.

Said's relevance to the academic enterprise of the researcher is therefore multi-faceted as he: (a) makes his invaluable contribution to the issues of secularization and modernity in Dar ul Islam; (b) more so, he posits that the path to secularization and modernization must be based on the recognition, articulation and de-construction of the Orientalist discourse of the West which constituted its "other" the Orient, as an outcome of the European will to power, thereby entrapping the Orient in a position of subservient powerlessness; (c) But ultimately, the silence of Said on the issue of whether Islamic discourse is in fact an able alternative discourse necessary to the process of deconstruction of Orientalism and the constituting of a new discursive realm in which the Orient has ceased to exist is the most deafening silence of his text "Orientalism."

Said, positioned geographically and discursively within the belly of the beast, launched a foray against the Orientalist discourse in the tradition of guerrilla warfare à la Che Guevara. But it was only and just that, a foray, a limited engagement and the targets struck in the initial foray have now realigned themselves and the hegemonic discursive structures continue to pump out its objects of knowledge: the fanatical Muslim mullahs and their passive followers, or in other words – the fundamentalists.

"Orientalism" the text could have only been a limited foray for Said himself has withdrawn himself, physically and discursively from the people his foray was supposed to have served. Said could not be a mental worker bent on creating discursive rupture through his articulated ideas, because he himself is not situated within the dominant discourse of the people he strives to serve. He is therefore condemned to engage in futile guerrilla warfare at the level of discourses, for he does not and cannot swim amongst the people he serves. Said is therefore contending against Orientalist discursive hegemonies in the hegemonic language of the Occident, with an absent, unconcerned and irrelevant Arab audience, because the only way they could be party to Said's enterprise is to be that secular, modern Arab – the quintessential schizoid impaled on the stake of discursive contradiction/ attrition.

Said must understand that he cannot launch an attack on the hegemonic discourses of Orientalism and relegate Islamic discourse to the scrap heap of history as an irrelevant and archaic weapon in the annals of modern warfare. The masses of Dar ul Islam continue by their praxis to insist that Islamic discourse is their preferred and chosen means of defining themselves, their perceptions, their experiences and informing their actions as humans.

Mental workers who insist on creating parapets from which the movements for change would be launched, built upon alien and antagonistic discourses would and will continue to pay the price for building structures with defective intellectual lumber, many with their lives. In part this chapter would look at instances of defective structures built by mental workers in Dar ul Islam utilizing lumber of European origin, which have failed when pressure is applied by Islamic discourse.

Said's ambivalence to Islamic discourse created structures which defined his enterprise as one entirely situated in the debate within western hegemonic discourses. The discursive location of Said's text meant that he, himself, within his text was inevitably involved in the dangerous act of representing Dar ul Islam as an anti-other/ Oriental signified of the Orientalist. In this act of representation, he was now creating his own field of representation that could only throw up alien mirages when viewed by the humans of Dar ul Islam, but for Said he saw only liberated ex-Orientals, secular, modern Arabs.

What was this discursive location? Said's text comes straight out of Foucault's worldview as of the epoch which culminated in Discipline and Punish, but this worldview has to be welded to the specificity of being an Oriental. Said's text is the pivotal work in which Foucault's discursive structures are applied to the task of deconstructing hegemonic discursive structures of the post-colonial periphery.

Said, by embracing Foucault's worldview, positions himself within a specific field within the western discursive structures and enables persons within these discursive fields to create critiques, which debate Foucault rather than Said. These debates do not interest the researcher for as a human of the periphery my main interest is to discover the insights, if any, offered by Said's interpretation of Orientalist discourse through Foucault's worldview. More so, the answers must be found for the glaring shortfalls of the text from the perceptions of a person of the periphery as outlined before.

The issue with Said's text would not be resolved through a futile debate over his Foucauldian lineage and the "correctness" of Foucault's worldview. In fact, the researcher commends Said for recognizing that when a person of the periphery is in need of insights, articulations and revelations of and about the hegemonic western discourses that kept us of the periphery in "objecthood" for too long measured in linear time, the best tools to grasp are those thrown up by the mental foundry of Foucault's worldview.

But alas within that statement lies the fundamental difference between the researcher and Said of the text. For Said, clearly was not seeking tools for analysis and articulation as he was shopping around for a non-Islamic discourse, which allowed him the means and the space from which to launch forays against the hegemonic Orientalist discourse of the West.

Said, the constituted other, could only purchase a Western alternate discourse founded on the ontological concepts which gave Said modernity, secularization and humanism, whilst allowing him the means to dismiss Orientalist discourse. Said could only find this discourse he so eagerly sought amongst the new philosophers of the Nietzschean re-awakening. Said's embrace of Foucault is therefore not surprising for it gives him the luxury of critique, the praxis of change whilst retaining and jealously guarding all the metaphysical essences he desires, which he yearns for and only found for himself in Western, white civilization.

He, Said desires: rationality, secularization and modernity. Ultimately, he posits that it is by only embracing modern Western capitalism that the Orient can acquire the means to stop being the Occident's other, the Oriental. Sadly, Said is but another mental worker of the periphery burdened with the "black mirage." For Said, Orientalism is the ultimate barrier that creates on a continuing basis "the other", the Oriental, that are fetters on the inevitable march of history, in its linear rationality, towards capitalism. Orientalist discourse is, therefore by extrapolation, irrational as it continues to create representations and objects of knowledge, which retard the hegemony of the discourses. Orientalist discourse is therefore trapped in an ideational inertia, seen in the works produced by American Orientalists in the post-world war two era.

Perhaps for Said, Foucault's worldview allows one the ability to break up the discursive log jam of the American Orientalist discourse, thereby allowing the creation of new organic strains of discourse, which would now address the issue of secularization and modernity in the Orient, but Said must now be allowed to speak from his text to throw light on his worldview. Said reveals: "The Arab world today is an intellectual, political, and cultural satellite of the United States. This is not in itself to be lamented; the specific form of the satellite relationship, however is." (Said 1978 Pg. 322). The import of the words quoted need no comment for they indicate Said's position in relation to Dar ul Islam and its relations with the "Great Satan." But Said continues revealing his worldview as he says: "In addition, the Arab and Islamic world remains a second-order power in terms of the production of culture, knowledge, and scholarship. No Arab or Islamic scholar can afford to ignore what goes on in scholarly journals, institutes, and universities in the United States and Europe; the converse is not true." (Said 1978 Pg. 323). The worldview is now clearly apparent, Said labors under the weight of the white worldview he continues to carry as one of the children of Sisyphus. To write a text, to give words to experiences, to create structures to deconstruct Orientalist discourse, and at the end of your enterprise you reveal that all you really want is to contribute to the creation of a neo-Orientalist discourse is in itself an agenda that evokes the only solution possible from the researcher, i.e. – Glock love.

We of the periphery rankle, rant and rave at the arrogant racism of the Orientalist, but Said you are worse for you inspired hope, you challenged us to grasp the intellectual mettle, we took up the gauntlet you threw down, only to realize that you are the worst possible form of peripheral intellectual existence. You are simply an intellectual mercenary in the service of the hegemonic Orientalist discourses of the day. Your role as the intellectual jamette is to draw us out, to ferret us out of our burrows and lead us to the fatal embrace of Orientalist discourse. You, Said, are the quintessential intellectual lagahoo who arouses us with the aroma of resistance and the promise of perceptual liberation, but as we walk together, you must always hide your Orientalist cow foot via the circular dualities of Foucault's danse macabre.

Some of us never expose your Orientalist cow foot until it is too late for us and we end up condemned to the netherworld of the third world intellectual, forever doomed to walk a perceptual limbo cut off from organic contact with the powerless and silenced, whilst always seeking to prove one's intellectual credentials and worth to the discursive structures of the North.

You see Said, there are Arab and Islamic scholars who can afford to ignore what goes on in the knowledge producing Orientalist structures of the North. To these Arab and Islamic scholars there is no need to create knowledge-producing structures to rival Oxford, Harvard or UCLA. Why? Because Said when you are situated and placed in your alternative worldview, the knowledge created by and in contradictory worldviews don't change the price of cocoa in your worldview. The Orientalist knowledge generated in the West is of no relevance to the Muslim seeking union with her God, as is the Coca Cola she drinks or the television and radio programs she experiences. For if they were, there would have been no Islamic Revolution in Iran and the consequent turmoil that has swept through the secularist Muslim states as Algeria, Egypt and Afghanistan.

Said ultimately from his Arab/ Saxon worldview can only see the overwhelming potency of the white man's Orientalist discourse, sadly as an Arab, but more so a Palestinian Arab, he sees no resistance and the discursive structures which were at the basis of the movements of resistance. Said refuses to give credence to movements of resistance, if and when those movements of resistance in themselves were not articulating or defining their discursive structures and positions in relation to the white man's Orientalist discourse. Resistance for Said is therefore creating discursive agencies and structures, which would throw up knowledges to rival the corpus of texts being produced by Oxford, Harvard and UCLA. The "Other" therefore resists Orientalism by situating its "otherness" within the discourse that defines the very "other." In other words, Said you are wandering aimlessly the wasteland of the black mirage. The linear dating of your text "Orientalism" did not allow you to textualise on the impact of the Iranian Revolution on your neo-Orientalist white worldview.

And the researcher eagerly awaits the experience of journeys through your texts, if any dealing with Iran without the Shah and the Intifada without Yasser Arafat. For you see Said the mullahs of Iran and the children of the Intifada offer up potent images of the worldview, burdened with Orientalists as Gibb, Massignon, et al. and neo-Orientalist house slaves as yourself, can still when it so determines create mechanisms to resolve contradictions which are uniquely the products of the worldview.

The potency of the worldview therefore excludes from its agenda the need to replicate, to debate with Orientalism via Orientalist idioms, to create parallel discursive structures, which would give succor to the neo-orientalist Arab elite liberating them from the anxieties of the diaspora. Ultimately, Said and the mental workers in exile within the belly of the beast lament the fact that the alternative discourse of resistance has created an agenda of resistance that does not see them, much less welcome them. For the strategies of resistance formulated by the discursive streams of resistance all have one central theme, i.e. – violent resolution of the contradictions.

The resolution of the contradiction involves in all cases addressing death, accepting death and using death as a discursive statement of liberated non-Orientalist space. The use of death to create resistance, to liberate space, both mental, spatial, geographical, and discursive, is the most potent weapon used to date by the powerless of the periphery in our incessant battles with the hegemony of the North since Columbus crossed the Atlantic Ocean. Islamic discourse has created its own unique reveries of death to create liberated space in which the assailed discourse blossoms and gathers voices, articulations necessary for asserting its hegemony. Said, as all compromised intellectuals of the periphery cannot accept, much less organically ground himself in such strategies of resistance, hence their flight to the North and exile in the belly of the beast. Said says therefore: "My project has been to describe a particular system of ideas, not by any means to displace the system with a new one." (Said 1978 Pg. 325).

Said was to publish in the 1980's the article "Orientalism Reconsidered" revealing his continued debate with his Orientalist texts, but subtle changes in his discursive worldview as he now drifts amongst the thinkers of the post-modernist western debate. Said trapped within his post-modern discursive black hole continues to address himself to debates which are of no relevance to the people burdened with Orientalist space and discursively designated.

In "Orientalism Reconsidered", Said makes not one single reference to the discursive battles of Dar ul Islam, to Said: the Orient. His spatial vision is blinkered, he is handicapped perceptually for his Orient resides only in the texts created by Orientalists, sadly Said has textualised himself and his fellow castaways on the shores of the land of Oz. The verdict on Said's enterprise stated above would now give way to Said's words. Words, which form the basis of the verdict given on Said's enterprise. Said states: "I have found it useful here to employ Michel Foucault's notion of a discourse, as described by him in the Archaeology of Knowledge and in Discipline and Punish, to identify Orientalism." He goes on: "My contention is that without examining Orientalism as a discourse one cannot possibly understand the enormously systematic discipline by which European culture was able to manage and even produce -the Orient politically, sociologically, militarily, ideologically, scientifically, and imaginatively during the post-enlightenment period." (Said 1985 Pg. 3). Again: "The relationship between Occident and Orient is a relationship of power, of domination of varying degrees of a complex hegemony." (Said 1985 Pg. 5). Said's text situates his work at the heart of Foucault's enterprise, thereby his insistence on viewing Orientalism through Foucault's panopticon but in addition in keeping with Foucault of Discipline and Punish he has to focus on the scientifico-juridical complex, the political economy of the body, the political technology of the body, the micro-physics of the body consequently the objects of knowledge, the products of power/ knowledge relations. He glaringly fails to articulate the power/ knowledge relations of Orientalism, which creates the Oriental as an object of knowledge by investing us with the soul, the effect of the microphysics of power on the body of the Oriental.

It is the researcher's position that even if Said wanted to, he cannot and could not articulate the power knowledge relations of the genealogy of the modern "soul" for he would have to create those structures in the Orient because they simply do not exist. And this is perhaps the most potent indication of the limits of Foucault's worldview outside of modern European capitalism. Capitalism did not, cannot replicate the social structures which Foucault interpreted in his enterprise in the periphery. The reason for this comes out of Foucault's enterprise itself, but Said cannot grasp that thread. Said's text continuously speaks about, mourns the undeniable historical fact for Said that it was the inherent weaknesses of Arab society that allowed these societies to be conquered by capitalist Europe. His enterprise is to understand the nature of Orientalism that fostered, created, threw up this European expansionism, this predilection to acquire geography and peoples in an imperial colonial necklace. Said is therefore at the outset seeking only one single, simple thing the European metaphysical "essences" that gives him the answer to his problematic.

In seeking this essence, this ontological predilection uniquely European, Said could not even be faithful to Foucault's genealogy of the modern soul. Said simply does not see the need to recognize, much less listen to the voices of Dar ul Islam, for in his perceptions he only sees Oriental/ Orient a hegemonic label stamped on Dar ul Islam by Orientalism. There are no struggles of resistance, no voices of Dar ul Islam, no contending discourse striving for its own hegemony. For Said only the oriental has voice, all other species are deaf mutes. For Said there was then total capitulation which makes his enterprise fatalistically nihilist in vision and worldview. Said simply then did not have the intellectual rigor, the testicular fortitude, to apply the genealogy of the modern soul to his Orient for fear that it would not only indicate the limits of its relevance as a method of mapping to the periphery, but more so the certainty that it would unearth for Said the existence of an alternate discourse forever trapped in the struggle for hegemony with his Orientalism.

An alternate discourse since the Iranian Revolution now in its ascendancy in its struggle with Orientalism. Perhaps Said refuses to recognize the potency of Islamic discourse in its struggle with Orientalism because he blames Islam for the so-called weaknesses, which allowed European penetration and conquest, especially from the 19th century onwards. To recognize Islamic discourse as the contending discourse is to then refuse to believe that modernization is possible, hence no liberation, no progress for Said. He can only turn his back from his Dar ul Islam and only see a conquered determined instance of Orientalism, nothing else. Ultimately for his enterprise there is no possibility of liberation, that is why he has no problem with the Orient continuing its subservience being the satellite of the United States.

A new re-defined "other", a post-modern Oriental state of existence is desirable when faced with feudal Islamic fundamentalism. For Said there is only the aimlessness of a fatalistic nihilism. Said continues: "My thesis is that the essential aspects of modern Orientalist theory and praxis [from which present day Orientalism derives] can be understood, not as a sudden access of objective knowledge about the Orient, but as a set of structures inherited from the past, secularized redisposed, and re-formed by such disciplines as philosophy, which in turn were naturalized, modernized and laicized substitutes for [or versions of] Christian supernaturalism. In the form of new texts and ideas, the East was accommodated to these structures." (Said 1985 Pg. 122). Again: "The four elements I have described- expansions, historical confrontation, sympathy, classification- are the currents in 18th century thought on whose presence the specific intellectual and institutional structures of modern Orientalism depend. Without them Orientalism, as we shall see presently, could not have occurred." (Said 1985 Pg. 120). Again: "this is not to say that the old religious patterns of human history and destiny and the 'existential paradigms' were simply removed. Far from it they were reconstituted, redeployed, redistributed in the secular frameworks just enumerated." "it also retained, as an undislodged current in its discourse, a reconstituted religious impulse, a naturalized supernaturalism. What I shall try to show is that this impulse in Orientalism resided in the Orientalist's conception of himself, of the Orient and of his discipline." (Said 1985 Pg. 121). Said uncovered his metaphysical "essence" which ensured Europe's ability to mutate their orientalist discourse to the state of it being a "doxology" thereby ensuring its discursive hegemony, continuity and survival. The "essence" is simply supernaturalism in its manifestations from Christian to natural supernaturalism, but more so its potency articulated through the person of the Orientalist in whom it was located.

Said therefore creates the linear historical continuum of Europe's orientalist enterprise, for European supernaturalism threw up: "a closed system, in which objects are what they are because they are what they are, for once, for all time, for ontological reasons that no empirical material can either dislodge or alter." (Said 1985 Pg. 70). Said's enterprise is now complete, he found the European "essence", the metaphysic construct, which informs Orientalism through linear time. For Said therefore there could be no historicist explanations for the form Orientalism took with the appearance of European industrial capitalism. He continually hints in passing that Orientalist discourse had the ability and did will European expansionism into existence. He is therefore a loyal student of Foucault's enterprise, especially so in his search for the ontological "essence" he found the holy grail, the will to knowledge, truth and power. Said now holds his ontological essence: supernaturalism and the holy grail: the will to truth, but where is the path that extricates the periphery from the field, the text of Orientalism? Is there the possibility of the represented "other" extricating ourselves from Orientalist discourse? If yes, what is the necessary praxis of liberation? Are we "the other" to effect change must now create an ontological "essence" a metaphysic that parallels, imitates, clones the European ontological "essence", thereby creating an ontological Orientalism in reverse? We then create a parody, for no matter how vigorous our methodology of cloning be, we of the periphery lack one salient reality necessary and vital to ensure the success of the exercise, i.e. – the technological veracity that ensures our ability to dominate, to invade, to appropriate space and the bodies that inhabit space.

Ontological Orientalism in reverse is a futile act of resistance on the level of attempting to stop a cruise missile with spitballs. And this is what Said fails to see with his search for ontological essences, for without the technological means that allowed conquest and occupation, Orientalism would have remained a stunted textual exercise locked up and circumvented by the intellectual ghettos, which ensured its irrelevant survival.

It was not Orientalism that ensured victory over the Native Americans and the Zulu nation but technology, because peripheral peoples have repeatedly shown through the numerous defeats in battle inflicted upon European colonial armies, that the only difference between them was the relative efficiency of European weaponry in exterminating life, i.e. – the force multiplying effect of technology. The white man's ontological predilections rather than ensuring his superiority in many instances, informed the blunders of his colonial journeys. In his conflict with, we the peoples of the periphery, his technologies of mass destruction have always ensured his continued hegemony.

That is why today we of the periphery are locked in a never-ending quest to acquire our own weapons of mass destruction, for it is with acquisition of these weapons and the means of delivery that Orientalism would finally meet a potent adversary. It is indicative of the discursive positioning of Ontological orientalism in reverse that its main proponents in the Orient are members of the Westernized, secularized, modernized ruling elites. Faced with constant pressure from Islamic discourse, they now hope to create space for themselves by hoping their ontological determinism embraces and absorbs the elements of Islamic discourse that constantly attack their marginal existence.

This class has concentrated on embracing the monster they created – fundamentalism, through the centrality of essences, in their discourses such as the "Arab language", the "Arab nation", the "Arab experience"; all unique, distinct and essences that ensure the inherent superiority of the Arab race. It is but an old strategy to utilize racist nationalism to fracture the all-embracing reality of the Ummah created by Islamic discourse. The proxies of the white man's Orientalism are simply continuing the struggle with Islamic discourse in the neo-colonial realities of today.

Sadly, Said answers the question with his acceptance of the need for the Orient to be satellites of the United States. As for Foucault, Said does not have a praxis of liberation for his worldview, as Foucault's, does not or cannot envisage the possibility of revolution given their metaphysical determinism manifested through the totality of and totalitarian rule of discourse. Their metaphysical determinism made discourse into the transcendental locomotive of history, and not even Foucault's archaeology or genealogy were capable of moving from recognizing and mapping these discourses and their objects of knowledge to the formulation of strategies to dethrone them, for Foucault looked over fields of European history and only saw the irrepressible march of ontological essences from Homer to Boy George.

Said located himself within this worldview from which he produced his text "Orientalism", but the need for liberation constantly presses the psyche of the people of the periphery, but in his text there is no liberation as in all his mentor's texts. The effect is noticeable in the text "Orientalism Reconsidered" for Said no longer speaks of Foucault and more so, he now cites: (a) the research going on in the periphery and for the periphery; (b) he cites a new mentor in passing, but for those of us exposed to the intellectual debates it is a major re-focus for he cites Frederic Jameson.

Sad to say in Jameson, Said would not and cannot find the strategy of and for liberation he craves. For what Said needs is first to remove the blinkers to deconstruct himself, thereby allowing him to see the solutions and strategies being created by peoples who are in no way silenced or deaf mutes. He must now find relevance; he must now swim amongst the people and make his pilgrimage to find the centre. If he cannot accept the validity of the discursive positions of the people from whence he came and who, like him, seek release from the European colonial yokes then he can only end his days a lonely castaway on the shores of Babylon. What then is Said's patrimony to the enterprises of the mental workers of the periphery? For the researcher, Said found his metaphysical locomotive of European history, this supernaturalistic essence carried around in the perceptive matrices of the European. This ontological essence, from Homer to Bill Clinton, ensures the survival, regeneration and re-constitution of a salient feature of the European worldview: Orientalism. For this researcher, I prefer a descriptive term of the European condition of more salient relevance to the periphery: racism. Said situated himself within Foucault's worldview and came up with the will to truth, will to knowledge and the will to power that drives the nature and structures of European discursive productions in its contact with non-white peoples of the Earth, i.e. – racism.

To dismiss the researchers' position on European ontological racism the apologists for Europe must dismiss Foucault's enterprise for it is through Foucault's worldview, we of the periphery have now finally deconstructed European racism. What we the victims of the white man's racism have always known through contact with Europeans in our daily lives, has now been confirmed by one stream of European discourse. Said says: "Being a white man, in short, was a very concrete manner of being-in-the-world, a way of taking hold of reality, language, and thought. It made a specific style possible." "Kipling himself could not merely have happened, the same is true of his white man. Such ideas and their authors emerge out of complex historical and cultural circumstances, at least two of which have much in common with the history of Orientalism in the 19th century." (Said 1978 Pg. 227). The specific styles of racism are all clearly discernible and are experienced by us, the non-whites, in our daily contact with whites. But what has always troubled us in the periphery is the fact that the common thread that runs through our history since that fateful day in 1492, over 500 years of history, is the resilience of racism in our relations with the White Man and the fact that it has been his most potent contribution to our patrimony in the post-colonial era of our history. The White Man's most potent legacy left to us is racism, sad to say we cannot use the past tense of the verb.

Said knowingly or unknowingly presents for us an entirely new angle to the issue for he posits a new field of knowledge, a new approach based on a post-Nietzschean worldview. Out of Foucault comes the concept of Ontological Racism/ Orientalism, which enables the periphery to reject the most potent blinkers to date embraced by mental workers of the periphery in our attempt to come to grips with the continuity, the resilience of European racism, i.e. – the historicist, determinist/ materialist blindfold.

The hegemony of Marx's worldview amongst mental workers of the periphery always ensured that we reject and continuously struggle against any worldview that saw racism as being ontologically constituted and driven. We must reject any metaphysical determinism and relentlessly seek causality in the material relations of society. Racism was for those carrying Marx's ghost the product of specific material relations, a superstructural instance. But the purveyors of this worldview were always at pains to explain why the continued survival and potency of racism in the White man's worldview, even though capitalism was now in the stage of "late capitalism". Therefore, the mode of production continued to change, to mutate, but the superstructural instance that is racism does not reflect these changes, the Ku Klux Klan is now joined by the neo-Nazis.

What we got from Western Marxism, both Critical Theory and Structural Marxism, was plain and simple apologetics, such as the over determination of racism as a superstructural instance, false consciousness, ideology and the structures that produce culture. But what the historicists could not answer were the specific questions thrown up by Caribbean history. Columbus in 1492 should have been devoid of conceptions of inferiority linked to skin type, physical appearances, cultural practices which were the possessions of non-white people and superiority based on whiteness. For the historicists he at best should have been only beset by the plague of 'androcentric ethno-centrism', whatever that is. For it is a very shady boundary that separates racism from ethno-centrism as constituted by a minority race on this planet. But the historical record shows that alongside the normal activities of conquest and plunder so common to male history on this planet, there was a parallel activity of destroying historical records which would have effectively challenged the ontological superiority, hence the discursive basis, of the White Man's enterprise and his mandate to rule inferior races. Why in the midst of conquest, selected agents of European discursive structures, mainly Catholic priests, were charged with and ruthlessly carried out the strategy of forcing the discourses they met into becoming ruthlessly suppressed esoteric knowledges?

The writings of the Maya were hunted out and destroyed, temple carvings were destroyed or removed to Europe and the living carriers of the oral traditions, the history of the peoples were hunted to almost extinction. Why was it a unique strategy of European conquest, regardless of the mode of production or historical epoch in which it was launched, to destroy, stamp out and suppress the knowledges of the people it conquered?

The armies of Alexander the Great torched the largest collection of written works in the history of man at that time at Alexandria in Egypt. The agents of intellectual European colonialism followed their armies into the New World destroying knowledge wherever they ventured. We of the Caribbean periphery have always asked why? The evidence points to one salient reason and that is, wherever the European ventured or ventures all systems of knowledge that challenge his ontological premise of inherent superiority have to be destroyed at best, at least esotericized. The esoteric knowledges give us the evidence that overwhelmingly confirms the paranoia of the white man's quest for hegemony.

For example, in the book "They came before Columbus" by Ivan Van Sertima, we of the periphery are shown that the existence of African peoples in the Caribbean before Columbus was confirmed by written reports of the Spanish conquest, which naturally were ruthlessly suppressed by Europe. In turn African accounts, including Egyptian, of voyages to and from the Western Hemisphere before Columbus were suppressed by Europe since the epoch of Columbus voyages. A people undertake the task to suppress knowledge like this for one plausible reason since the 15th century onwards and only one: ontological racism. The inherent superiority of the white man and his enterprise is simply dashed, destroyed on the rocks of the reality that Africans preceded the white man to the Western Hemisphere. The growing mass of evidence which points to a vibrant link and syncretic cultural fusion between Egypt, starting between 800 BC - 700 BC, and continuing with West Africa as late as the 14th century and areas of the western hemisphere struggles to gain white academic recognition. Then there are the extensive voyages of the Chinese Admiral Zeng He to the Western Hemisphere from 1406 to 1433 without any colonial imperial agenda.

To refuse to accept the positions of the esoteric knowledges is but another attempt to deny the discourse of the silenced and peripheralized voice. The esoteric knowledges of the periphery are now becoming vociferous, and with each revelation another nail in the coffin of the historicist worldview is placed. Historicism has failed the periphery by simply maintaining the hegemony of the white man's worldview. It denied us the means to "gaze" upon his metaphysical/ ontological essences that constitute his worldview, and for this it must be relegated to the la basse of the periphery.

The lesson to be learnt from Said's enterprise is that in any enterprise that seeks to investigate any specific reality or experience of the periphery, the mental worker cannot evade fixing the gaze at the level of discourse. To do this inevitably leads to the discovery of: (a) the ontological essences that inform the discursive structures; (b) the power relations that ensure discursive hegemony. Said in the text specifically focuses on a resilient discourse of Europe and explained its hegemonic dominance across historical epochs through its ontological essences, which are central to the European worldview. The ontological essences constitute the European worldview and racism is an organic part of this worldview because the European metaphysic calls it into perpetual existence. To end European racism there is but one strategy to deconstruct and re-constitute the ontological essences of the European worldview.

No minority race that has enjoyed world hegemony for so long would ever undertake such a vision quest. For to do so the esoteric knowledges of the periphery would surface and flourish and continued European world hegemony would not be guaranteed. But more so, Europe cannot be expected to commit race suicide thereby destroying the "White Man" and turning Europe into, but a lonely geographic expression. We of the periphery are only left with the task of understanding, and with the knowledge this brings setting about the task of unearthing and giving voice to esoteric knowledges of the periphery, some of which are hidden within the Islamic discourse.

That is why Said cannot be forgiven for the painful failures of his enterprise, for he himself refused to carry his enterprise to its consummate end, for as that particular creature of colonial domination the black skin white mask, the Sino, Indo, Afro, Arab/ Saxon he refuses to walk away from his white worldview, thereby accepting the peculiarities and ambivalence of what it is to be the peripheral in the "White Man's" hegemony. Said cannot commit worldview suicide for he is convinced that there is nothing "positive", "progressive", "modernist", "secular" in the periphery he left as a child for the embrace of Babylon. But sadly, his categories of disdain, dismissal and deep psychic pain are all white in origin, but he can never be white, and so he withers under the weight of self-contempt, self-hatred and self-immolation: an existence that cannot be a brave new example for those of the periphery.

Said's enterprise is a living lesson for those of us, the mental workers of the periphery. His enterprise produces insights, incisive tools of exploration, discovery and understanding, but it cannot point to praxis of change and liberation. For Said to do this he must embrace his peripheral essences and thereby journey to find the centre. The centre, which teaches that there is a means of change and liberation in the periphery that is reachable and attainable for those of us who so seek.

Said owes it to himself to give voice to the esoteric knowledges of the periphery. His pilgrimage brings to mind the journey of discovery and re-definition a pilgrimage evoked in the mind of Malik al-Shabazz (Malcolm X). Thoughts of acute relevance for the enterprise at hand and the journeys of the peoples of the periphery. Malik al-Shabazz speaks: "The black man needs to reflect that he has been America's most fervent Christian.... and where has it gotten him? In fact in the white man's hands, in the white man's interpretation...where has Christianity brought this world?" "Only one religion Islam had the power to stand and fight the white man's Christianity for a thousand years! Only Islam could keep white Christianity at bay." (Haley 1976 Pg. 486). "Indeed, how can white society atone for enslaving? for raping, for unmanning, for otherwise brutalizing millions of human beings, for centuries? What atonement would the God of Justice demand for the robbery of the black peoples' labour, their lives, their true identities, their culture, their history and even their human dignity?" (Haley 1976 Pg. 488). "He will make use of me dead, as he has made use of me alive, as a convenient symbol of "hatred"- and that will help him to escape facing the truth that all I have been doing is holding up a mirror to reflect, to show, the history of unspeakable crimes that his race has committed against my race." (Haley 1976 Pg. 500). The words of Malik al-Shabazz were not silenced with his murder, and these words uttered in the 1960's have resurfaced in the 1990's because the vision that informed these words has never lost its incisive grasp of the racism that pervades the white man's discursive structures. It is a telling summation of the gulf that exists between enterprises of the mental workers of the people of the periphery and discourses of the silenced that a non-academic mental worker was able to sum up the realities of peripheral existences in terms, which only now are being articulated by mental workers.

Malcolm X saw the realities of black inner-city existences in the 1960s and explained these realities through theoretical frameworks only now being embraced by the mental workers of the periphery. The single salient difference between Malik al-Shabazz and the academics is the organic link he possessed with the silenced and powerless. It was because of the potency of this organic link he paid the ultimate price: his life.

The white man's discourse/ worldview constituted him a nigger and he continuously strove to deconstruct himself, to liberate himself from the fields of knowledge that continuously constituted him a nigger. In his enterprise of liberation he understood, practiced and taught that liberation commences first at the level of the individual and consciousness. The worldview he discovered that for him satisfied his need for healing, for wholeness, for the love which enabled him to embrace all of humanity regardless of race was Islam. For he posited that being a nigger he was totally severed from the solidarity of being human. Malik al-Shabazz therefore accepted and posited Islam as the alternative discourse of liberation for the Afro-American.

In this lies his relevance for the enterprise at hand but more so, it compels the people of the periphery to repeat his journey and within ourselves work out our own vision quest, our alternative worldview that is the only basis for our praxis of liberation. For liberation from the burdens of colonial domination is a must, a necessity, an organic demand for we have labored too long under the burdens of self-hatred and self-immolation.

At this juncture in the journey of discovery, re-discovery and research the pilgrim recollected words of the long silenced native American. Words which showed the native American's inability to not only comprehend the ways of the White Man but more so, their inability to create their own discourse of ontological racism in reverse as a discursive weapon of resistance.

Malcolm X of the Nation of Islam drew sustenance and visionary definition from a specific discourse of ontological racism in reverse. The worldviews of the Native Americans did not allow them to create similar discursive structures. To create a discourse of ontological racism in reverse, the Native American would have been forced to abandon their worldview, their discursive structures and adopt those of the white man. In their thousands they willingly accepted their fate: death and so died grounded in their worldview.

The lessons to be learnt from the words that follow are legion, but perhaps the most potent one is the fact that the Native American has shown that the resilience of your discursive structures is not the product of the material relations of society/ the mode of production. The Native Americans, who were at the fringes of metal producing technology with the coming of the "white man", were able to first propel themselves into a situation where they rapidly absorbed and adapted to the white man's material culture and secondly continued to adhere to worldviews which resisted the white man's physical and psychic onslaughts to the point of death.

The Native American resistance to the "white man's" genocide is therefore an object lesson in the resilience of alternative ontological/ metaphysical structures of the periphery. The insights it affords point to the survival of the knowledges of the silenced and powerless, and the transmission of discourses through esoteric knowledges. But now let the silenced speak: "Where today are the Pequot? Where are the Narragansett, the Mohican, the Pokanoket, and many other once powerful tribes of our people? They have vanished before the avarice and the oppression of the white man, as snow before a summer sun. Will we let ourselves be destroyed in our turn? Without a struggle, give up our homes, our country bequeathed to us by the Great Spirit, the graves of our dead and everything that is dear and sacred to us? I know you will cry with me, Never! Never!" Tecumseh of the Shawnees. (Brown 1976 Pg. 1). "The whites were always trying to make the Indians give up their life and live like white men, go to farming, work hard and do as they did- and the Indians did not know how to do that, and did not want to anyway... If the Indians had tried to make the whites live like them, the whites would have resisted, and it was the same way with many Indians." Wamditanka of the Santee Sioux/ Dakota. (Brown 1976 Pg. 38). "I have heard that you intend to settle us on a reservation near the mountains. I don't want to settle. I have to roam over the prairies. There I feel free and happy, but when we settle down we grow pale and die. I have laid aside my lance, bow and shield, and yet I feel safe in your presence. I have told you the truth. I have no little lies hid about me, but I don't know how it is with the commissioners. Are they as clear as I am? A long time ago this land belonged to our fathers; but when I go up to the river I see camps of soldiers on its banks. These soldiers cut down my timber; they kill my buffalo, and when I see that, my heart feels like bursting; I feel sorry.... has the white man become a child that he should recklessly kill and not eat? When the red men slay game, they do so that they may live and not starve." Satanta, Chief of the Kiowas. (Brown 1976 Pg. 235). "The Earth was created by the assistance of the sun and it should be left as it was....the country was made without lines of demarcation, and it is no man's business to divide it.... I see the whites all over the country gaining wealth, and see their desire to give us lands which are worthless....The Earth and myself are of one mind. The measure of the land and the measure of our bodies are the same. Say to us if you can say it, that you were sent by the Creative Power to talk to us. Perhaps you think the Creator sent you here to dispose of us as you see fit. If I thought you were sent by the creator I might be induced to think you had a right to dispose of me. Do not misunderstand me, but understand me fully with reference to my affection for the land. I never said the land was mine to do with as I chose. The one who has the right to dispose of it is the one who has created it. I claim a right to live on my land, and accord you the privilege to live on yours." Heinmot Tooyalaket of the Nez Perce. (Brown 1976 Pg. 300). Finally, the lament of genocide: "I did not know then how much was ended. When I look back now from this high hill of my old age, I can still see the butchered women and children lying heaped and scattered all along the crooked gulch as plain as when I saw them with eyes still young. And I can see that something else died there in the bloody mud, and was buried in the blizzard. A people's dream died there. It was a beautiful dream...the nation's loop is broken and scattered. There is no center any longer and the sacred tree is dead." Black Elk bearer of the esoteric knowledges of the Sioux/ Lakota. (Brown 1976 Pg. 419). The quotations reveal diversity in the worldviews articulated, but one central reality pervades: the fact that the actions of the White Man was for the Native American reprehensible as it flouted and trampled every perceptive field of interpretation which made up their worldview.

Satanta could only say that the white man's actions were those of a child. Where then is the ontological/ metaphysical constructs of racism, or ethnocentrism? Why didn't these voices of the Native American articulate their rejection of the white man's genocide through the spoken words of plain and simple racism? It would have been very simple for Black Elk, Satanta and Heinmot Tooyalaket to establish their innate superiority through the differences they perceived between their actions/ perceptions and experiences and those of the white man. Why didn't they articulate their 'chosen people' status through their link to their metaphysical concepts/ constructs of the supernatural? Why didn't they then formulate ontological essences, which assured their innate superiority and their ultimate victory in the psychic realm of definition of self? Based on this the white man would have become the Native American's other, the great Satan. These are all questions, which arise from the hegemonic ontological essences of the discursive structures of the European. But the very said questions did not and could not be thrown up by the ontological structures of the Native American worldviews.

The most potent evidence for this is found in the movement called the Dance of the Ghosts. By 1878, the Teton Sioux/ Lakota clans were defeated in battle having paid dearly for the humiliation of the white man at the Little Big Horn. The survivors of this massive onslaught on the clans of the plains were locked up in reservations, a broken and defeated people. By the final quarter of 1890 a movement of rebirth swept through the nations of the plains based on the teachings of the Paiute Messiah, Woroka. Woroka's discourse was centered on a mixture of Christianity and Native American revival and restoration. Woroka proclaimed himself to be the

Native American messiah à la Christ, being all-powerful and all-knowing. The transformation was to be effected through the dance. All Native Americans were required to dance until transformation, renewal and restoration of the Native Americans' physical and mental realities and sensibilities by the Great Spirit. The Native Americans danced and there was no renewal, no restoration, but still there was no creation of ontological racism in reverse to give succor to the dehumanized. Why? Because the carriers of the esoteric knowledges today of all Native Americans, whether they be in the frozen tundra of the North, the plains of the central expanses or the tropical jungles of the South, continue to insist that their worldviews do not contain the ontological structures which allow the formulation of racist discourse.

Ontological racism in reverse amongst the peoples of the periphery is therefore the result of carrying around in our perceptive fields the metaphysical constructs borrowed from the "White Man." It is a learned perceptive habit, reflexive and reflective linkages from our colonial domination under the hegemonic order of the "White Man's" discursive structures. To decouple individual perceptions and action from a racist worldview requires the adoption of an alternate worldview, which does not allow the creation of ontological structures, which create, replenish and renew racist worldviews. The task is Herculean and Pol Pot's enterprise in Kampuchea comes to mind, the creation of a new society based on and informed by a new alternate worldview, realized through the wiping out of two generations of Cambodians infected by and with the worldview slated for destruction and blotting out from their psyches.

In the end whatever the ideal, genocide is still genocide, however clothed in the designer garb of European Marxist rhetoric. Pol Pot simply determined that all Cambodians, save and except his new ruling elite, was expendable in his march to modernity à la his Western Marxist mentors. Yet another potent example of the immense mountains of bones and anguish collected in worship of the "white man's" worldview; and in the periphery the ritual offerings continue without ceasing. It is now fitting to end the journey of discovery and re-discovery through Said with visionary incisiveness laid down in, with and via the written word as expressed by Derek Walcott. The text of the poem is titled:

AT LAST

To the exiled novelists.

You spit on your people,

Your people applaud,

Your former oppressors laurel you,

The thorns biting your forehead are contempt,

Disguised as concern,

Still you can come home, now

Before, in your finical gut the bowels of compassion petrify to a gallstone

And your ink deliquesces into bile.

In your eye every child is born crippled, every endeavor can you hear the achievement of this chimpanzee trying?

We are through with that pastoral of palm- splashed zebras soundlessly circling nostalgic veldts with the caved in balafong and the snapped strings of savannah grass,

Let your fur shrouded Aryan horseman melt into the snowstorm,

Till the page is again blank, and, under the snowdrift of the white page, of the white ocean, all is buried, generations, generations.

The snows have hardened, the page is cold, it is glazed like the snow -lashed eyes

and the freaked, parted mouths of your horsemen,

like the dice of skulls rolling under lilting sea - floor

Generations, generations

they did not cross for us to abhor them,

they did not all die for your prose,

those who perished in the snows or under the snow- torn billows,

nor do they need to forgive their children who tear at the scabs of their names.

We have passed through the fever,

when we heard our voices

when the bells of the anopheles

were ringing in the ears

over the rice fields

over the sea comes

when the morning sunlight

shivered with malaria,

and the night sea grew tepid

with weeds, like a bush bath.

We have sweated cold sweat

remembering generations

while you, who have risen

from their sweat -soaked capra

from the tangled night bed

folded over like snowdrifts

should know that the sun

is no longer ill,

an orange infested with ants,

that this landscape was never

forgiven or forgiving,

while the pelican beats

to the rock of Soledad

to a beat which is neither

poetry nor prose.

I have sweated it out,

generations, generations,

I am growing hoarse

from repeating the praise

of the ape and the ass,

the enslaved, the indentured,

who are nothing. Grass, then

dung. Paths for the good

to walk over. Men.

And now, let it come to fruit,

let me be sure it has flowered

to break from the bittersweet root

and the Earth that soured,

the flower bursts out of my heart,

the cleft in the rock, at last

flowers, the heart breaking past

unforgiven and unforgiving,

the net of my veins I have cast

here flashes with living

silver at last, at last!

(Walcott 1976 Pg. 88)

Walcott has spoken, commanding the imagery of experiences in the periphery, thereby establishing the salience, rigor and versatility of our experiences as people of the periphery. He therefore insists that we turn away from; we discard the worldviews of the oppressors to ensure our wholeness, our humanity. In a combination of Walcott's imagery and the idiom of the inner-city Afro- American, we say it's time to dis the Aryan horseman and his palm splashed zebras. (See my deconstruction of Derek Walcott's poetry that followed this work.)

A Structural Marxist's Exile in the Islamic Periphery

The researcher experienced this Western Marxist in the line of Althusser to Jameson in two anthologies of writings from Dar ul Islam. In the article published in 1988 titled "The Neo patriarchal Discourse: Language and Discourse in Contemporary Arab Society" the author Hisham Sharabi reveals the discursive structures where he places his enterprise as a mental worker of the periphery. What then is the relevance of Sharabi's enterprise in these texts for the mental workers of the periphery? The answer is simple, for Sharabi like Said, is but another example of the ongoing attempts by mental workers of the periphery to explain why the periphery continues to refuse the inevitability of modernization and modernism. The lesson is that even though these zebras situate themselves in different spaces of the "white man's" discourse, they have one aim in common and arrive at the same conclusions.

Said walked in the spaces created by Foucault in his text "Orientalism", Sharabi walks in the spaces created by Althusser and now Jameson, the fields of knowledge are supposedly dissimilar, the matrices through which experiences, perceptions are sifted, are supposedly dissimilar and contradictory. But there is a commonality in the motivation of both Said's and Sharabi's works, which extends to the sharing of the same worldview and perceptions on the commonly shared problematic of their works, i.e. – Dar ul Islam. What is therefore shared by Said and Sharabi is the White Man's racist discourse which posits "homo Islamicus" as the thing, the "other" thrown up by a backward metaphysical religion which holds its adherents in feudal bondage. The question for Said and Sharabi is: why the continued survival of this unscientific dinosaur in the age of secularized, scientific modernism and modernity? For Sharabi it no longer is a question but a lament, a continual tirade, by the vacuous psyche created by racism. Sharabi writes as a crusader, the modernist White Knight forever locked in battle with a decadent backward order that is tottering but refuses to mutate, thereby opening the door for modernism.

For Sharabi modernism à la the European model, is the only model that is available and has the potency to put Islam in its proper place. This then becomes the basis of the formidable weakness of Sharabi's works, for he appropriates perceptions and experiences via his imported matrices of knowledges and interprets the objects trapped in his fields of knowledge via his imported irrelevant worldview. Sharabi therefore creates an enterprise of little or no relevance to a praxis of liberation in the spaces he focuses his gaze upon. He is trapped in a plastic tower erected in tribute to the "white man's" discourse, which he clings to militantly refusing to "see" his very irrelevance as a thinker in Dar ul Islam.

But we would let his text indicate his irrelevance to the periphery. He shows the central core of his work – "The Neo patriarchal Discourse; Language and Discourse in Contemporary Arab Society" when he says thus: "This fact has been instrumental in preserving the social and cultural divisions of Neo patriarchal society and in maintaining the epistemological compromise of the Arab Awakening over a period of two or three generations, thus blocking the possibility of a genuine epistemological break with traditional patriarchal discourse. No breakthrough toward full modernity was possible." (Sharabi 1988 Pg. 159). Sharabi was therefore seeking to explain why there was no epistemological break that opened patriarchal Arab society to the liberating push/ wave of modernity. This question of Sharabi did not fall from the sky, the very question was thrown up by a specific discourse within the discursive structures of Europe. The question is the product of a specific worldview and Sharabi's answer to the question came out of the discursive worldview of his choice, which also produced the question.

The worldview begs both the question and the answers generated by the fields of knowledge thrown up by the worldview. It is but a dance of circularity whose aim is to create knowledges in themselves and for themselves. The tragedy of Sharabi's text is that the worldview is alien, imported, and belongs to the colonizer. The alien worldview creates fields of knowledges through its matrices of appropriation, which are only relevant to the persons entombed in the alien worldview. But the persons who created the perceptions and experiences, the manner/ methods used to create knowledges are irrelevant to their specific worldview, thereby invalidating the relevance of the knowledges created on their experiences. Therefore, by and through their experiences, the people of the periphery, are appropriated, passed through matrices of sifting and the end product, knowledges, are but distorted, perceptually handicapped mutants of their original selves. To the people of the periphery, the knowledges created by an alien worldview has then the supreme problematic: their inability to pin down causality. This ever-present failure on the part of the "white man's" Orientalism to predict events in the periphery, but more so to create knowledges that allowed the colonizer the space created by the acquiescence of the colonized rather than the space created by technology, is the paramount indictment against the supposed hegemony of the white man's worldview in the periphery.

Sharabi sadly continues in this tradition of creating knowledges relevant to the discursive structures and their debates in the metropole; but in Dar ul Islam, Sharabi's discourse simply does not change the price of cocoa. How then does Sharabi's worldview serve itself by producing knowledges that validates its discursive existence?

To answer the question of "Why no epistemological break?" The worldview answers itself through Sharabi thus: (1) Through positing the centrality of language. "Language is simultaneously a social institution and a system of values." "In its narrow sense, discourse is a form of language." "The sense in which I use the term discourse includes this denotation but goes beyond it to assimilate the objective realities." (Sharabi 1988 Pg. 149). What are these objective realities? "In Frederic Jameson's precise terms these objective realities refer to "realities" or objects in the real world, such as the various levels or instances of a social formation, political power, social class, institutions, and events themselves." (Sharabi 1988 Pg. 149). But Sharabi's worldview also posits the centrality of language within a social totality thereby enabling the statements, which follow: "The "language" of the Neo patriarchal discourse is classical Arabic, in which the knowledge [beliefs, concepts, substantive information] and self- knowledge [modes of self-understanding and self-relating] of Neo patriarchal culture becomes formulated and produced in the shape of discourse." (Sharabi 1988 Pg. 149).

What then is the nexus between language/ discourse and modernity? Sharabi begins to build his case for his brief is founded on the specificity of classic Arabic. He says: "If language limits thought, classical Arabic limits it in a decisive way. This is not only because of the essentially ideological character of the classical, with its rigid religious framework, but also because of its inherent tendency to "think itself" that is, to impose its own patterns and structures on linguistic production." (Sharabi 1988 Pg. 150). Classical Arabic therefore produces discourse, which accomplishes the following: "The sort of discourse this language produces mediates reality through a double ideology; the ideology inherent in the "trance of language," produced and reproduced by the magic of catchwords, incantations, verbal stereotypes, and internal referents, and the ideology supplied by the "encratic" language produced and disseminated under the protection of political and religious orthodoxy." (Sharabi 1988 Pg. 150). Sharabi's text is in itself Orientalist; as such he is involved in self-deprecation and self-immolation. How? Because he says thus: "It is a discourse especially suited for the projection of a particular kind of being, for organizing the irrational, and for activating the imaginary." (Sharabi 1988 Pg. 150). Sharabi is therefore now positing that the homo Islamicus is the creation of the linguist hegemony of classical Arabic projected through the specificities of the discourse it creates. Sharabi's enterprise is simply to update the Orientalist craving for causality/ instrumentality in the periphery. Sharabi's discursive choice to grant the holy grail to Orientalism is the new "insights" offered by structuralist Western Marxism from Althusser to Jameson.

Whether it is via the positivist bourgeois worldview or the various lines in anti-bourgeois Marxism in the European discursive structures when applied to Dar ul Islam there is commonality of the gaze and the knowledges produced. They both create a specific unique being, homo Islamicus, a constituted object of knowledge created by the white man's worldview and for the validation of the said worldview. The problem arises when the proponents of the worldview must now create a praxis on the knowledges thrown up. Whether it is a colonial governor, a neo-colonial official from the United Nations and its arms as the WHO, a political activist, and an educator etc. etc., as long as you must have a praxis based on contact with "it", the homo Islamicus, your actions informed and motivated by your alien worldview is going to be constantly tested to determine its relevance, its potency, its ability to predict human action in the crucible of power relations.

And this is where the alien worldview is constantly found wanting, persistently short of a length. Sharabi's text is but another example for he sets up his case, but when called upon to articulate its veracity his means to this end is to present a stream of "evidence" gathered from the realm of psychological discourse. He has no problem in resorting to psychology to explain the resilience of Islamic discourse, for the worldview in which he situates himself embraced Freud in their overpowering need to explain the fundamental question: why no proletarian revolution in Europe?

To explain the constituting of homo Islamicus through the discourse thrown up by Classical Arabic, the language, is perfectly within the discursive methodology of Sharabi. The problematic of creating a body of causal and deductive knowledges, based on an "object of knowledge" brought into existence by an alien and challenged worldview that constituted homo Islamicus is real. This then is the key to the failure of the exercise to create a reflectively acquiescent colonized object. For the researcher posits that the only objects of knowledge in the colonial nexus were the dependent Saxonized marginalized persons, who were directly dependent upon the colonial economic structures for their creation, sustenance and survival. Those of us whose specific class positions showed the marginality of our relations to the colonial mode of production therefore traversed a matrix of spaces, which were expressed as a horizontal continuum consisting of those spaces under the hegemony of an alternate worldview locked in contradiction with the colonial discourses. In this space perceptive structures reflected the hegemony of the alternate worldview, but also the constant pressures of the invading discourses of Europe.

At the next end of the continuum was the space under the hegemonic control of the European discourses. In this space the zebras, Afro, Indo, Sino/ Saxons were constituted, the quintessential objects of knowledge, the building blocks of the colonial discourse and the source of knowledges which informed their perceptions and their power relations. These objects of knowledge were fixed in orbit as satellites revolving around their constituting nexus, white colonial rule. They were, therefore objectively and subjectively, in their relations to the colonial mode of production marginal to its existence. Why? Because their existence did not create, preserve nor ensure the survival of the white colonial enterprise. Their existence was simply to validate the knowledges created by the discursive structures, which constituted the zebras to validate the knowledges in the perpetual circular danse macabre.

In a reality where colonial discourse was not enjoying ascendant hegemony, the need to validate colonial discourse was perpetually overwhelming. To continually practice discursive masturbation was the only means to achieve discursive hegemony, at least in the minds of the carriers of the discourse. Therefore, the marginal proto classes, the lumpen petty bourgeoisie, the zebras of the colonial empires were ushered into being. For they served no other purpose but discursive masturbation. They had no praxis, no respect, no validity in the spaces controlled by the alternate discourses of the colonial world. Rather than aiding the colonial quest for hegemony, they became the living examples of the Uncle Tom's, the house niggers, Gunga Dins and Hop Sings of the white man's spaces. As they traversed the colonial spaces in their western attire, their western language, western worldviews they were ridiculed as parodies of the white model and traitors to their race and culture. Their marginality, their irrelevance became the most potent example of why not to embrace the spaces under the white man's hegemony. Since they were not organically important to the striving for hegemony by the white man's worldview, what then was their importance save as the products of discursive masturbation?

The third space encompassed the boundaries along which the discourses in contradiction met on a daily basis in the constant push and pull of power relations between colonizer and colonized. Both discourses were always seeking hegemony, in a strategic war for territorial supremacy. Of central importance for the ferocity of struggle on a daily basis were the technological machinery of conquest and resistance present and the level of integration of the specific territory into the world colonial capitalist system.

The power relations, which were common to the space under contention, were in fact the discursive products of central importance to both discourses in contradiction. More so the colonial discourses perpetually sought to constitute objects of knowledge within the confines of this netherworld of contact and conflict. But the major hindrance was both the fluidity of the space that enclosed discursive attraction and the mobility of the individuals entrapped by the power relations of this space. It was the prerogative of the colonized to retreat spatially, mentally, or both from the power relations and hence from contact with the discursive structures of the colonial discourse. In Dar ul Islam, to retreat was to embrace Islam fervently in the Casbah, which fringed urban colonial spaces, or to spatially move to rural areas where the colonial presence was a garrison surrounded by a sea of resistance.

Pilgrimage, both mentally and spatially or both, was then the proven means of resistance, hence the colonizer's undying quest under colonialism to squeeze to a trickle the annual Haj to Mecca. Spatial and mental pilgrimages of retreat are common to all peoples subjected to colonization, and in response to the colonial master devised ways to curb, to hinder, to harass this constant move to escape contact with their discursively constituted power relations. Therefore, in this space constituted by and through discursive attrition, both colonizer and colonized met, battled for hegemony and broke off contact at specific moments. But the worldviews that grew out of this battle for hegemony/ retreat/ pilgrimage thence renewed contact are seen today in the worldviews of the periphery.

The commonalities of these worldviews are the longing for the products of modernity, but intense suspicion of the western means to produce the products lusted after. The refusal to accept the white man's world system as the path to modernity, but the inability to overcome the intense belief in the superiority and desirability of all things western. The willingness to accept the western worldview in times of prosperity, but in times of material deprivation and hopelessness we overwhelmingly turn to alternate worldviews.

Peoples of the periphery who traversed this space of discursive attrition had by necessity to enable themselves the means to ensure their mental and spatial fluidity, hence their adaptability necessary to survival. Our survival as peoples of the periphery depended then, as now, on our ability to create multiple marriages of worldviews, which ensured our means of adaptability to a quantum of power relations, which we perceived we would meet in our pilgrimage through our peripheral life.

Our success in surviving under oppressive conditions for over five hundred years of European domination bears testimony to our resilience as humans. But more so peripheral peoples of the world as a direct result of colonial domination have been forced to become people of Diasporas. We migrate to survive physically, mentally, economically and spiritually. But the bottom line is that we are forced to migrate to survive, and this is an experience unique to peoples of the periphery.

Our success in migrating, establishing beachheads and eventually Diaspora is testimony to our enabling structures of worldviews held in perceptive matrices. We are multi-perceptive individuals constantly moving to balance, to add, to discard experiences held in these mental matrices. Without this multi-perspective body of windows to see, to gaze upon different worlds constituted by different worldviews we would have perished long ago, as did the Arawaks/ Taino and Caribs/ Kalinago of the Caribbean.

Hisham Sharabi's method to prove the backwardness of Islamic discourse through European structuralist thought is not unique in its hatred of things "native". His discursive masturbation by presenting psychological instrumentalities drawn from a being, homo Islamicus, constituted by the white man's worldview is also in keeping with his worldview. Sharabi simply constitutes a being that would give up the psychological instrumentalities, which prove his worldview. Sharabi a member of the Palestinian Diaspora is then the living expression of a non-white plagued with hallucinatory whiteness, an existential condition which precludes him to problematise himself and his race to the benefit of massa and his zionist operatives.

We therefore at minimum have a case where someone who is a Palestinian uses an alien, white supremacist worldview to constitute objects of knowledge for discourses of paltry relevance to the peoples of the text. In Hisham Sharabi's text we now have the example of western Marxism serving the discursive needs of white supremacist, zionist and Arab Orientalists. Sharabi's attempt to create a postmodern Orientalism, as Said attempted, indicates the continual striving of the Western discourses to understand, to constitute, to subject, to coerce, the peoples of the periphery, in this case specifically the Palestinians. But one reality continually surfaces, that is the blatant racism of the exercise seen in Sharabi's nineteenth century descriptions of Islamic discourse. On the other hand, if we of the periphery were a vanquished people there would be no need for the Sharabis of the world.

The fact of the matter is that the Palestinian Intifada constituted Sharabi as a mental worker of relevance, not the other way around. And Sharabi's relevance is not to the Palestinian children who use stones to resist bullets, but to the persons who point, aim and squeeze the triggers at children armed with stones. The murderers of children need to be reassured, to be convinced that who they are killing is a less than a human being, a homo Islamicus. A fanatical fundamentalist who would destroy the zionist homeland, the by-product of a backward and oppressive religion, an automaton.

Sharabi, by insisting that Islamic discourse in itself and for itself cannot embrace modernity, is adding to, serving the very worldview that threw up the Nazi's and the Final Solution as a Palestinian hitman in the service of massa and his zionists. What he is saying is that the only way to open the doors to modernity in areas under the hegemony of Islamic discourse is to secularize the society, separate state from Islam, education from Islam, personal relations from Islam etc. Secularization has failed miserably in Dar ul Islam, the best example of failure being the assassination of Anwar Sadat and the Iranian Revolution.

What then is left for Sharabi to suggest as an alternative means/ method of secularization? Maybe the final solution à la Sabra and Chatila or Auschwitz? Islamic discourse beckons with insistent persistency for the text has for too long evaded the necessary embrace, the grappling that enables understanding and insight.

V.S. Naipaul's Islamic Journey.

But as part of a textual foreplay, the researcher would end this field of text with experiences of V.S. Naipaul's: "Amongst the Believers: An Islamic Journey". The researcher's quest for understanding and insights of the Iranian Revolution inevitably led to grappling with Naipaul's discourse on Islam, for Naipaul is a product of the very same crucible as the researcher. The crucible is the same but the worldviews, hence the perceptions are in contradiction, for Naipaul relentlessly measures the periphery against his yardsticks and we are always found wanting to the extent where we are dismissed with scant contempt. The key to the debate with Naipaul is the sources of his yardsticks, the discursive structures that inform these yardsticks.

Sad to say Naipaul's yardsticks are all solidly situated in the racist worldview of the "white man". In effect Naipaul is therefore the quintessential zebra, the Gunga Din of the periphery, and he always demands our attention in the periphery for he unashamedly dares to articulate the worldview of the black skinned, white masked elites of the periphery. Naipaul's discourse is therefore one of modernity, and the reasons why we of the periphery are doomed to inhabit festering overcrowded barracoons or the areas of darkness of the periphery. He is the most versatile, perceptive and articulate product of the colonial discourses charged with the task of haranguing, of opening wounds in our psyches through exposing our endemic failures in our attempts to grasp modernity.

But Naipaul did not stop with the persistent harangues dealing with our ludicrous instances of grappling with modernity, he goes on to postulate that the peoples of the periphery are unable to follow the white man's path to modernity because of innate ontological hindrances. For him colonial domination was not a hindrance or an evolutionary setback, for he is the supreme example of a person, of the periphery carrying the "white man's" Orientalist/ racist burden.

Naipaul refuses to gaze upon the futility of human existence under colonial domination, whilst pouring scorn on the perceptions of the people condemned to labour under the legacy of colonial domination and neo-colonialism. Sad to say, he is the most potent and virulent spokesman for white racism and neo-colonialism today. His works burden us, the people of the periphery with a worldview that absolves the "white man" from all guilt for his volumes of injustices against us, past and present.

Naipaul blames the victim for the crimes of history, past and present, and succinctly states repeatedly that we are to blame for the repeated violations carried out on us. If we submit to his discourse and in our submission call out for deliverance, for modernity, he even denies us the emancipation found only in the white man's worldview. For he posits that we lack the means, the worldview to grasp, to attain the white man's emancipation. For Naipaul we are therefore ontologically, if not racially flawed.

The master race concept, brought back through a black back door, for the existence of ontologically flawed peripheral peoples determines the existence of a non-ontologically flawed black race. Naipaul is in "essence", in his ontology, in his metaphysics: nihilist. For he can and could never be white, no matter how intense his harangues of us are, his ontology used against us is also a weapon against himself. Naipaul cannot live in a world without the mirror image and his image is a black reflection, even though he "sees" white in his images. Naipaul, as Michael Jackson, is condemned to live in a world of surreal nihilism for there is no escaping one's genetic coding. In the world of racism your genetic coding is destiny, and Naipaul is doomed to live into the twenty first century the fatalism, and self-immolation endemic to the zebras of the periphery.

Let Naipaul now speak: "Islam was a complicated Religion, it wasn't philosophical or speculative. It was a revealed religion, with a prophet and a Complete set of rules. To believe, it was necessary to know a lot about the Arabian origins of the religion, and to take this knowledge to heart." "Islam in Iran was even more complicated. It was a divergence from the main belief; and this divergence had its roots in the political-racial dispute about the succession to the prophet, who died in 632 AD. Islam almost from the start, had been an imperialism as well as a religion." (Naipaul 1982 Pg. 7). Naipaul's concepts of Islam stated above all indicate their origin within the texts of the white man's American style, especially Orientalism. His journey amongst the believers was ultimately perceived through Orientalist matrices or fields of knowledge, what followed in the book was in no way shocking. Kittens born in an oven cannot be by any stretch of the imagination, loaves of bread.

Naipaul goes deeper: "It was the beauty of Islamic that I heard a third Iranian speaks. But what was he doing, studying law in an American university? What had attracted these Iranians to the United States and the civilization it represented? Couldn't they say? The attraction existed; it was more than a need for education and skills. But the attraction existed; it was more than a need for education and skills. But the attraction wasn't admitted, and in that attraction, too humiliating for an old and proud people to admit, there lay disturbance expressed in dandyism, mimicry, boasting and rejection." (Naipaul 1982 Pg. 13). Naipaul saw in the Iranian petty bourgeoisie singing praises to the Revolution on American network television in the immediate post-revolution days his "other". Unlike Naipaul, there was no looking back to the peripheral origins with nostalgia seeking definition and positioning in the world order. He admits his attraction for the civilization, is not burdened with nostalgic "betweenity", therefore he could never and cannot suffer under the burdens expressed through "dandyism, mimicry, boasting and rejection." The key statement in the text quoted is: "What had attracted these Iranians to the United States and the civilization it represented?" This theme reverberates through the linear length and breadth of Naipaul's text on the believers.

Let us now hear Naipaul on the fundamentalists: "The West, or the universal civilization it leads, is emotionally rejected. It undermines; it threatens. But at the same time it is needed, for its machines, goods, medicines, warplanes, the remittances from the emigrants, the hospitals that might have a cure for calcium deficiency, the universities that will provide master's degree in mass media. All the rejection of the west is contained within the assumption that there will always exist out there a living, creative civilization, oddly neutral, open to all to appeal to, rejection therefore is not absolute rejection. It is also for the community as a whole, a way of ceasing to strive intellectually. It is to be parasitic; parasitism is one of the unacknowledged fruits of fundamentalism. And the emigrants pour out from the land of faith; thirty thousand Pakistani's shipped by the manpower export experts to West Berlin alone, to claim the political asylum meant for the people of East Germany." (Naipaul 1982 Pg. 168). "Step by step, out of its Islamic striving, Pakistan had undone the rule of law it had inherited from the British, and replaced it with nothing." (Naipaul 1982 Pg. 169). The text quoted above indicates for us Naipaul's scorn for our enterprises of the periphery, which seek to experiment with alternate discursive structures. To replace British law with experiments in the Sharia in Pakistan is the consummate nihilist exercise for "nothing" replaces substance, relevance, civilization signified by British law.

Fundamentalism is essentially parasitic for it rejects a "universal civilization" out of fear for its potency, its relevance for "it undermines", "it threatens." For as a dog returns to its vomit, the fundamentalist returns to the "universal civilization" seeking its material specificities for the fundamentalist is unwilling to strive to create the means to produce the western material specificities lusted after.

Why? Because the periphery afflicted with fundamentalism, and by inference Islam, does not "strive intellectually" and is therefore "parasitic." To justify their parasitism, their ontological deficiencies they deny the fact that this "universal civilization" is driven by, is the creation of the West, the Great Satan. This denial is accomplished through the representation of Western "universal civilization" as a "living, creative civilization, oddly neutral, open to all to appeal to."

For Naipaul there is therefore but one civilization, and it is in itself an exercise in futility to deny its hegemony, whilst drawing from its material products. He therefore insists that it is futile, a game of charades to need the technologies of the West, whilst seeking to reject the worldview of the West. For Naipaul to seek Western products is but a potent indicator of our inability to replace, to render the west subservient and in our position of dependence we cannot reject the Western worldview for the alternative to it is simply "nothingness."

To experiment with the structures of an alternate worldview is not a revolutionary/ quantum leap on the linear path to modernity for Naipaul. It is but a retrogressive step, a backward looking backwardness, a longing for a pre-modern tribal existence, which is always ahistorical, even anti-historical. Naipaul states: "In the fundamentalist scheme the world constantly decays and has constantly to be re-created. The only function of intellect is to assist that re-creation. It re-interprets the text it re-establishes divine precedent. So history has to serve theology, law is separated from the idea of equity, and learning is separated from learning." "The Islamic fundamentalist wish is to work back to such a whole, for them a God given whole, but with the tool of faith alone - belief, religious practices and rituals. It is like a wish – with intellect suppressed or limited, the historical sense falsified - to work back from the abstract to the concrete, and to set up the tribal walls again. It is to seek to re-create something like a tribal or a city state that -except in theological fantasy never was." (Naipaul 1982 Pg. 167). Islamic fundamentalism, and by extension Islam, rejects the European worldview of the ever progressive forward linear march of ideally European civilization and by doing so subjects history to theology. The rejection of history as the locomotive of human civilization is then the ontological essence that accounts for the backwardness of the periphery and ultimately the futility and nihilism of peripheral existences.

The ontological essence of fundamentalism therefore condemns its adherents to view human society and its history as being segregated into epochs characterized by adherence or non-adherence to the laws of Islam. Islamic history is not then a continuous linked linear line characterized by material progression. Again, another example of pontificating on a people's worldview under the belief that it is universally recognized in the various agglomerations of human experiences, the "white man's" worldview is hegemonic. Given the nature of the Islamic worldview; adherents of this worldview can only view their world as epochal predicated on the hegemony/ or desertion of the discourse by its adherents. To judge a worldview on criterion drawn from an entirely contradictory worldview and pronounce one fit to be hegemonic and the other only worthy of the scrap heap of history, is to be ethnocentric at best.

When there is a conjuncture of power and powerlessness, involving specific race types then what we have is blatant racism. We therefore have in Naipaul, a non-white of the periphery articulating a white racist worldview against the peoples of the periphery, the most profound example today of the Indo/ Saxon, the Gunga Din, of the literary discourses of the "white man's" worldview par excellence. Naipaul's brilliance, his literary insights, his command of the "white man's" language are all irrelevant to the people of the periphery who relentlessly strive to preserve our alternate discursive structures.

We, who hold fast to our alternate religions, our alternative languages they call "dialects," our alternate festivals, our alternate cuisines, our alternate sociologies, all summed up by, but not larger than our alternate worldviews; to us Naipaul is vastly irrelevant. Because he does not and cannot address our realities, save and except to harangue us into submission to his white worldview. For many of us he writes in a language alien to us, articulating a worldview that at best we are ambivalent towards.

Naipaul and his texts cannot change the price of cocoa and is therefore of little relevance to us in our daily struggle for physical and psychic survival. He berates, and belittles our experiences, our perceptions, he cannot give succor and healing, and therefore he is relevant only to his white masters and the marginalized petty-bourgeois zebras of the periphery.

For the petty-bourgeois zebras, Naipaul is the consummate tormentor for he ridicules their attempts to create the hegemony of modernity in the periphery since the end of colonial domination. He uses himself as the yardstick by which he measures the actions of the adherents of modernity in the periphery and inevitably they are always found wanting, as in the case of the Iranian exiles extolling the virtues of the Iranian revolution on American television. This is his constituency in the periphery, to them he would always be of salient importance, unlike Walcott who is separated by his worldview from the petty-bourgeois zebras, but more so as is the case of the researcher, by the fact that Walcott is a genetic zebra.

We, the genetic zebras of the periphery, have no need to acquire the white man's worldview to pronounce ourselves modern, fit to gain entry to the petty-bourgeois elites. The white genetic credentials we carry in our arteries enable us to embrace, to grapple, to dance with alternate worldviews for we are spared the monumental task of whitening a black body, which would fundamentally always remain black. The racist discursive structures teach us from our earliest moments of perceptive experience that we occupy a netherworld between spaces marked for the two discursive race types: white and non-white. We are therefore left to roam the discursive spaces of racism, the choices we make on how we would define ourselves are always predicated on our experiences of "in betweenity", on the marginality of living in the discursive space where sexual contact between the races are situated, that space that houses the dougla, the half-breed, the mestizo, the chingo, the mulatto, the mongrels.

We, the half-whites of the periphery, have no need to Saxonize our worldviews in a bid to acquire definition and positioning in our human existence, whether we want to accept it or not, part of our genetic ancestry grounds us in the white man's world and the obverse, is the fact that we are grounded in non-white alternate worldviews. It is therefore fitting at the end of the textual journey through the spaces created by the writers presented to now sit back and reflect on the preponderance of racism in the spaces traversed which corralled instances of the periphery.

This textual journey began with a journey in search of insights, but at the end of this specific pilgrimage there is but one salient lesson learned: which is the continued potency of racism within the discursive structures that informed the spaces and their contents journeyed through so far in this work. The unchallenged potency of racism that throws up objects of knowledge through its discursive structures of power/ knowledge can then inform only one conclusion from the texts traversed. This is the position that in the discursive structures of the hegemonic European worldview the basis for, the locomotive of the racist discourse, is a metaphysical construct that specifically defines the European perception as a race in itself and for itself. What then is posited by way of review of the textual spaces is a will to power, a will to truth that defines the race perceptions of Europeans that is expressed through racism.

The race will to truth, the will to power/ knowledge throws up discursive structures which are racist, which constitute objects of knowledge who are racist in relations to the "other" and in relations within themselves when the person is the "other." The racist discursive structures must ensure race hegemony and can be utilized by any race that has the positional situation that enables that race the means to constitute objects of knowledge through these discursive structures.

In post-colonial societies the racist discursive structures are strategic constituents of the power relations thrown up by the hegemonic discourses of the day, dependent legacies of colonialism. These discursive structures, inherited and adopted unchallenged by the ruling elites of the post-colonial era, continue to constitute racist objects of knowledge but the white colonial master is now one step removed from the power relations of the discursive structures. Non-white people are constituting non-white objects of knowledge through white centred racist discourse.

The end result of this is the constituting of objects of knowledge differentiated not by their non-white state, but their difference in being non-white, their specificities in being non-white. The end result is a society pervaded with racism between non-white peoples, but the discursive structure of the racism self-immolates both the powerful and the silenced. In the periphery we therefore have the parodies of capitalism, modernity and racism.

Non-white peoples attack, maim and kill each other physically, psychologically or both, through racist structures that ensure the hegemony of the "white man's" worldview. And this is the fundamental reason why black on black racism in the periphery is the Pandora's box of the zebras who are the powerful and the vocal. The people of the periphery who situate themselves in the alternate worldviews of the periphery have rejected this black on black racism by their actions for generations. The East Indians who are Spiritual Baptists or Orisha devotees and the Africans who are Hindu's, Kali Mai devotees or Krishna devotees by their actions show their rejection of black on black racism.

More so, the growing quantum of Douglas, that is spreading panic among the black racists as they rant and rave over "douglarisation", is the most potent instrument of the powerless in their rejection of black on black racism. The dougla, the half-breed is therefore a product of a silenced discourse in its ongoing war with racism and the racist discursive structures. It is therefore fitting to end this specific journey with the mixed blood/breed who dares to articulate an alternate worldview: Walcott.

Frescoes of the New World II

My Anna, my Beatrice

I enclose in this circle of hell,

in the stench of their own sulfur of self hatred,

in the steaming, scabrous rocks of Soufrie're,

in the boiling, pustular volcanoes of the south,

all o'dem big boys, so, dem ministers,

ministers of culture, ministers of development,

the green blacks, and their old toms,

and all the syntactical apologists of the third world,

explaining why their artists die,

by their own hands, magicians of the new vision,

Screaming the same shit.

Those who peel from their leprous flesh, their names,

Who chafe and nurture the scars of rusted chains

like primates favoring scabs, those who charge tickets,

for another free ride on the middle passage,

those who explain to the peasant why he is African

their Catamites and eunuchs banging tambourines

whores with slave bangles banging tambourines,

and the academics crouched like rats

listening to tambourines

jackals and rodents feathering their holes

hoarding the sea-glass of their ancestors' eyes

sea-lice, sea-parasites on the ancestral sea-wrack

whose god is history. Pax.

Who want a new art

and their artists dying in their old way.

Those whose promise drip from their mouth like pus

Geryons gnawing their own children.

These are the dividers,

they encompass our history,

in their hands is the body

of my friend and the future,

they measure the skulls with calipers

and pronounce their measure

of toms, of traitors, of traditionals and Afro Saxons

they measure them carefully

as others once measured the teeth

of men and horses, they measure and divide

Their music comes from the rattle of coral bones

their eyes like worms drill into parchments,

they measure each other's sores

to boast who has suffered most,

and their artists keep dying,

they are the saints of self-torture,

their stars are pimples of pus

on the might of our grandfathers,

they are hired like dogs to lick the sores of their people

their vision blurs, their future is clouded with cataract,

but out of its mist, one man

whom they will not recognize, emerges

and staggers towards his lineaments.

(Walcott 1973 Pgs. 127-128).

And finally, the recognition, the acceptance, the utilization of the sin of our common white ancestor to erect matrices of perception to trap insights, to build discourses of understandings, of tolerances. Walcott speaks:

The Train

On one hand, harrowed England,

iron, an airfield's mire,

on the other, fire gutted trees, a hand

racking the carriage windows.

Where was my randy white grandsire from?

He left here a century ago

to found his "farm,"

and, like a thousand others,

drunkenly seed their archipelago.

Through dirty glass

his landscape fills through my face.

Black with despair

he set his flesh on fire,

blackening, a tree of flame.

That's hell enough for here.

His blood burns through me as this engine races,

my skin sears like a hair shirt with his name.

On the bleak Sunday platform

the guiltless, staring faces

divide like tracks before me as I come.

Like you grandfather, I cannot change places,

I am half home.

(Walcott 1969 Pg. 24).

The Revolution that Failed

177

Introduction

The text that follows is Part 2 of the revised version of my book published in 2004 titled "Exiting a Racist Worldview" which deals with the writings of selected leaders of specific revolutionary movements opposed to the order of power of white supremacy applied to specific social orders. The revolutionary movements chosen are: the Haitian Revolution for the liberation of the enslaved from the order of power of French white supremacist colonial imperial domination of the colony of Saint Domingue of the island of Hispaniola, the Caribbean and the African movement for the liberation of the African minority in the USA in the late 1960s and early 1970s. These are followed by a deconstruction of skin bleaching in the English speaking Caribbean in the 21st century. Specifically, the discourse of Toussaint L'Ouverture of the Haitian revolution is deconstructed to expose his order of power and worldview riven and driven by hallucinatory whiteness, which explains the affirmation of his oeuvre by massa across time/ space as he was the progenitor of a specific type of non-white leader who was committed to preserving the white order of power of massa over formerly colonized non-white peoples of the ex-colonial world, typified by Nelson Mandela of post-apartheid South Africa. The deconstruction of the discourse of L'Ouverture reveals then, how a non-white plagued with hallucinatory whiteness exercising state power conceptualizes and formulates this order of power and the instruments of power requisite to exercising hegemony in a social order. L'Ouverture conceptualized and applied a model of colonial power that maintained white power with an accommodation for a non-white elite rooted in the Haitian military with L'Ouverture as the resident dictator. Massa learned well from the L'Ouverture model in his design of a neo-colonial dictator for life sourced from different strata of the social order, especially the military. This model was applied when Massa found a willing non-white leader, Nelson Mandela, to launch the servile post-apartheid South Africa model they desired. George Jackson (1941-1971) was a prominent non-white theorist of the African revolution in the USA, utilizing historical materialist discourse, of the 1960s and 1970s in the USA. Jackson's discourse is deconstructed to expose his historical materialist concept of revolution that will be launched by a minority non-white race in the white supremacist order of power of the USA where whites are the majority. This deconstruction of Jackson's discourse reveals the grave flaws of historical materialism which constituted the possibility of an African revolution that overthrows the white order of power. A possibility that was myth, external of the discourse that constituted it and proved to be false, unattainable. Jackson's discourse of revolution can only generate a praxis of revolutionary adventurism at best which fits into and flows with the nihilism that pervades the practice of Africans in Amerikkka, that is a potent indicator of servility. Jackson's discourse presented in his prison letters was in transition, which he himself did not fully pursue for fear of falsifying his absolute of revolution which made it inevitable in Amerikkka, and we are still waiting. Jackson's revolution failed and this deconstruction reveals why. Finally, skin bleaching in the 21st century in the English speaking Caribbean is examined as a potent indicator of the collapse of the neo-colonial order of massa established with independence from the English massa. The black nationalism of the independence movement has maintained the white order of power, the servility to white power and the hallucinatory whiteness that afflicts all of us in the Caribbean. Black nationalism cannot deliver us from the self-hate and servility to whiteness, it cannot be the instrument of liberation from servility at the level of the idea, from hallucinatory whiteness. Skin bleaching in the 21st century is then embraced as one solution to our self-hate by now changing our skin color to reflect what we want to be, not what we are. In the 21st century the assault on our non-white bodies and minds has been evolved and intensified by massa new discourse of assault on the female non-white body which embraces skin bleaching with cosmetic surgical interventions with emphasis on the face, buttocks, breasts and vagina and the range of solutions for the wrong hair. What is noteworthy is the prescription by massa of a 21st century body image for African women as desirable which was originally described by white supremacist science as the most potent instances of the inherent inferiority of the African woman, their buttocks and vagina. With non-African women today doing the buttocks, breasts and vagina jobs to now carry these markers on their non-African bodies speak to the issue of signals of desire and of sexual potency now being displayed by non-African women. Massa insisted that the buttocks and the vagina of the African woman were that of an inherently inferior being which gave them a propensity for sexual potency and desire that have been long washed out of the white woman. The African woman is then the living epitome of black ugliness summed up in her buttocks and vagina, but she is the repository of sexual potency and desire which a white woman cannot have for she will not be white. Massa then has the African woman for multiple purposes one of which is sweetness he cannot expect from a white woman. An African woman is then property, rape bait, a multifaceted woman who possess her labor power, reproductive power and her sexual power. Skin bleaching in the 21st century in the neo-colonial world has now been combined with enhancing the symbols of African female sexual potency. When an African woman applies the full works to her body what then is the message she is sending to the massa of the world? When white and other non-African women apply the same works to their body what is the message she is sending to African men and women and to massa? A white woman can now match and beat the African woman in sexual potency which means that she must have nothing that we don't have for she is inherently inferior, hence we restore our lost sexual potency surgically and retain our inherent superiority. White feminist white supremacy!

The Failed Revolutions

The single binding commonality of all the liberationary movements going up against white supremacy is the failure of the revolution arising from the ability of the order of power of white supremacy to engage with and mitigate the threats posed by transforming the outward appearance of the white order of power with the help of leaders of the races in ferment. White supremacy engages with pliable non-white leaders to transform the discourse of domination whilst intensifying the power it wields over each non-white body it holds in subjection intensifying the deprivation, oppression, humiliation and self-hate which intensifies the power white supremacy wields over non-white bodies and the oppression and underdevelopment that results. In this post revolution white order of power there is a common non-white race response to the oppression, underdevelopment and self-hate seen from Haiti to America to South Africa which is the embrace of a discourse of criminality as the fitting, effective strategic response to white oppression applied from Haiti, to America and South Africa. This embrace of a discourse of non-white criminality as the effective strategic response to their living conditions aids, abets and heightens white oppression of these non-white races. Embracing criminality is a gift to the white order of power, a self-fulfilling prophecy fulfilled, which justifies relentless militarized policing of these races in marginalized spaces. It fills the prisons with the males of these races criminalizing large swaths of its male population with its deadly impact on the family, the clan, the community and the social order intensifying their marginality. It escalates the non-white on non-white violence to epidemic levels which intensifies the dislocation and marginality of their communities effectively destroying the gaze upon the need for political action, knowledge and education. In addition, this criminal element is not adverse to hiring themselves out to the white order of power to maintain order in the communities for massa, in turn benefiting from their service to massa by being allowed to build criminal empires in marginalized spaces. Criminality as a survival strategy then targets within the communities all those who are perceived as presenting a threat to an order of power that benefits them and they will take out the threats posed. The potent abiding lesson is then in its quest for world hegemony white supremacy is relativistic, it sees no distinction between legality and illegality; law, the rule of law is then a propaganda fetish unleashed to deceive, to make comfortable, inactive and always accessible to its instruments of power targeted bodies. The white order of power is also flexible, it has but one intent: to assure white hegemony by any means necessary. This discourse is now under challenge from doctrinaire white supremacy of the 21st century formulated by the Luddites of Jim Crow/ Nazi white supremacy who insist that there are lines that white supremacists must not cross, compromises that must not be made, even though they ensure white world hegemony.

These 21st century Nazis insist that the white war machine will deal with all recalcitrants.

The fundamental reality that must be grasped is that hegemony is attained through subservience at the level of the idea which in turn drives servile action. Therefore liberation itself has to commence at the level of the idea, for this is the only path to formulating and launching liberationary action again and again. This is the potent act of embracing criminality which redounds to the benefit of the white order of power and is so treasured as an instrument of power by massa. Criminality fosters a servile mind, there is no path to liberation possible in criminality, massa loves our embrace of criminality as he fills his private jails, which are the new sweat shops exploiting dirt cheap labor. This is the neo-liberal sweat shop utilizing disposable labor where you are not burdened with the cost of the reproduction of labor which is borne by the marginalized spaces from which they are drawn, and there are no labor rights to increase the cost of labor, this is unbridled capitalist exploitation in the 21st century, back to the source.

The Haitian Revolution (1791-1804), The Discourse of Toussaint L'Ouverture (1743-1803)

This is a deconstruction of selected writings of L'Ouverture to unearth his discourse and the worldview it drove of the order of power of a liberated Haiti and its place in a world under white supremacist hegemony in the 19th century. This deconstruction is then seeking to determine if L'Ouverture himself was liberated at the level of the idea seen in his writings whilst involved as a leader of the Haitian Revolution, which speaks to explaining his actions during this period of his life. The base reality is the need to interrogate L'Ouverture's practice as a lesson to heed in the quest to build liberationary movements that will topple the white order of power and its world hegemony.

L'Ouverture was born on the Habitation Breda plantation in St Domingue, rising to the rank of principal manager of the livestock of the plantation which placed him in close contact with massa on a daily basis and exerting power delegated to him by massa over the enslaved Africans and Mixed race persons on the plantation Breda, especially those assigned to the livestock division of the plantation. Livestock was expensive to replace and was a most important part of the production process of the plantation from the fields to the production of raw sugar, semi refined sugar, molasses and rum. The organic link between Toussaint Breda and massa was seen in Toussaint being freed in 1776, choosing to continue working as a free man on the plantation whilst purchasing plantations and enslaved persons to commence his career as massa, in his own right. In August 1791, Boukman and Jeannor at Bois Caiman commenced the Haitian Revolution of the enslaved. From 1791 to 1793 Toussaint adopts the role of revolutionary agitator which evolves to revolutionary military commander engaged against the French forces in Haiti. In February 1793 the French revolutionary forces declared war on Spain, Toussaint now fights on the side of Spain in Haiti. In August 1793 the Commissioner of revolutionary France in Haiti abolishes slavery unconditionally, Toussaint continues fighting on the side of Spain changing his name to L'Ouverture calling for war to attain liberty and equality. L'Ouverture will continue fighting for Spain until the French assembly abolished slavery in the spring of 1794. Thereafter he became a firm defender of the French Revolution and republicanism using the power relations between the republican and revolutionary forces in France to guarantee his licit power in Haiti, which became the basis of his drive to become the dominant player in Haiti, militarily, politically and economically. General Etienne Laveaux and Commissioner Sonthonax will give L'Ouverture the military power to govern on a daily basis, which gave him the space to reveal his vision of the new Haitian order of power, of a social order rooted in a revived plantation economy where the old massa class is rejuvenated and expanded, now joined by the new class dominated by a military elite dominating the social order. L'Ouverture would repeatedly release edicts which forced the former slaves against their will to work on the plantations of their former massa invited to return and claim their properties by L'Ouverture in conjunction with the the new slaver massa. Those who resisted, revolted against L'Ouverture's new order of power paid with their lives at the hands of the new military massa led by L'Ouverture. A distribution of land to the former slaves to create a new economy of small landowners was utterly rejected and suppressed with violence by L'Ouverture. L'Ouverture banished from Haiti Commissioner Sonthonax in April 1797 and persuaded General Laveaux to return to France in October 1796 creating a vacuum in the chain of command which gave L'Ouverture unrivaled power on the ground in Haiti. This quest of L'Ouverture for maximum power in Haiti was not sustainable given the fact that in April 1797 the stalwarts of the old order, the Ancien Regime won the majority in the National Assembly expressing its intention to restore the order of power of the nobility, aristocracy and the monarchy, which naturally meant the reconquest of Haiti and the reimposition of enslavement. The champion of this cause that appeared was the commander of the French military Napoleon Bonaparte. L'Ouverture's agenda to reimpose the plantation system through forced labor that was supposedly free with the use of violence alienated the masses in an environment of hostility from France and the drive to create a unified bloc of white slave owning nations committed to destroying Haiti, especially Britain and the USA. The other salient reality is the fact that there was no shortage of competent military leaders to effectively defend Haiti against the holocaust that was to come, especially Dessalines with Christophe in the wings awaiting his opportunity. In April 1798 when L'Ouverture negotiated the departure of the last of the British invaders from Haiti which gave him control of Port -au- Prince finally, he simply went on a roll, drunk with power with no apparent consideration of the strategic realities at hand. There is already race war between Africans and Mixed troops in the military, L'Ouverture in November 1798 orders all non-enlisted Africans to report for forced, obligatory paid work on the plantations of their former massa and the new massa. In October 1798 L'Ouverture expels Commissioner Hedouville from Haiti sending a potent message to the right-wing politicians and Bonaparte who is L'Ouverture's commanding officer. Before he leaves Hedouville hands over all the power of the commissioner to General Rigaud, a mixed race Haitian soldier who immediately engages with L'Ouverture in a game of musical power chairs which by June 1799 evolves into open warfare. Massa is now playing divide and rule once again in Haiti thanks to L'Ouverture's personal agenda. In October 1798 L'Ouverture sends a trade delegation to the USA which generates the paranoia amongst the French politicians that L'Ouverture is seeking to invite the USA into Haiti, this is confirmed by the US and British action to blockade the French navy from Haiti. L'Ouverture is now on a roll convinced that he has played massa divide and conquer game better than massa. In August 1800 he defeats Rigaud in battle who flees to France, in October 1800 L'Ouverture releases his decree enforced by the military of forced labor on the plantations which ensures the labor supply to the plantation system. The adopted nephew of L'Ouverture voices opposition to his uncle's decree calling for land reform which will create a body of small landowners, rejection of the return of their old massa and forced work for their old massa and open revolt against the intransigence of L'Ouverture and this new servility to their old massa, one of whom was killed in the course of the revolt. L'Ouverture arrested, charged, tried and executed his nephew Moyse as an example to all Haitians. In January 1801 L'Ouverture invades and seizes Santo Domingo now making him the maximum leader of

Hispaniola. In May 1801 L'Ouverture makes public a constitution for Hispaniola which he unilaterally produced and proclaimed which made him governor/ dictator for life. L'Ouverture's actions to January 1801 are driven by a reckless desire for power that knows no limits, refusing to acknowledge the grave strategic reality Haiti/ Hispaniola faces from a united white supremacist slave owning federation dedicated to destroying Haiti.

In November 1799 Bonaparte seizes power with a coup as the right-wing Directory collapses establishing a new order of power which evolves from a military dictatorship to a military monarchy. Bonaparte makes it clear in his new constitution that France will restore slavery in its colonies. Bonaparte must now bide his time working on attaining the necessary strategic impetus in which to invade Hispaniola. He has to work out the logistics of invasion and more importantly garner this federation of white supremacist slave owning white nations which is accomplished between July to October 1801 when both Britain and the USA called for the French destruction of Haiti and pledged their support and input, with Jamaica becoming the operational base for the British. In February 1802 the French invasion fleet arrives in Haiti which exposes the reality that L'Ouverture cannot defend Hispaniola, quickly loses control of Santo Domingo and resorts to a scorched earth policy of retreat in Haiti in face of the blockade backed invasion. What use is your favored plantation renaissance in light of this strategic reality? In April 1802 Christophe deserts to the British with 1,200 fighting men with him, whilst in May 1802 L'Ouverture offers to surrender to the French whilst Bonaparte orders the reinstatement of slavery in the colonies even though Haiti is not yet conquered and in July 1802 word from Guadeloupe confirms that slavery has been restored there. This reality was the potent galvanizing instrument that mobilized the masses to engage with the French to the death, L'Ouverture no longer commanded the the means to mobilize the Haitian masses as in the past. In August 1802 L'Ouverture is renditioned from Haiti to France and placed in Bonaparte's Guantanamo without trial where he died in 1804. There was no leadership void created with the renditioning of L'Ouverture which favored the French invader as the masses were resolute in their commitment to die fighting, refusing to be once again enslaved, and Dessalines harnessed this commitment of the masses to birth a free Haiti aided and abetted by the incompetence of Bonaparte and his foot soldiers.

The white discourse of L'Ouverture the Black Spartacus was formulated by Laveaux and Sonthonax, a discourse that L'Ouverture embellished and was swallowed by so-called radical revolutionaries and black power advocates and regurgitated to this day in a deliberate attempt to create a massa version of the Haitian revolution, servile, shattered and keeping the Haitian masses locked in chronic underdevelopment because their ancestors dared to liberate themselves from massa through revolutionary violence. In his dealings with Bonaparte L'Ouverture will reveal in living color the contradictions of his discourse and the worldview it drove. When faced with the French invasion of Haiti under the leadership of Bonaparte, L'Ouverture embraces defensive aggression then shucking and jiving as a dutiful soldier of France holding unquestioned allegiance to France and Bonaparte. L'Ouverture places himself within the grasp of the French forces and willingly obeys the order to report without a military entourage which enables an incident free, seamless rendition to France. With his rendition L'Ouverture continues his shucking and jiving in writing to Bonaparte as if expecting military justice to be afforded him as he was a loyal soldier of France and Bonaparte. L'Ouverture is delusional, refusing to embrace and act upon the reality that he is a non-white presenting a grave threat to white supremacist hegemony and the slave economy of the Caribbean and North America. Faced with the French invasion he refuses to enter into the full guerrilla mode of resistance waiting on the yellow fever to strike the invaders and the breakup of the massa international coalition against Haiti. Both soon followed decimating the invasion force and setting up the retreat of the French from Haiti, at this time L'Ouverture was already dead in Bonaparte's Guantanamo. Faced with its grave existential crisis of the invasion L'Ouverture turned his back on Haiti, failed Haiti immersed in his refusal to lose all that he personally accumulated since 1793, gambling on a delusional discourse of French white supremacy and his value to it. Refusing to understand that this brand of white supremacy wanted no compromise, no non-white front man to work in their favor. They demanded a return to the raw naked slave order of white might, having no interest in a neo-colonial Haiti in 1803. L'Ouverture was then ahead of his time, the father of all non-white neo-colonial lackeys of massa, but totally irrelevant to the order of power of white supremacy in 1803.

Deconstruction of the correspondence of Toussaint L'Ouverture

1. Proclamation 29 August 1793

This is L'Ouverture's first public proclamation to the masses of Haiti where he utilized this opportunity in writing to present his discourse of the Haitian Revolution and his pedigree as a bona fide leader of the Haitian Revolution. L'Ouverture states as follows: "I am Toussaint L'Ouverture perhaps my name has made itself known to you. You know, brothers, that I have undertaken this vengeance, and that I want liberty and equality to reign in St Domingue. I have worked since the beginning [of the revolt] to make that happen, and to bring happiness to all, Unite yourselves to us, brothers, and fight with us for the same cause. You say that you are fighting for liberty and equality? Is it possible that we could destroy ourselves, one against the other, and all fighting against the same cause? It is I who have undertaken [this struggle] and I wish to fight until it [liberty] exists...among us. Equality cannot exist without liberty. And for liberty to exist, we must have unity." (Nesbitt 2008 Pgs. 1-2). In this his first public proclamation L'Ouverture uses his new name rather than his former name Breda, signifying his rejection of the slave past, even though in 1776 he became a free African who then proceeded to purchase land and enslaved workers forming the Toussaint Breda slave plantation. L'Ouverture's discourse presents his Manichean duality constructed as follows: enslavement/ liberty, enslavement/ inequality, liberty/ equality, enslavement/ disunity/ liberty/ equality/ unity. There is then no attaining the desire for liberty and equality without the unity of the masses, but this unity is rooted in the hegemony of a dominant leader, a hegemonic leader, a maximum leader. At this time in the history of the Revolution there was a multiplicity of leaders with no single cogent vision and strategy to attain the desired liberty and equality, L'Ouverture is then offering himself as the new visioned, strategising maximum leader; they would soon become very familiar with his practice/ praxis. L'Ouverture's discourse insists that liberty/ equality is not attainable without unity attained on the basis of the hegemony of a single maximum leader who proved to be autocratic at best.

L'Ouverture in his first public statement presents his play for maximum leadership of the Revolution exemplified by his spanking brand-new name, but alas Breda lives as he expresses openly his white supremacist discourse and its worldview that he was socialized into at the Breda plantation under the hegemony of massa. L'Ouverture in 1793 is plagued with hallucinatory whiteness, burdened with a white supremacist discourse by which he views and orders the world he perceives and acts upon, an example of black skin, white mask seeking power to wield power over non-white peoples of the Haitian Revolution, which inevitably must benefit massa for he remains servile to massa at the level of the idea in spite of the Revolution he desires to lead. The equality/ unity L'Ouverture writes of when made manifest will reveal its autocratic, elitist, racist order of power that is firmly rooted in massa's white supremacist order of power, a neocolonial order of white power which renders the African and Mixed masses of Haiti servile with a non-white autocrat wielding dictatorial power.

2. Letter to Biassou 15 October 1791

In this October 1791 letter Breda is writing to a prominent commander of the Haitian Revolution who has attached to his command Jean-Francois and Dutty Boukman. Breda is literally sucking up to Biassou seeking to find favor with him, solicit his patronage and most of all exert influence towards building his power base in the leadership of the Revolution en route to realizing his desire for power. Breda is also soliciting inputs from the Spanish to aid his cause and expresses in the letter his disdain for Jean-Francois and his white supremacist contempt for the unwashed, uneducated, unkept Haitian masses who are openly fighting in the Revolution, dying for the Revolution, unlike him. Breda states: "To M. Biassou, Brigadier of the King's Army at Grand Boucan My veery dear friend In keeping with the request I just made of the Spanish and daily awaiting the thing I asked for," (Nesbitt 2008 Pg. 3). Biassou, his command personnel and Breda are all dependent upon Spanish inputs in order to make war on the French plantation order of power rooted in enslavement.

But the Spanish are also white supremacist slave owners as the French, which raises the potent question of with defeat of the French with Spanish support then what? Consorting with the Spanish is then a double-edged sword that creates an opportunity for British intervention to capture the territory for the British empire. Breda continues: "As for Jean-Francois he can still go in a carriage with his ladies, but he hasn't done me the honor of writing to me for several days. I am very surprised by this." (Nesbitt 2008 Pg. 4). Breda does not attack Dutty Boukman choosing instead to focus on Jean-Francois inferring that Jean-Francois is too much involved with his ladies to enable him to effectively execute the duties of his command. Breda is then an informer seeking to undermine the relationship between Biassou and Jean-Francois, towards exploiting the space created to enable him to increase the power he wields in the Biassou command structure to eventually replace Biassou with himself. The most potent revelation of this letter is Breda's expressed discourse of the former enslaved Africans who are now the foot soldiers of Biassou's command as follows: "If you want tafia I will send you some when you'd like, but try to use it sparingly. The troops must not be given this so they won't get out of hand." (Nesbitt 2008 Pg. 4). The formerly enslaved African has to be strictly managed for they are as little children driven by desire as Jean-Francois is, with little concern for discipline and hard work. Any form of indulgence by the leadership such as regular large rations of tafia distributed to the troops will bring out the worst in the African, their childishness, indiscipline and propensity to violence, spare the rod and lose control of the African. Breda is then articulating massa discourse of the shucking and jiving nigger which speaks to his white supremacist discourse and worldview. At this time is Breda's plantation still in production and if so, what are the terms and conditions he affords labor on this plantation as he is drawing down on his stock of tafia produced on his estate? Tafia was a high proof rum alcohol that was not aged in oak barrels from where we got the tradition of puncheon rum in the Caribbean. Breda signs the letter "General Doctor" which points to Breda's strategy at this time to not sign correspondence to the command of the revolution and massa with his name, clearly an attempt to mask his revolutionary activity until the right time that suits his agenda. He is then a general in Biassou's command carrying the name Doctor given his reputation as an animal whisperer on massa Breda plantation and the physician that is here to heal Haiti from its afflictions.

3. Letter to the General Assembly from Biassou, Jean-Francois and Toussaint Breda

Breda's nineteen-year-old nephew's name, Belair, was on the document with Breda signing for Belair, which means to the massa general assembly of St Domingue Breda did not even use General Doctor, choosing instead to put Belair in play. The revolutionary discourse of this letter with its assault on white supremacy expressed as enslavement of non-whites is the treatise by which to judge the actions of L'Ouverture when exercising the power he enjoyed and exercised over the Revolution from 1793 to 1803. The letter states: "For too long, gentlemen by way of abuses that one can never too strongly accuse of having taken place because of our lack of understanding and ignorance – for a very long time, I say we have been victims of your greed and your avarice. Under the blows of your barbarous whip we have accumulated for you the treasures you enjoy in this colony; the human race has suffered to see with what barbarity you have treated men like yourself – yes, men – over men you have no other right except that you are stronger and more barbaric than we; you have engaged in [slave] traffic, you have sold men for horses, and even that is the least of your shortcomings in the eyes of humanity; our lives depend on your caprice, and when it's a question of amusing yourselves, the burden falls on men like us, who are most often are guilty of no other crime than to be under your orders." (Nesbitt 2008 Pg. 6). The discourse driving this statement is unmistakably white supremacist abolitionist anti-enslavement discourse. The impact of this servility at the level of the idea is the embrace of the concepts of what is the "black man" conceptualized and constituted by the Manichean dualities of white supremacist discourse. There is no formulation and unleashing of an independent non-white discourse which rejects the white supremacist Manichean dualities thereby choosing to express non-white existential realities under enslavement grounded in the non-binary circular cosmology of non-white civilizations. This servility at the level of the idea to white supremacist discourse means that Revolution brings no liberation at the level of the idea, hence no mitigation of the spectrum of trauma arising from racist enslavement. The self-hate continues in spite of the success of the Revolution in ending enslavement creating new massa, non-white massa astutely abiding by the white supremacist order of power. This new massa, servile at the level of the idea with "freedom" is the basis upon which the neo-colonial condition is rooted in.

The letter continues as follows: "We are black, it is true, but tell us, gentlemen, you who are so judicious, what is the law that says that the black man must belong to and be the property of the white man? Certainly you will not be able to make us see where that exists. It is not in your imagination – always ready to form new [plantation] so long as they are to your advantage. Yes, gentlemen, we are free like you, and it is only by your avarice and our ignorance that anyone is still held in slavery up to this day, and we can neither see nor find the right that you pretend to have over us, nor anything that could prove it to us, set down on the earth like you, all being children of the same father created in the same image. We are your equal then, by natural right, and if nature pleases itself to diversify culture within the human race, it is not a crime to be born black nor an advantage to be white. If the abuses in the Colony have gone on for several years, that was before the fortunate revolution that has taken place in the motherland, which has opened for us the road which our courage and labour will enable us to ascend, to arrive at the temple of liberty, like those brave Frenchmen who are our models and whom all the universe is contemplating." (Nesbitt 2008 Pgs. 6-7). The letter recognizes black as being inferior to white as it was black ignorance which enables massa to enslave the non-white and keep then in bondage. This ignorance was not broken by enlightened action of the non-whites in Haiti, rather it was broken by the enlightened action of the "motherland" France and the whites who made Revolution in France against the Ancien Regime. The Haitian Revolution has then no indigenous non-white momentum, all it has is what it has learnt from massa who assaulted their ignorance giving them the idea of making revolution. The Haitian Revolution is then the product of a conjuncture within the terrain of French white supremacist discourse which sought resolution via armed conflict. The enslaved non-white in Haiti was then incapable of analysing and formulating strategies of resistance arising from their existential experiences and realities, they simply were incapable of agency, less than human. Only when massa in the motherland engaged with revolution then the enslaved non-whites were taught the white, massa methodology by which to overthrow massa in Haiti. The document expresses the ignorance of the enslaved non-whites in a discourse rooted in Christian cosmology, betraying the hegemony racist Christian discourse and cosmology has over their worldview to the extent where in the document there is no presence of a non-white discourse and its cosmology. Non-white writers are speaking to massa using only white supremacist discourse which denies the very humanity of the writers as it elucidates the inability of the non-white enslaved to make revolution without the white model of the "motherland." A servile position which cannot grasp the reality that this revolution in the motherland was not about ending the hegemony of the discourse of white supremacy, but rather over which political factions will now exert hegemony over the order of power of white supremacy in France, white supremacy remains constant up to today. Which means that Haiti must be destroyed by any means necessary from 1791 to the present, which has been accomplished with the vitally necessary compliance of the servile of Haiti, those plagued with hallucinatory whiteness, as witnessed in this document.

The letter continues as follows: "For too long we have borne your chains without thinking of shaking them off, but any authority which is not founded on virtue and humanity, and which only tends to subject one's fellow man to slavery, must come to an end, and that end is yours. You, gentlemen, who pretend to subject us to slavery have you not sworn to uphold the French Constitution? What does it say, this respectable constitution? What is the fundamental law? Have you forgotten that you have formally vowed the Declaration of the Rights of Man, which says that men are born free, equal in their rights; that their natural rights include liberty, property, security and resistance to oppression? So then, as you cannot deny what you have sworn, we are within our rights, and you ought to recognize yourselves as perjurers; by your decision you recognize all men as free, but you want to maintain servitude for 480,000 individuals who allow you to enjoy all that you possess. Through your envoys you offer liberty only to our chiefs, it is still one of your maxims of politics to say that those who have played an equal part in our work should be delivered by us to be your victims. No, we prefer a thousand deaths to acting that way against our own kind. If you want to accord us the benefits that are due to us, they must also shower onto all of our brothers." (Nesbitt 2008 Pg. 7). In spite of the French Constitution and the Declaration of the Rights of Man, massa in St Domingue and France is treating with the Haitian Revolution as a slave revolt which must be suppressed, and slavery preserved in the French colony. Cognizant of the realities of the Revolution, massa is then offering a pardon and freedom to the leaders in exchange for giving up the masses in revolt for punishment and a return to enslavement. The freedom offered to the leaders gives them the opportunity to be like Breda before the Revolution: to acquire property, slaves and to amass wealth through exploitation of their enslaved. This offer is rejected outright in the letter all in the name of liberty and equality through joint action and unwavering solidarity of non-whites. But this does not preclude the leaders under the order of power of the Revolution from amassing wealth through military rule of the social order and forced labor on the plantations of the new military dictators of the Haitian Revolution. The discourse of the letter is then grounded in grave hypocrisy. The central, core concept of this section of the letter is fatally flawed which reflects the delusion of hallucinatory whiteness, which is the grave error that the Declaration of the Rights of Man and the French Constitution gave rights to non-whites thereby rendering enslavement illegal. The Declaration of the Rights of Man gave no rights to white women, much less to non-white men and women who were the property of white persons. The fact that emancipation was only legal by act of the National Assembly and was easily restored by such an act proves that there was no constitutional barrier to enslavement. Your "motherland" that made revolution and emancipated you from your ignorance, which enabled you to undertake revolution against massa, was never anti-enslavement in its constitution. Emancipation was the outcome of political power relations of the epoch which abolished slavery, then restored it, then finally abolished it ever in perpetuity. In spite of the loss of their colony of St Domingue to

Revolution the politics of the era restored enslavement throughout the empire until its end. This potently indicates that this 'motherland" viewed enslavement as part of its white male revolution, its white entitlement until its abolition. This letter which is the product of white discourse and its worldview is delusional as it speaks to a reality that has no traction with reality on the ground. It is an early specimen of the worldview and ideational production of delusional hallucinatory whiteness. The specific action taken to govern the Haitian Revolution on the ground is then expected, normal given this mindset of its leaders, for it boils down to desire and its satiation, as exemplified by L'Ouverture himself.

The letter now presents the demands of those in revolt against enslavement by massa as follows: "First, general liberty for all men detained in slavery. Second, general amnesty for the past. Third, the guarantee of these articles by the Spanish government." "If like us, you desire that the articles above be accepted, we will commit ourselves to the following first, to lay down our arms, second, that each of us will return to the plantation to which he belongs and resume his work on condition of a wage which will be set by the year for each cultivator who starts work for a fixed term." (Nesbitt 2008 Pg. 8). The letter demands liberty for all the enslaved, an amnesty for those taking part in the Revolution and a guarantee that the Spanish king accepts this deal with the Revolution. After embracing the Spanish to make war on the colony and the French revolutionary forces at the point of a peace deal the threat posed by the slave owning Spanish is now recognized. This then is a pledge that in the event of Spanish hostility to the new order of power of post-enslavement St Domingue the French will join with the Haitian revolutionary forces to neutralize the Spanish threat. In exchange for peace, freedom and justice the Haitian revolutionary forces shall disarm themselves and return to work on the plantations they rebelled and made war against as bonded wage workers. L'Ouverture and the rest of the signatories are then insisting on state control of the nascent, emerging free labor market thereby shackling it, distorting its development to the detriment of free labor. The ultimate aim is therefore ensuring that massa and the new non-white massa will enjoy coerced, servile "free" labor; where the state will now regulate the cost of labor to massa for a period of one year. L'Ouverture is insisting that free African labor in a labor market must be placed in bridles, controlled and dominated for the good of the plantation order of power. Liberation, liberty and equality is defined by the unfitness of the African labor force to be "responsible" in a free labor market. The ongoing African push back against this position championed and implemented by L'Ouverture would alienate him from the radical sections of the free African population who were adamant on land reform and becoming landowners in their own right. The invasion of Bonaparte to restore slavery marked the end of the hegemony of L'Ouverture over the leadership of the Revolution. The apologists make the excuse of shucking and jiving massa to attain strategic ends justifies the refusal to accept what the masses desire for their future development. Shucking and jiving using a white supremacist discourse which you have internalized and act upon is reworking massa's worldview to benefit both massa and yourself. In so doing the operational discourse you have embraced is relentlessly attacking your humanity and you respond with self-hate, eventually you turn on your own race in your attempt to earn the affirmation of massa, that is hallucinatory whiteness in action. This article to bond free labor to the plantation on which they were enslaved directly benefits L'Ouverture and the most brutal, decadent, serial killer massas who survived the Revolution and returned to claim their property, whilst intensifying the spectrum of trauma plaguing the former enslaved Africans who will now be forced to return to the trauma delivery site and interact with the persons who traumatized them as bonded workers. One is then forced to return to the plantation with the old massa in charge and his crew of brutal drivers intact, but now you are unarmed as you under the instruction of your leaders disarmed yourself. The entire process of coercing labor is then hinged on a new military structure created utilizing chosen leaders and detachments from the Revolutionary army charged with coercing the free African population. This was the first experiment towards creating the neo-colonial order of power unleashed with the end of colonial rule of its colonies.

4. Letter to General Laveaux 18 May 1794

L'Ouverture continued waging war on the French colony of St Domingue with the Spanish until the French outlawed enslavement in February 1794. Thereafter, L'Ouverture became the darling of the French as he was made General of the Western Army and cultivated a close working relationship and personal friendship with the French interim Governor – General Etienne Laveaux.

L'Ouverture states as follows: "It is true, General, that I have been led into error by the enemies of the Republic and humanity," "I fell into their nets, not without knowing what I was doing; you will remember that {...] my goal was only that we unite to combat the enemies of France and to bring an end to an internal war among the French of the colony. Unfortunately, for all concerned, the paths toward reconciliation that I suggested were rejected." (Nesbitt 2008 Pg. 9). L'Ouverture is guilty of consorting with the enemies of the Republic and humanity, i.e. – the slave holding Spanish. L'Ouverture embraced the Spanish after his attempts to end the internecine war amongst the French in the colony failed as his structure for reconciliation between the warring parties was rejected. There was then no Revolution from 1791 to 1794 in St Domingue, this was simply a civil war between French citizens. Are the enslaved in revolt, waging war to exterminate massa and their order of power rooted in enslavement, actually involved in a French civil war? This isn't shucking and jiving, this is delusion which reveals his worldview. Clearly, St Domingue orbits around L'Ouverture, a narcissist standing in the way of the formerly enslaved African and Mixed-race people realizing their fullest potential denied by enslavement.

L'Ouverture now deals with his embrace of the Spanish king and waging war on the French colony as follows: "At the time, the Spanish offered me their protection and freedom for all those who fought for the cause of kings. Having always fought to achieve the same liberty, I accepted their offer seeing myself abandoned by the French, my brothers. But a somewhat late experience opened my eyes to these perfidious protectors..." "Let us unite forever, therefore, and, forgetting the past, let us seek henceforth only to crush our enemies and to avenge ourselves against our treacherous neighbors." (Nesbitt 2008 Pg. 10). In your quest for liberty and equality, as France was not willing to emancipate the enslaved, but you were not actually enslaved and instead benefited from it, you embraced the Spanish king with the colonial imperial empire premised on enslavement and extermination of especially Natives. When mercenaries as you all broke the back of the French order of power in St Domingue did you expect that the former enslaved will be free? But you were already free, making war on an order of power you benefited from and would have benefited from its restoration under Spanish hegemony. When French white supremacy moved to restore enslavement, which white power was then available for you to solicit their embrace? None! Hence your capitulation in 1802 to Bonaparte by abandoning a prolonged guerrilla war led by you. This task then fell to Dessalines.

L'Ouverture now speaks to the prowess of his military leadership, the hegemony he exercises over an area under the control of Haitians fighting for the Spanish king and the enlightened nature of his governance as follows: "It is true that the national flag flies over Gonaives and its surroundings, and that I have routed the Spanish and emigrants from the area." (Nesbitt 2008 Pg. 10).The national flag for L'Ouverture is the French tricolor, there is no Haiti, Haitian nationalism and self-determination, which means he has surrendered to French white supremacy once again in his life in a position that benefits his economic interests, but now his desire for political power trumps all as he plays the game with the French colonial order of power, hence his attachment to Laveaux. L'Ouverture continues as follows: "But my heart is broken to contemplate the event that occurred against a few unfortunate whites who were victims in this affair. I am utterly unlike many others who witness scenes of horror in cold blood. I have always held humanity in common to all, and I suffer whenever I cannot prevent evil. There were also a number of uprisings in the workshops, but I rapidly returned things to order and all are working as before." (Nesbitt 2008 Pg. 10). L'Ouverture is once again peddling the white supremacist discourse of the unregenerate, in-disciplined, barbarous childlike nigger, the threat they pose to massa and the need for massa to embrace L'Ouverture's protection given his propensity to discipline and punish errant niggers to massa benefit as he was never a nigger, he is a Breda, free, literate, cultured and a former slave owner. L'Ouverture will never slaughter whites simply for the sake of revenge against mass murderers or the family of mass murderers, exemplified by his invitation for massa to return to the colony, reclaim and re-start their plantations, and he will deliver to them servile, bonded ex-slaves to work for their former massa for wage levels determined by L'Ouverture. L'Ouverture never fails to point to his hardline approach to niggers in rebellion, recalcitrant and in-disciplined and his unflinching ability to unleash the hardline suppression to restore massa order. He then unleashes the non-white military to discipline errant niggers who are supposedly free, to the benefit of massa. L'Ouverture is then massa premier, apex driver on a neo-colonial plantation. L'Ouverture ends this letter by stating: "Salvation in the fatherland." (Nesbitt 2008 Pg. 10). White supremacist France and its colony now founded on free/ unfree labor and a predominantly non-white military order of power is the "fatherland" of L'Ouverture, hence his perceptual collapse and surrender when the massa invaded to restore enslavement in expectation of grave and prolonged resistance from the Haitian masses and their maximum leader, L'Ouverture who failed to comply with massa expectations. Hallucinatory whiteness can never be an effective discourse of resistance against white supremacy at the level of the idea, much less drive an effective and successful military resistance that reaps the benefit of liberation.

5. Letter to Laveaux 7 July 1794

In this letter L'Ouverture is reporting to Laveaux on his battlefield victories against Jean Francois, who has refused to abandon service to the Spanish king as L'Ouverture did. At this time both Spain and Britain had invaded the colony intent on conquest and breaking the back of the non-white movement for liberation. L'Ouverture comments on the passage of the act to abolish slavery by the National Convention in its final year of existence, 1794 to 1795. The sting in the tail followed with the rise to power of the National Directory (1795-1799) with its right wing white supremacist agenda which included the restoration of enslavement in the French colonies. L'Ouverture states as follows: "I also read of the September sessions of the last year of the National Convention and the decree they issued for the abolition of slavery. This is reassuring news for friends of humanity, and I hope that in the future all will feel more at ease and that, if we are able to enjoy peace and tranquility, the colony will flourish to an unparalleled degree. Salvation in the fatherland, and its success." (Nesbitt 2008 Pgs. 11 12). There is no peace and tranquility to come from the politics of France as instability in the National Convention gives sway to the rise to political power of a nascent bourgeois in alliance with elements of the nobility intent on erasing the measures implemented by the radical republicans of the National Convention, such as the abolition of slavery. There is then no salvation for non-whites in this new order of power being formed in the social order of revolutionary France, there is no "fatherland" for non-whites in this French order of the white supremacist order of power, which spawned the dictatorship of Bonaparte. L'Ouverture will get this message delivered to his door in the colony with the French invasion to break the back of non-white power in the colony with a return to the order of power of massa rooted in enslavement.

6. Toussaint L'Ouverture to his brothers and sisters in Varettes 22 March 1795

This is a signal piece of correspondence of L'Ouverture which reveals his willingness to utilise propaganda in an effort to seduce the masses in an effort to render them servile to his agenda. In this case the propaganda is the love of freedom and liberty of the National Convention and the obligation placed on the masses to abide willingly to L'Ouverture's agenda without question, protest or push back. This correspondence reveals L'Ouverture's discourse of governance of the masses with the instruments to power formulated and unleashed to ensure his hegemony. L'Ouverture states as follows: "I learned with infinite joy of the return of the citizens of Upper Varettes within the Republic. There they will find the happiness they had fled at the instigation of the soldiers of tyranny and royalty. To give them support, to console them of their past faults and to lead them to abjure the errors they nourished insidiously, is for all republicans an absolute duty and the sacred maxim of the French." (Nesbitt 2008 Pg. 13). The inhabitants of Upper Varettes were seduced by those serving the Spanish king to depart the jurisdiction of the republic led by the National Convention, thereby rejecting the happiness assured by the republic to the masses. They have now returned voluntarily and it's the duty of all French republicans to rehabilitate and reintegrate them into the republic to ensure they are fit and proper to enjoy and contribute to the happiness assured by the republic. L'Ouverture is demanding from the returnees deep seated contrition and self-regeneration leading to devotion to the French republic, primarily him.

L'Ouverture continues as follows: "The French are our brothers, the English, the Spanish, and the royalists are ferocious beasts who only caress to suck at their leisure, until they are satiated, the blood of their women and children." "Your duty is now to contribute with all your moral and physical might to strengthen your parish and to make flourish therein the principles of holy liberty. If it is otherwise, do not hope for any further sign of our fraternity. Think well about what I am saying." (Nesbitt 2008 Pg.14). L'Ouverture unleashes his white supremacist Manichean binary discourse demonizing the enemies of France who are the natural enemies of the masses of Upper Varettes. The duality: France – inherently good, vitally necessary for the liberty and progress of the non-whites of the Upper Varettes vs. Britain, Spain and the French royalists – being inherently evil and potent adversaries of liberty and progress enjoyed by the masses of Upper Varettes. L'Ouverture's binary discourse went into crisis with the election of the National Directory in control of the National Assembly of France and collapsed with Bonaparte's invasion of the colony in February 1802. The French in control of the state were now intent on reinstating enslavement in all French colonies, thus dismantling L'Ouverture's discourse of the beloved French and his credibility on the ground.

L'Ouverture now reveals his order of power which is prosecuting a specific social order that L'Ouverture insists is what the colony needs with no consultation of the masses. Dictatorial power denies the masses voice and choice, for no one has voted for L'Ouverture as the dictator of the colony of free humans of all races. L'Ouverture states as follows: "It is in these circumstances I have ordered and order the following: Second Article – The conservation of citizens' properties is assured by the constitution; consequently, all the commanders of the parishes, camps and posts of the line are ordered to respect and preserve these, and this, under their personal responsibility." (Nesbitt 2008 Pg. 14). The former enslaved entered freedom landless and the only way to acquire land legally was with the agreement of its owners, of massa. Enslavement was abolished, but the continued dominant ownership of property in the colony by massa, his religion and the state continued with the full support of L'Ouverture. L'Ouverture's worldview called for a landless non-white labor force forced to work for wages set by the state for massa on his plantations. There was no room for the vision of a colony of small land holders cultivating the land, feeding the nation and providing inputs for value added production for local consumption and export. This was freedom from enslavement, not from exploitation for the benefit of massa. There was then no concept of social justice in L'Ouverture's discourse making him a traitor to his race not a revolutionary, potently indicated by this instruction which orders the military to police issues of land occupation, ownership and tenure, thereby militarizing the social order and the state with L'Ouverture as the substantive military dictator of his commission. L'Ouverture continues as follows: "Fifth Article – All farmers, twenty-four hours after the publication of the present proclamation, shall return to pursue all forms of agricultural labor in the plantation to which they are dependent, except those contiguous with enemy territory. The cultivation of plantations bordering the enemy, if they are not soldiers, will report to other plantations to participate in labor" (Nesbitt 2008 Pg. 14). These landless former enslaved are farmers only when they own the land they are cultivating. Those occupying former plantation lands will be faced with eviction by the military whenever the massa returns claiming her/ his property or the new owner appears. They are also powerless to block depredations by the military elite seeking land to create their own personal landholdings. This article then forces landless labor and landless farmers to report for work on plantations of their massa, a measure that Jim Crow of Amerikka would view with lust. L'Ouverture continues as follows: "Sixth

Article – Work is necessary, it is a virtue, It is the general good of the state. Every lazy and errant man will be arrested to be punished by the law. But service is also conditional and will be paid a just wage." (Nesbitt 2008 Pg. 15). L'Ouverture is again using white supremacist discourse of the lazy shiftless nigger who has to be taught how and forced to work for his own good. All the former enslaved who refuse to work for their former massa, want to own land towards self-determination, masters of their destiny are for L'Ouverture lazy shiftless niggers who will be rounded up and punished according to the existing slave laws on the books of a former slave colony. L'Ouverture loves to speak to equality and liberty under the French fatherland/ motherland whilst using slave law to coerce free labor to servility to white capital. L'Ouverture is now assiduously building an edifice of wage disguised bondage to ensure the sustainability of massa plantation system using a military dictatorship and slave law as the preferred instruments of power to so do. L'Ouverture with this action, which he repeated until 1801, set in motion the creation of an order of power that blighted Haiti to this day.

7. Letter to Jean-Francois 13 June 1795

As of June 1795 L'Ouverture and Jean-Francois are still at war with each other. Jean-Francois in his continued service to the Spanish king is involved in convincing the masses to pledge allegiance to the Spanish king thereby walking away from the French Republic and L'Ouverture. L'Ouverture's letter to Jean_Francois of 13 June 1795 is in fact L'Ouverture's input to the debate with Jean-Francois over allegiance to the Spanish king versus the French republic. L'Ouverture states as follows: "2. You claim in your second article to show that we have been misled, while we hope to convince you that anyone who is a subject or vassal of kings is no more than a vile slave and that a republic alone is truly a man. 3. Consequently we are free by natural right. It could only be kings, whose name alone expresses what is most vile and despicable, who could dare claim the right to reduce into servitude men made like them and whom nature has made free." (Nesbitt 2008 Pg. 16). In light of the rise to power of the National Directory, the dictator Bonaparte, then emperor Bonaparte, committed to the restoration of enslavement in the colonies in the bowels of the French republic meant that every human having a natural right to freedom was a myth perpetuated by massa and championed by L'Ouverture for his personal agenda. There was than an organic common discourse linking the Spanish king and the French republic, the discourse of white supremacy which L'Ouverture in his hallucinatory whiteness, his delusion, was incapable of discerning the evolution of the order of power in France to one that embraces the return of enslavement. The invasion of the colony by Bonaparte to restore slavery was then the end of L'Ouverture's relevance, credibility and hegemony as a maximum leader.

8. Letter to Dieudonne 12 February 1796

Dieudonne was born in the Kingdom of Kongo and sold into slavery in St Domingue, unlike L'Ouverture who was born in St Domingue enslaved to Breda. In 1796 Dieudonne operated in the mountains that border with Port au Prince in command of some 3,000 armed soldiers and openly expressed his disdain on what was transpiring with the rise to power of the National Directory in France and its impact on the order of power in St Domingue, which L'Ouverture single handedly contributed to given his assault on the power on the commissioner dispatched to the colony by the National Directory. Dieudonne's grave problem was his distrust of the mulatto Rigaud who was handed the power of the commissioner following L'Ouverture's assault on him eventually expelling him from the colony. Dieudonne is negotiating with the British to embrace their cause against the French given his problem with Rigaud, which is a race war between African and Mixed-race persons. L'Ouverture is now intervening to woo Dieudonne to embrace the French cause in spite of his paranoia over Rigaud. If successful L'Ouverture will assault Rigaud's power base in his quest to destroy Rigaud and expel him from the colony. Faced with the National Directory and Bonaparte, L'Ouverture chooses at this time until 1801 before the invasion to actively, aggressively pursue the consolidation of his hegemony over the colony. This lust for power of L'Ouverture consolidates the unity of white supremacy in France and in the North

Atlantic intent on restoring slavery under the order of power of massa in St Domingue.

L'Ouverture states as follows: "And so it is impossible for me to believe the slanderous rumors that have been spread about you that you have abandoned your fatherland to join the English, the sworn enemies of our freedom and equality." "Governor Laveaux who is the father of us all and in whom the motherland has placed her trust, must also merit yours, I think as well that you will not refuse it to me, a black like yourself, …" "For my part, I believe that this is only possible by serving the French Republic, it is under its flag that we are truly free and equal." "If it is possible that the English have managed to fool you, believe me, my dear brother, abandon them, unite with the good republicans, and, all together, let us rid our land of the royalists." (Nesbitt 2008 Pgs. 18-19). L'Ouverture unleashes his discourse of massa white supremacist Manichean dualities in an attempt to seduce him to swear fealty to L'Ouverture, enabling L'Ouverture to counter coup and bolster his power base even further. L'Ouverture unleashes the duality of republican/ royalist, French republican/ all royalists/ English and the duality of race and trusting your race, hence black/ mixed.

L'Ouverture continues as follows: "I have no doubt that you are a good republican; as such, you must unite with generals Rigaud and Bauvais who are good republicans, since our country has rewarded them for their services." "Remember, my dear friend, that the French Republic is one, and indivisible, that that is what constitutes its strength and that it will vanquish all its enemies. Believe me, my dear friend, forget all individual animosity, reunite with our brothers Rigaud and Bauvais." (Nesbitt 2008 Pgs. 19-20). This is an instance of the structure of L'Ouverture's discourse of seducing to manipulate a human he has targeted. This structure is rooted in white supremacist symbolism, concepts, cosmology and worldview which is essentially racist, anti-non-white peoples. L'Ouverture states that the French republic is an absolute, indivisible, a secular god which granted the non-white enslaved liberty and equality. Any monarchy, in spite of its claim of divine right, is not and cannot be an absolute, indivisible, hence it cannot grant freedom and equality to enslaved persons that persists across time/ space, only the French republic can and did. To consort with the royalists means the eventual loss of liberty and equality granted by the French republic, hence it is lunacy for Dieudonne to embrace the English royalists thereby forsaking the motherland/ fatherland of the French republic. L'Ouverture attests to the republican credentials of Rigaud and Bauvais therefore Dieudonne in embracing the French republic to ensure his freedom and equality across time/ space must now bond with Rigaud and Bauvais with L'Ouverture as the mediator or shot caller when necessary.

Developments in the politics of the French republic from the rise to power of the National Directory, then collapse of the republic, the usurpation of power by the Bonapartist coup d'etat and his self-proclamation of himself as emperor. The French republic was not then an Absolute as it collapsed and was replaced by a new structure of white supremacist royalist discourse intent on reinstating enslavement. White supremacist France being the motherland/ fatherland of formerly enslaved non-white peoples was falsified by the action of white supremacy proving the depth of the delusion that pervaded the mind of L'Ouverture, delusion spawned by hallucinatory whiteness. This is why in 1801 with the French invasion to reinstate enslavement L'Ouverture resisted in a vain attempt to prevent the French force from landing, but with successful landings he simply ceased resistance and made himself readily available and accessible for his rendition from the colony to detention in France without due process of law where he died. The manner in which he responded to the invasion indicates and illustrates the collapse of his discourse and its worldview, leaving him a castaway in his own skin, alienated from his white worldview with no non-white worldview to replace it, alienated and in a state of anomie, schizophrenic to the core.

9. Letter to Laveaux 20 February 1796

In February 1796 in the northern mountains near Port-de-Paix a labor rebellion driven by an alternative discourse of post enslavement self-development and self-determination to the hegemonic discourse of L'Ouverture triggered by the dismissal of Etienne Datty, the leader of the plantation workers of this area occurred. L'Ouverture writes to Laveaux boasting how he speedily and mercilessly used various instruments of power to put down this worker rebellion and restore his order of power. This then is L'Ouverture's version of events preserved for posterity because of the hegemonic power he wielded whilst the counter discourse of the workers by dint of their powerlessness is erased, buried, has no history, for history is only his story, namely those who exercise power. L'Ouverture states as follows: "I told them that if they wished to preserve their liberty they would have to submit to the law of the Republic, and be docile and work, that it was only in this way that they would benefit from their freedom. Furthermore, I said that if they had any claim to make that they would never obtain it in this manner, and that God had said: Ask and ye shall receive, knock and my door will be open to you, but that he has not said to commit crimes to obtain what one needs." (Nesbitt 2008 Pg. 22). L'Ouverture speaks to the workers in rebellion as massa, using white supremacist discourse to exercise power over non-white workers, forgetting that he is also non-white, until such time massa Bonaparte exercises power over L'Ouverture renditioning to detention without recourse to law. The very law that L'Ouverture is pointing to that criminalizes the refusal of workers to be servile, unquestioning, silent and work. L'Ouverture is again insisting that slave law of the colony renders servile free labor which is an existential condition that is not exactly wage slavery of the industrial European model, but a variant of slavery unleashed on free labor to render it servile and productive in the interest of massa in an imperial colonial context. L'Ouverture is again insisting to the workers that they are free thanks to the benevolence of the French republic as such they are obligated to massa benevolence to work as good servile, productive workers for massa and L'Ouverture's benefit. For the law that grants freedom does not grant self-determination, for liberty has to be responsible in order to cultivate sustainable freedom which means abiding by L'Ouverture's structure of self-determination for the freed workers, which means forced plantation work. L'Ouverture then unleashes massa white Christianity in the tradition of massa in his attempt to render them servile to his will. L'Ouverture speaks to the masses as if they are children, simpletons who must be guided, herded along the path designated for them by power wielded by

L'Ouverture. The masses are then nominally free as they are still powerless in the power relations of the colony free of enslavement. Their liberty, freedom is then a weapon being used to deny them self-determination, to render them servile as there is no rule of law established on the freedom of the citizenry, only slave law which recognizes only the power of massa to dominate the enslaved by any means necessary. This then constitutes power relations which force the masses to utilize violence to mediate conflict with those who wield hegemonic power, which remains the reality of the social order of Haiti to this day.

L'Ouverture is now giving his version of what the workers told him was the reason for their rebellion as follows: "Alas, general they wish as well to make us slaves; there is no equality here, as it seems there is with you." "We are looked down upon, they vex us at every turn. Thy don't pay us what we are owed for the food we grow. They force us to give away our chickens and pigs for nothing when we go to sell them in the city, and if we complain, they have us arrested by the police, and they throw us in prison without giving us anything to eat, and then make us pay to get out. You see, general, that one is not free if he is treated like this." (Nesbitt 2008 Pg. 23). The workers understand the nature of the power relations they are enmeshed in and above all their powerlessness in an order of power where massa is now joined by the military and the colonial state to ensure the powerlessness of the newly emancipated from enslavement. In a colonial imperial context, there can be no limits to the power of the colonial state which is now conspiring with massa and the new non-white military to render them servile productive workers devoid of rights though free. Freedom in this context only means freedom from being massa chattel/ property, it cannot mean having your freedom assured by law placing limits on the exercise of power. From then to the present in Haiti the order of power is unchanged. L'Ouverture is now boasting to Laveaux of his hard unrelenting line he adopted in response to this statement form the masses, indicating to massa that he has no soft heart for niggers in need of punishment, forever worthy of the trust of massa as his head driver. L'Ouverture states as follows: "I used this expression to make them understand that they could have all the reasons they wished and still they were in the wrong because they had

rendered themselves guilty in the eyes of God, of the law, and of men."
(Nesbitt 2008 Pg. 24). There is no redress forthcoming by L'Ouverture
under law for the complainant workers as the order of power of massa
remains hegemonic with a vengeance. L'Ouverture insists that there is no
redress for them under law, whilst he plays the role of the enlightened
military massa despot who is dispensing patronage because he is of the same
race as them. L'Ouverture is playing them for his own benefit and that
of massa hoping to make himself indispensable to massa as the controller
of unruly niggers. In his role as controller of a race with a propensity for
violence L'Ouverture stresses on his willingness to lie to them, to seduce
them by any means necessary to ensure their servility to the order of power
of massa. Case in point as follows: "What will I tell the National
Convention when it will ask me for an account of what you have just
done?" (Nesbitt 2008 Pg. 24). In 1796 the National Convention no longer
wields political power in France as its term has expired replaced by the
National Directory intent on restoring slavery in the colonies. Since it was
the National Convention that abolished slavery and L'Ouverture has utter
contempt for the unwashed masses he is then haranguing them for their
rebellion by insisting that it places their liberty in jeopardy in the National
Convention and only L'Ouverture can redeem the situation, hence the
need for their obedience to him. L'Ouverture continues with the
demeaning, patronizing con job as follows: "How can I assure them, after
this, that they will work to deserve this decree and will prove to France
and all nations that they are worthy by their submission to the law, by
their work and their docility, that I can answer for them all, and that
soon, with the help of France, we shall prove to the entire universe that
St Domingue, worked by free hands, will recover its wealth? Answer me
this. My shame will show that I have deceived them; it will prove to them
what the enemies of our freedom have tried to make them believe, that
blacks are not fit to be free, that if they become free they will no longer
work, and they shall steal and kill." (Nesbitt 2008 Pg. 24). L'Ouverture
is openly, unashamedly lying to the workers in rebellion that their action
against oppression, powerlessness and inequality, a new state of denial of
self-determination can result in the revocation of their freedom and a
return to bondage ordered by the National Convention. A delusional

construct formulated to deceive the workers back into servility which illustrates potently the narcissism and depravity of L'Ouverture as it masks the reality of French politics in February 1796 and to come. L'Ouverture's massa contempt for the non-white masses expects that they will be seduced by this discourse and willingly embrace their servitude for the sake of preserving their "freedom". This arrogant racist discourse repeatedly unleashed by L'Ouverture set the stage for the collapse of his hegemony over the masses when his beloved French motherland/ fatherland invaded to restore enslavement and he meekly surrendered to his white superiors as a true house nigger, the Grand Steven of St Domingue.

L'Ouverture now reports to Laveaux that he indicated to the workers that he was now willing to use force against them thereby giving them the choice to work against their will or die abiding by their will, in the very best tradition of massa dealing with slave revolts. L'Ouverture states: "but that it was up to them to prove that they wanted peace and tranquility by all of them returning immediately to their respective plantations and starting back to work, and this was entirely up to them." (Nesbitt 2008 Pg. 24). In response to the certainty of death at the hands of L'Ouverture, the African massa, they resorted to shucking and jiving the new massa as they did the first massa, biding their time to effect his demise which came in 1802 at the hands of his beloved French and his massa. Reading L'Ouverture without reading Fanon is the basis of the L'Ouverture apologists, whilst the opposite is the basis for convicting him of grave crimes against his race and the masses of Haiti.

10. Letter to Laveaux 23 May 1797

In April 1796 L'Ouverture is promoted to Lieutenant-Governor of the colony. In July 1796 Commissioner Sonthonax promoted L'Ouverture to general of division giving him total control of the Northern Department of the colony and the most powerful military commander of the colony. The rise of L'Ouverture to military power has to be viewed in light of the promotion of Bonaparte to Commander-Chief of the French Army in October 1795 which meant his promotion was approved by Bonaparte. In October 1796 L'Ouverture moves now to convince Laveaux to depart for

France as the representative of the colony to the National Assembly which gave L'Ouverture control of the colonial state. Laveaux was supposed to defend the interests of the colony against the rising tide of reaction and the intention to restore enslavement in all French colonies. L'Ouverture was then cognizant of the threat posed by French politics of the day, yet he chooses to launch a coup d'etat capturing the colonial state to then set himself up as dictator for life in 1801, thereby unifying the white supremacist North Atlantic in an alliance to remove him and restore enslavement in the colony. In April 1797 the slavery restoration agenda wins a majority in the French National Assembly. In August 1797 L'Ouverture expels Commissioner Sonthonax from the colony given their livid disagreement over L'Ouverture's forced plantation labor proclamation. This expulsion which he had no power to do under law followed Sonthonax's promotion of L'Ouverture in May 1797 to commander in chief of the French army in the colony with Bonaparte in the loop. In October 1798 L'Ouverture expels the French commissioner Hedouville from Haiti sending the right message to the national directory and Bonaparte which stresses the necessity of an invasion of the colony to remove L'Ouverture and restore slavery. In November 1799 the National Directory collapses, Bonaparte seizes power via a Bonapartist coup d'etat proclaiming himself dictator/ First Consul which is validated by a new constitution, which also declares that the colonies will be governed by special laws separate and apart from France as they are not seamlessly part of France, or organic to French civilization. Loosely translated Bonaparte will now put the niggers in St Domingue back in their place defined for them by the discourse of French white supremacy. Two dictators: one white the other non-white, one in the motherland/ fatherland, the other in the prized colony, one has the right to rule whilst the other is just a nigger upstart that must be put in his place. The die was then cast, the necessity of the invasion was written in stone, whilst L'Ouverture in his narcissistic desire for power did everything in his power to make it real to then unleash a bi-polar response to the invasion when it appeared in the colony, further proof of his schizophrenia driven by hallucinatory whiteness.

L'Ouverture writes to Laveaux in France continuing with his formulated shuck and jive for massa of his fealty, loyalty to France and his integrity. He is now using the success of his efforts to remove from the colony the Spanish and British invaders and their local allies as the basis of demanding investment from France to develop the colony to its maximum potential to the benefit of France. This is the context then for his unrelenting enforcement of his forced labor programme, in spite of the push back against it from the masses. L'Ouverture states as follows: "The colony's survival is guaranteed. Please convey to the Legislature the nature of my efforts and my sincere attachment, describing to them how such an important portion of France as this colony must no longer be deprived of the aid she owes it, and that the enemies of France and general liberty have kept from it by distorting the true position of St Domingue. Its preservation, let me repeat is assured, and [France] can count upon my irrevocable zeal as its true defender." (Nesbitt 2008 Pg. 30). In L'Ouverture's mind Laveaux is his white lobbyist in France charged with delivering L'Ouverture's shuck and jive for the new white supremacist massa holding power in the legislature. L'Ouverture's discourse aims at insisting that the freed African and Mixed race workers of the colony do not enjoy or command the power to be indolent, lazy and slothful as is expected of niggers by massa, for L'Ouverture has defined and polices liberty in such a manner with forced labor on the plantations to ensure the return to wealth generation and accumulation in this colony that will outstrip the level generated under enslavement in the past. L'Ouverture's unrelenting success in ridding the colony of its invaders and their local allies and the discipline he has forced upon the newly freed niggers to ensure the return of the plantation system of production then merits an alliance between the French ruling elite and the dictator of the colony, L'Ouverture. L'Ouverture has then by his action mitigated the two grave risks to the colony: the enemies of France who invaded the colony, and the formerly enslaved who were deluded by their idea of general liberty and what labor relations they were willing to embrace and not to. To back up this bold proposal in his bid to retain his dictatorial power over the colony and expand rapid wealth generation in the colony through forced labor on the plantations to the mutual benefit of France and himself he sent his children to France in the care of Laveaux, thereby providing hostages to massa to seal the deal. But the nascent French bourgeois, the remnants of its nobility and Bonaparte wanted no deal and those children of L'Ouverture in France were used as instruments of massa to convince L'Ouverture not to resist the invasion, transported from France for that purpose by massa.

11. Letter to the French Directory November 1797

The L'Ouverture apologists cite this letter and the proclamation of 29 August 1793 as the potent proof of L'Ouverture's credibility, integrity and commitment to the ideals of the Haitian Revolution, what the deconstruction reveals is as follows. L'Ouverture states as follows: "when finally the rule of law took the place of anarchy under which the unfortunate colony had too long suffered, what fatality can have led the greatest enemy of its prosperity, and of our happiness still to dare to threaten us with the return to slavery? The impolitic and incendiary speech of Vaublanc has threatened the blacks less than the plans meditated upon by the property owners of St Domingue." (Nesbitt 2008 Pg. 32). L'Ouverture is reacting to the speech made by Vaublanc, member of the Assembly, in which he called for the re-imposition of enslavement in the colonies with his standard discourse. What is new about this discourse is his paranoia over the St Domingue massa pulling the political strings in the background to roll back time in the colony. In doing so he reveals no appreciation of the depth and expanse of the move towards the re-imposition of slavery within the French oligarchy and their political lackeys. L'Ouverture now recognizes that his economic prosperity under free labor discourse is not cutting it, but he never acts upon a realization that the re-imposition has nothing to do with wealth generation and prosperity, but everything to do with white supremacy and the sanctity of the white order of power. To recognize and act upon this reality necessitated the preparation for an invasion and a long guerrilla war which L'Ouverture was unwilling and refused to do, hence his capitulation with invasion. The only option left to L'Ouverture by militarized white supremacy is to indicate that there will be no willing embrace of enslavement by the non-whites of the colony which means a return to civil war and further destruction of the colony. But when the invasion became manifest L'Ouverture quickly lost his appetite for prolonged guerrilla warfare, choosing instead to be a dutiful soldier of France under the command of dictator Bonaparte.

L'Ouverture now employs again his discourse of mutual assured destruction but massa is not deterred and proceeds with the plan to restore enslavement in the colony. L'Ouverture states as follows: "My attachment to France, the gratitude that all the blacks conserve for her, make it my duty to hide from you neither the plans being fomented nor the oath that we renew to bury ourselves beneath the ruins of a country revived by liberty rather than suffer the return of slavery." (Nesbitt 2008 Pg. 33). L'Ouverture talks the talk but when faced with the conjuncture created by the actual French invasion, he certainly refused to walk the talk. The experience of Haiti today, and through the epochs since they defeated the French invader, firmly confirms that massa did win the battle in the end with the full complicity of the ruling elites and oligarchs of Haiti from L'Ouverture to Moise.

L'Ouverture now switches instinctively to his discourse of shucking and jiving showing his fidelity to France by admitting that he gave up his children as hostages to France. L'Ouverture continues as follows: "It is to the solicitude of the French government that I have confided my children. [...] I would tremble with horror if it was into the hands of the colonists that I had sent them as hostages, but even if were so, let them know in punishing them for the fidelity of their father, they would only add one degree more to their barbarism, without making me fail in my duty." (Nesbitt 2008 Pg. 34). The question is: what duty? The duty to France born out of your fidelity to France or making the ultimate sacrifice whilst fighting to repel the invader? L'Ouverture did not make the ultimate sacrifice even though he repeatedly promised mutually assured destruction. He resisted then chose to follow orders as a good dutiful French soldier aiding and abetting his rendition to France, where he died in a cold dark dungeon, not in battle in Haiti. L'Ouverture then placed his children in France, in the den of massa, as hostages attesting to his fidelity as a dutiful

French soldier to create space for his political quest for hegemonic power over the colony in the run up to 1801, which culminated with the proclamation of **his** constitution for the French colony.

L'Ouverture unrelentingly repeats the said discourse of mutually assured destruction that shall follow a French invasion which amounts to bravado which has no impact on massa, for the white world order of power is sacrosanct and shall be defended by any means necessary across time/ space which drives the unrelenting strategy to destroy the Haitian Revolution. L'Ouverture states as follows: "Blind as they are, they cannot see how this odious conduct on their part can become the signal of new disasters and irreparable misfortunes, and far from it helping it regain what in their eyes liberty for all has made them lose, they expose themselves to total ruin and the colony to its inevitable destruction. Could men who have once enjoyed the benefits of liberty look on calmly while it is taken from them!" (Nesbitt 2008 Pg. 34). L'Ouverture's discourse has no traction in the mind of the white supremacist, for no price is too high to pay to erase the first non-white order of power rooted in liberty in the era of white supremacist imperial colonial domination. L'Ouverture is speaking as a plantation capitalist rooted in free but servile non-white labor with an order of power dominated by the black military under the control of L'Ouverture. French white supremacy has rejected this L'Ouverture centered non-white order of power and their conviction to destroy it is bolstered by the desire of L'Ouverture to deepen and consolidate his personal power over the colony, contrary to the sentiment of massa. Bonaparte failed in his bid to destroy this non-white order of power through invasion, occupation and conquest, but white supremacy after the failure of Bonaparte never relented to this day in its duty to destroy the Haitian Revolution subjecting it to the white world order of power. Hence blockades became the order of the day, invasion, occupation, reparations and occupation of the financial structure of Haiti extracting wealth for export to the North Atlantic for the supposed purpose of paying off debt Haiti had failed to service as agreed upon.

Again, L'Ouverture beats the same said drum as follows: "But if, in order to re-establish servitude in St Domingue this were to be done, I declare, that this would be to attempt the impossible. We have known how to confront danger to obtain our liberty, and we will know how to confront death to preserve it. This, Citizens and Directors, is the morality of the people of St Domingue, these are the principles I transmit to you on their behalf." (Nesbitt 2008 Pgs. 34-35). L'Ouverture is then informing the French political elite that the masses of Haiti will fight to the death in order to preserve their liberty from enslavement. In this context what then is L'Ouverture's commitment to this principle of the masses that he has articulated to the French political elite? Resisting the invasion was soon replaced by following the orders of the invader as a dutiful French soldier rejecting the alternative of a prolonged guerrilla war, seizure and destruction of his property and wealth and possibly death in battle. This choice showed that he in fact had no balls to make the ultimate sacrifice in battle in Haiti to ensure that mutually assured destruction became manifest. Rather he chose to obey white orders, shuck and jive, cast himself as the ultimate non-white victim and write reams of paper actually expecting that he would be a recipient of white justice under the rule of white law. Utter mind crippling delusion constituted by hallucinatory whiteness.

12. Bonaparte's Letter to St Domingue 25 December 1799

Bonaparte has seized power via coup d'etat with the collapse of the National Directory, proclaimed himself dictator and adopted the title of First Consul of France. A new constitution has been written and adopted to legalize the power of Bonaparte for it has killed the republic of the revolution. Bonaparte's letter is devoted to Article 91 of the new constitution which establishes a distinction in law between the order of power of the metropole versus that of the colony, where the order of power of the colony is distinct, separate and apart from that of the metropole. The order of power that L'Ouverture has constituted to enable his hegemony over the colony is now in the sights of the dictator Bonaparte as there can be only one dictator in the metropole and the colony, Bonaparte then refuses to share power with L'Ouverture over the colony. The re-imposition of slavery is then the sleight of hand distraction of L'Ouverture to mask the fundamental contradiction between Bonaparte, the grand white dictator and L'Ouverture the upstart, uppity non-white dictator of massa colony, hence the need to change the legal status of the colony. The contents of this letter of Bonaparte to the colony is then his Christmas 1799 present to the colony which means it must be read in the context of December 1799 not in the context of events that followed. Bonaparte states as follows: "Article 91 states that French colonies will be ruled by special laws. This disposition derives from the nature of things and the differences of climate." "The Consuls of the Republic, in announcing to you the new social pack, declare to you that the SACRED principles of the freedom and equality of blacks will NEVER SUFFER among you the least attack or modification. If there are ill-intentioned men in the colony, if there are those who still have relations with enemy powers, remember BRAVE BLACKS, that the French people alone recognize your freedom and the equality of your rights." (Nesbitt 2008 Pg. 37). The pragmatic of December 1799 demands that Bonaparte seek to placate all fears of the imminent abolition of the emancipation proclamation of the National Convention as there is no unified front of the North Atlantic that isolates the non-whites of the colony from North Atlantic support in a war against France. Then there is the cost of war against the colony which has to be financed by the state through debt issuance to finance houses who then hold this debt, which is mounting from the Ancien Regime to the Revolutionary Wars. The financiers are then calling the shots for Bonaparte and will determine if and when there is an invasion. The scale of the invasion force indicated that the strategy was overwhelming force to score early victories through conventional warfare. This failed from the outset, whilst the incompetent French leadership had no capacity to reformulate new strategies on the spur of the moment. The collapse of the French, the return to war with Britain, the British re-entry into the colony hoping to do what the French could not, meant the retreat of the French as they simply could not finance an indefinite war in the colony and those in Europe arising from Bonapartist adventurism. The strategy was then retreat, grant independence and continue the war by other means such as the demand for reparations from the Haitians. The salient question then is what did the dictator of the colony do from December 1799 to early 1802 in preparation for the coming holocaust?

13. Proclamation on Labor 1800

In 1800 L'Ouverture unleashes his first of two signal actions which illustrate the bi-polarity, the schizophrenia of his discourse that is constituted by hallucinatory whiteness, by now proclaiming as the law of the colony free labor that is bonded to the estate of their former massa working for wage levels determined by L'Ouverture. This is nothing new for L'Ouverture as in the military districts he commanded he was applying this rule, but in 1800 it became the law of the colony. The first blow against the freedom and equality of the non-white worker of the colony did not come from Bonaparte, it instead came from L'Ouverture sending a clear message to massa that the free non-whites of the colony can be compelled back into enslavement for they have already surrendered to L'Ouverture. Massa learnt this lesson well for his future engagements with Haiti, hence the need for a stream of non-white maximum leaders/ dictators who are subservient to them/ massa.

L'Ouverture is speaking of the centrality of agricultural work to the stability of the social order of the colony but this agricultural work is defined in an exclusivist manner, only plantation work for wages is acceptable to L'Ouverture. Under the dictatorship of L'Ouverture there will be no land reform, no distribution of land to the landless former enslaved citizens of the colony. L'Ouverture is breathing new life into the plantation system by intentionally keeping free labor landless, bound to the plantation it was enslaved upon working for wage levels set by L'Ouverture. Those who occupied land in the Revolution will have no title, no security of tenure and this reality exists in Haiti to this day. L'Ouverture states as follows: "It is the mechanism of all states, and if each member of society works, the result is public tranquility; troubles disappear along with idleness, which is the mother of vice, and each enjoys in peace the fruits of his labors." "they say, they are free, and so spend their days running about aimlessly, thus setting a very bad example for the other farmers, while all the while generals, officers, their subordinates and soldiers are engaged in permanent activity to protect the sacred rights of all." (Nesbitt 2008 Pgs. 38-39). Those who refuse to work on a plantation are lazy, a grave threat to the social order and must be then forced to work. L'Ouverture is then envisaging workshops for the lazy and idle, in addition to the plantation, thereby establishing an order of power which restricts the upward mobility of landless free labor into spaces dominated by the provision of goods and services to the social order. L'Ouverture then envisages a social order in which opportunity is the exclusive right of massa and the new non-white military elite and their kith, kin and associates. L'Ouverture's worldview remains that of massa which he was before 1791 and this exclusivist and gravely discriminatory discourse of the order of power of Haiti remains hegemonic to this day where all the oligarchs and their families are non-African.

14. Self-Portrait 1801

In this ode to his self-importance, this masturbation to climax in praise of his narcissism L'Ouverture repeats again his grave lie which is a construct to mask the fact that in 1791 he was a free African and a massa, hence he was never emancipated from enslavement but in fact he lost his wealth generating structure with emancipation and thereafter was relentlessly seeking to replicate it by pursuing power he could not possess, collect and exert under enslavement. L'Ouverture was then the classic opportunist narcissist riding the backs of the non-white race in rebellion for his own benefit blessed with the head start massa gave him over the mass of the enslaved in rebellion. L'Ouverture begins this ode to self-importance by insisting that he was illiterate at the time of the commencement of the Haitian Revolution. L'Ouverture states as follows: "I felt that I was destined for great things. When I received the divine portent, I was fifty-four years old, I did not know how to read or write." (Nesbitt 2008 Pg. 40). L'Ouverture was a trusted functionary of the Breda plantation rising to the rank of manager of the livestock which constantly exposed him to written language and the opportunity to learn to read and write on the Breda plantation in order to better serve massa. When granted his freedom L'Ouverture had now the right to become literate if he was not and the Catholic Church was there to teach him to read and write in exchange for his soul. Much more importantly as a free African in a white supremacist apartheid social order, L'Ouverture could not evolve into a successful plantation and slave owner taking part in the daily power relations of the social order being illiterate as there were white and mixed-race individuals operating in the social order to strip persons as L'Ouverture of his property and wealth through various instruments exploiting his illiteracy. L'Ouverture is spinning a web of lies to bolster his credibility with the formerly enslaved masses.

L'Ouverture ends his self-portrait of deception by repeating a core discursive concept of his discourse: his gratitude to France for his emancipation from enslavement as follows: '…at the moment the powerful French Republic proclaimed the general freedom of the blacks. A secret voice said to me: 'Since the blacks are free, they need a chief', and it is I who must be the chief predicted by the Abbe Raynal. I returned transported by the sentiment, to the service of France; France and the voice of God have not deceived me." (Nesbitt 2008 Pgs. 40-41). L'Ouverture insists that he is the one chosen to lead the former enslaved of St Domingue to the new life of liberty and equality under the banner of French republicanism as predicted by the French white supremacist abolitionist Abbe de Raynal. L'Ouverture is then a creature of white framed and constituted destiny for liberty and equality was a white gift to him and the former enslaved non-whites of St Domingue. L'Ouverture is then beholding to massa and never shirks his responsibility to massa, exemplified by his quest to return the colony to prosperity by shackling free labor to the benefit of massa. But L'Ouverture was a free, non-white, slave and plantation owner before emancipation whose wealth generation system was destroyed by the revolt of the enslaved in St Domingue, he was not emancipated by the French for he was not enslaved at emancipation, he was part of the body of massa, property owners including humans as chattel. What rebellion then emancipation gave L'Ouverture was the opportunity to play at being a radical, uncompromising enemy of enslavement whilst he played the game to collect and exercise personal power towards exerting hegemony over the colony and in this he was facilitated, encouraged and enabled by the republicans, until Bonaparte moved to end his dictatorship for two man rat cyah live in one hole. L'Ouverture's quest for power was always to the detriment of the formerly enslaved non-whites for they must pay the price of heightening personal underdevelopment and trauma in their free

state inherited from enslavement, so it is in Haiti up to today in the 21st century. The French massa then set up L'Ouverture for the fall as with the Bonapartist invasion L'Ouverture was paralyzed at the level of the idea. Incapable of, with his action, indicating that he was in fact liberated from the dominance of massa over his mind, discourse and worldview. L'Ouverture must support the end of slavery for this new order was his opportunity to satiate his desire for grand power. A return to enslavement destroys this quest of his as under the white supremacist apartheid order of power L'Ouverture cannot wield the power he did under freedom and the republic.

15. Letter to Napoleon on the 1801 Constitution 16 July 1801

L'Ouverture wrote to Bonaparte on the process he adopted to formulate and promulgate the 1801 constitution of St Domingue to correct the mistaken version of events of the French Minister of the Navy given to Bonaparte. On 5 February 1801 a General Assembly was convocated by L'Ouverture to create the constitution devoid of a member who was a formerly enslaved, for L'Ouverture certainly was not, hence L'Ouverture was in effect the voice of the formerly enslaved rendering them silent in this process, which is potently visible in the articles of the constitution. The constitution is rabidly white supremacist to its core, marginalizing and policing all African discourses, worldviews and action into the embrace of illegality in a bid to silence them. This reality is prevalent in Haiti to this day. On the 16 July 1801 L'Ouverture is informing Bonaparte that the process was completed and is sending the document for his approval when in fact the constitution was completed and promulgated unilaterally in May 1801 in the colony. L'Ouverture is then playing dangerous power games with the grand dictator of the French empire, sending the signal that he is in fact the maximum leader of the colony. Two males playing the sick game of who can piss the furthest.

L'Ouverture states as follows: "should have submitted to you my proclamation of 5 February 1801 on the convocation of a Central Assembly, which would be able to set the destiny of St Domingue through wise laws modeled on the mores of the inhabitants. I today have the satisfaction of announcing to you that the final touch has just been put to this work. I hasten to send it to you in order to have your approval and the sanction of my government." (Nesbitt 2008 Pg. 42). St Domingue in 1801 is then a colony dominated by white people not by non-white people as the mores of the document are in fact anti-non-white mores. A fitting indication of the discourse and its worldview of L'Ouverture for the overwhelming majority who are non-whites are free and equal citizens of the French empire which is a contradiction in terms.

L'Ouverture continues as follows: "Given the absence of laws, and the Central Assembly having requested to have this constitution provisionally executed, which will more quickly lead St Domingue to its future prosperity, I have surrendered to its wishes." (Nesbitt 2008 Pg. 42). The creation of L'Ouverture, the Central Assembly, now becomes the excuse to promulgate the constitution in the colony then send it to Bonaparte for his approval attempting to mask his subterfuge with a web of lies. Bonaparte the first of and only French dictator replied in February 1802 with the landing of his invasion force, which signaled the collapse of L'Ouverture at the level of the idea. Between July to October 1801 Britain and the USA informed Bonaparte they are against independence for St Domingue even though Britain is at war with France. On March 27, 1802 Britain, Spain, France and the Batavian Republic sign the Treaty of Amiens declaring peace in Europe for fourteen months. Britain had then given Bonaparte fourteen months to erase the revolution in St Domingue and the dictatorship of L'Ouverture. Britain immediately entered into the war for the conquest of St Domingue by using its colony of Jamaica as its forward operating base for its military, intelligence apparatus and logistics to support the French assault. The French military command was constantly moving between Jamaica and St Domingue soliciting British aid, funding, supplies and logistics especially so as the campaign collapsed under the weight of incompetent leadership and yellow fever which was also endemic in Jamaica. During the fourteen months the British were fully committed to the task of conquering the colony and ridding it of freedom for the formerly enslaved, but at the end of the fourteen month window of opportunity war recommenced in Europe and the French were no longer welcome in Jamaica. The abiding lesson of this fourteen months of peace between the warring massas was the operational capacity of the British covert network in St Domingue which was managed from the colony of Jamaica. The covert network was in intact before the war for freedom and expanded considerably with emancipation. The British were then constantly informed of the game L'Ouverture was playing which came to a head with the promulgation of L'Ouverture's constitution in May 1801, this gambit of L'Ouverture in May 1801 driven by his desire for dictatorial power in the colony was then the parting of the way in May 1801 resulting in 1802 in a peace treaty of fourteen months in duration, which laid no foundation for lasting peace between the warring massas. This was simply a device to enable a concerted assault on St Domingue and L'Ouverture which the ever-incompetent Bonaparte failed dismally to exploit. This was then a potent lesson to all non-whites intent on taking on the white world order of power, massa can never be our friends as they view us as less than human and must exercise hegemony over us. So much for the L'Ouvertures and Mandelas of the non-white world. When faced with a potent non-white threat massa creates the race solidarity to end this threat, with their most potent weapon being the sell-outs and informers amongst us always shucking and jiving to win the hollow applause of massa, hallucinatory whiteness gives them no other viable choice of action.

16. The Haitian Constitution of 1801

"Article 1. states as follows: "St Domingue in its entire expanse, ...form the territory of a single colony, which is part of the French Empire, but ruled under particular laws." (Nesbitt 2008 Pg. 48). L'Ouverture in this constitution of 1801 has presented the discourse that will determine the structure of these said "particular laws," which simply is his discourse collected and expressed with its instruments of power. The colony is part of the French Empire but the constitution is his, hence the particular laws are his. In May 1801 L'Ouverture threw down the gauntlet for massa, calling massa out and massa responded as he must, for this call out came from a member of an inferior race.

"Article 3: There cannot exist slaves on this territory, servitude is thereby forever abolished. All men are born, live and die free and French." (Nesbitt 2008 Pg. 48). All non-whites formerly enslaved are born, live and die free, which does not exempt them from forced labor on their former massa or new massa plantation and must be forcibly taught to be French which means the suppression of all discourses, worldviews and cultures that constitute them non-French which means the death of Kweyol, Vodun and the entire gamut of discourses that constitutes non-white difference. L'Ouverture was then intent on constituting the formerly enslaved as non-whites plagued with hallucinatory whiteness. This position is potently illustrated by the description common in Caribbean media of Haiti as a French speaking nation, Kweyol simply does not exist, thus silencing the overwhelming majority of the Haitian population. This assault on African discourses and worldviews in Haiti continues to today.

"Article 6. The Catholic, apostolic, Roman faith shall be the only professed public faith." (Nesbitt 2008 Pg. 48). All African derived belief systems are then driven underground and will be policed and suppressed when power so determines this to be necessary, thereby establishing L'Ouverture's thought police and the marginalization of non-whites who reject officially sanctioned religion. The slave state exists in spite of the proclamation of emancipation because it serves power, L'Ouverture's dictatorial power.

"Article 14. The colony being essentially agricultural cannot suffer the least disruption in the works of its cultivation."

Article 15. Each plantation shall constitute a manufacture that requires the gathering the cultivator and the workers; it shall represent the quiet haven of an active and constant family, of which the owner of the land or his representative shall be the father."

Article 16. Each cultivator and each worker is a member of the family and is entitled to a share of the revenue. Every change in domicile on the part of the cultivator threatens the ruin of the crops. In order to repress a vice as disruptive to the colony, as it is to public order, the Governor issues all necessary policy requirements in the circumstances and in confirmation with the bases of the rules of police of 12 October 1800, and of the proclamation of the following 9 February 1801 of the Chief General Toussaint L'Ouverture." (Nesbitt 2008 Pg. 48). Labor power relations in a labor market premised on free labor is subverted by the discursive concept of the power relations of the unit of production, the plantation, is that of a family with the owner of the plantation or his proxy as the paternalistic patriarchal father/ head of the family. The newly emancipated are then underdeveloped children who are in dire need of a paternalistic massa, the patriarch to instruct them on all that is expected of good workers in L'Ouverture's new order. The power relation then retains its white power basis as under enslavement which ensures that the assault on the non-whites with hallucinatory whiteness continues along with the spectrum of trauma. The centrality of the plantation to the economy of the colony justifies the intervention of the governor to regulate all aspects of the operation of a plantation especially the supply of labor, the cost of labor and the mobility of labor ensuring the hegemony of the owner over the worker, capital over labor, white over non-white, class and race have then combined into a new order of power which is the product of emancipation which constitutes free labor. Both owner and worker are entitled to a share of revenue, not profits, workers and massa are entitled to wages and salaries but the profits belong solely to massa. Before the constitution is promulgated L'Ouverture is already policing the mobility of free labor to the benefit of the new massa in a free labor market.

"Article 17. The introduction of cultivators indispensable to the re-establishment of and to the growth of agriculture shall take place in St Domingue. The constitution charges the Governor to take convenient measures to encourage and fashion the increase in manpower, to stipulate and balance the diverse interests, to ensure and guarantee the execution of respective engagements resulting from this process." (Nesbitt 2008 Pg. 49). L'Ouverture has to woo white investment back to St Domingue, to guarantee the return of plantations to its rightful owners abandoned or seized since the Revolution and occupied by non-white squatters. Above all L'Ouverture has to ensure the public safety of massa on their resumption of operations in St Domingue, hence the need for dictator L'Ouverture who is also a plantation owner who is operating in the new St Domingue. L'Ouverture is guaranteeing to investors more than an immobile servile labor force at an affordable wage, he is guaranteeing an order of power that keeps the former enslaved in the place he allocated to them in the order of power. Article 18 aims to reconstruct the order of mercantile capitalism through the ban on imports of goods and services which compete with those produced in the colony. This is an attempt to destroy the explosion of the smuggling of goods into the colony that followed the Revolution and the collapse of the plantation order in the colony and the end of the slave trade. This then is a blow to the smugglers of St Domingue in favor of the merchant houses of France, a blow to the non-whites who found space in this economy in which to prosper and grow their wealth and the indigenous shipping, ship chandlery and ship building industries. The smuggling link with Jamaica was now outlawed, a link that was vital to the cause of the Revolution.

On the post of Governor specifically the appointment of the first Governor under the 1801 constitution states as follows:

"Article 28. The Constitution nominates the citizen Toussaint L'Ouverture, Chief General of the army of St Domingue, and, in consideration for important services rendered to the colony, in the most critical circumstances of the revolution, and upon the wishes of the grateful inhabitants, **he is entrusted the direction thereof for the remainder of his glorious life."** (Nesbitt 2008 Pg. 51). L'Ouverture is patterning his action on the precedent set by the coup d'etat of Bonaparte failing in his delusion to appreciate the vast difference between the power relation that enabled Bonaparte to seize power via a coup d'etat proclaiming himself First Consul of France and L'Ouverture proclaiming himself dictator for life in a colony under the hegemony of white supremacy and white supremacist Bonaparte. By this reckless, narcissistic action L'Ouverture called out massa, Bonaparte and the white world order of power thereby raining down death and destruction to thousands of non-white formerly enslaved citizens of the colony and set in train a war on the non-white inhabitants of the colony then Haiti that continues to this day. Desire for power, predominance, eminence and the benefits of power knew no bounds with L'Ouverture such was his immersion in self-importance with all its dysfunctions. Article 30 of the constitution expresses in livid detail this morbid narcissism of L'Ouverture.

"Article 30. In order to strengthen the tranquility that the colony owes to the steadfastness, activity, indefatigable zeal and rare virtues of General Toussaint L'Ouverture, and as a sign of the unlimited trust of the inhabitants of St Domingue, the constitution attributes exclusively to this general the right to designate the citizen who, in the unfortunate event of the general's death, shall immediately replace him. This choice shall remain secret; it shall be cosigned under sealed envelope to be opened only by the Central Assembly, in the presence of all active generals and chief commanders of departments of the army of St Domingue." (Nesbitt 2008 Pgs. 51-52). The 1801 constitution not only legalizes the dictator for life status of L'Ouverture over the colony of St Domingue, it gives him the right to determine his replacement in the event of his death from the grave. L'Ouverture has then established the de facto independence of St Domingue from France whilst legally it remains a vassal of France. Reckless narcissistic adventurism for which the masses of Haiti pay up to today. L'Ouverture is not satisfied with being dictator for life as the constitution now legalizes the hegemonic power of the military over the state seen in Article 32.

"Article 32. the said Governor, jointly with active duty generals and chief commanders of departments, shall meet at the ordinary place of hearing of the Central Assembly, in order to nominate, concurrently with members of the Central Assembly, the new Governor or to continue the administration of one who is in place." (Nesbitt 2008 Pg. 52)."

"Article 33. Failure of a Governor to convoke [the General Assembly] constitutes a manifest infraction of the Constitution. In such circumstances, the highest ranked general or the senior general of equal rank, who is in active service in the colony, shall rightfully if provisionally, take control of the government." (Nesbitt 2008 Pg. 52). L'Ouverture's constitution places the only legal armed group in the colony wielding a monopoly on armed violence in the colony at the heart of governance of the colony, which enables the ability of the armed forces to exercise hegemony over the daily governance of the colony. With a legislature denied the ability to formulate and pass legislation, for its only use was to rubber stamp the legislation of the governor. There is no mention of universal adult suffrage in this constitution, there is only talk of elections. L'Ouverture's constitution then reveals the position that the only group in the society capable of assuring good governance is the military, which naturally means all governors following L'Ouverture will be from the military or have the express support of the military.

On the armed forces the constitution states as follows: "Article 52. The Armed Forces are essentially obedient, they can never deliberate; they are at the disposition of the Governor who can mobilize them only to maintain public order, protection due to all citizens, and the defense of the colony." "Article 53. They are divided into the paid colonial guard and the unpaid colonial guard." "Article 55. The state police force of the colony shall be part of the Armed Forces." (Nesbitt 2008 Pg. 56). The armed forces are also responsible for policing, hence militarized policing and under the direct power of the governor answering to no one else in the constitution. The governor is then the monarch who rules over the colony with no limits to the power of the governor embedded in the constitution. The governor is the creature of the military as the military is the only organized disciplined armed legal group in the social order with the power to coerce the weak, unarmed groups in the social order and most of all the governor is not a creature of direct elections on a limited franchise much less on universal adult suffrage. L'Ouverture never faced an electorate in his career in governance using a limited franchise, much less universal adult suffrage, yet he relentlessly crows about his popularity with the masses. The power of the military is enhanced by article 67 which indicates that it is an instrument of power to discipline the social order in favor of the governor. "Article 67. There cannot exist in the colony corporations of associations that are contrary to public order. No citizen association shall constitute a civil organization. All seditious gatherings shall be dissolved immediately, first by way of verbal order and, if necessary, by armed force." (Nesbitt 2008 Pg. 59). The governor has the unlimited power to define what is seditious and what is not and unleash the military to suppress said seditious activity. The formerly enslaved are now free, but enslaved to the new overarching massa, L'Ouverture, who enjoys no limits to his power by the rule of law, thereby establishing a constitutional dictatorship. So much for his unrivaled love for and commitment to liberty and equality and his hatred of enslavement.

Article 73 speaks to the order of land ownership of enslavement under the new order of power, but the constitution is silent on the issue of land reform and addressing the chronic landlessness of the formerly enslaved. "Absentee owners for whatever reason, conserve all their rights to properties belonging to them and situated in the colony it suffices, to remove any sequestration that might have been impossible, to reintroduce their titles of ownership and, in default of title thereof, supplementary acts whose formula is determined by law. Exempt from this disposition are, nevertheless, those who might have been inscribed and maintained on the general list of emigrants of France; their properties shall continue, in this case, to be administered as colonial domain until their removal from the list." (Nesbitt 2008 Pg. 60). Those who own land, developed or undeveloped, and are not domiciled in the colony have their rights to ownership under law recognized and protected. This enables them and their agent/s to claim their property and remove those who are squatting or have seized said property claiming rights as a sole owner as their own. Forced labor and wage levels determined by L'Ouverture is then backed up by eviction from former estates of massa rendering them landless which gives them a limited menu of choices: accept forced labor, migrate in search of opportunity into the urban areas forming the free underclass or embracing criminality as a vocation. The property belonging to the listed enemies of France will then be nationalized under the rule of the constitutional dictator and shared out for development by the constitutional dictator to those favored by him, towards the creation of a landed military ruling elite generating wealth through forced labor. This elitist autocracy remains the driving force of the Haitian social order to this day.

The final article of the constitution, Article 77, calls on L'Ouverture to promulgate this document before it is sanctioned by the dictator of the French empire as follows: "Article 77. the necessity promptly to re-establish agriculture and the unanimous wishes pronounced by the inhabitants of St Domingue, the Chief General is henceforth invited, in the name of public good to proceed with its execution in all areas of the territory of the colony." (Nesbitt 2008 Pgs. 60-61). This is the excuse for L'Ouverture promulgating this constitution in May 1801 before even dispatching it to the dictator of the French empire, de facto independence with a dictator for life in charge of the so-called French colony. If massa failed to answer this call out by L'Ouverture with overwhelming force they have then abdicated control of the colony to L'Ouverture which is supporting its de facto independence, hence the alarm of the British and the Americans.

17. Letter from Napoleon Bonaparte 18 November 1801

L'Ouverture receives this letter on 8 February 1802 delivered by his children who had returned to the colony from their sojourn in France. The French fleet led by Leclerc arrived in the colony in February 1802 which means that Bonaparte released L'Ouverture's children as hostages and made the strategic imperative clear in this letter that peace in Europe now enables him to deal with the colony. Bonaparte informs L'Ouverture that general Leclerc was appointed by him the first magistrate of the colony making Leclerc the limit to L'Ouverture's dictatorial power in the 1801 constitution. L'Ouverture was not replaced as the Chief General or as Governor of the colony, what he was now faced with was a First Magistrate, brother in law of the First Consul, leading a naval fleet and some 21,000 men at arms with the military and constitutional power to take control of the colony. In his letter Bonaparte informs L'Ouverture that he sent back his children to him in the colony, which means that the hostage situation is now ended, Bonaparte has no strategic use for them, therefore his brother-in-law, the fleet and the men at arms are there to remove L'Ouverture. L'Ouverture's children brought the message to him that it was futile to resist, simply capitulate, the products of good white supremacist French education. Amidst the stoking of L'Ouverture's ego in his letter, Bonaparte was then giving clear signals of his intention to wipe the slate clean in the colony which included L'Ouverture's grab for power. Bonaparte states as follows: "the constitution you made, whilst containing many good things, contains some that are contrary to the dignity and sovereignty of the French people, of which St Domingue forms only a portion." (Nesbitt 2008 Pg. 63). There are portions of the 1801 constitution that pose a threat to the French white order of power in France and its empire and St Domingue's reality constituted by L'Ouverture is a grave threat that is not countermanded by the economic contribution it makes to France. Bonaparte is then thrashing L'Ouverture's discourse of the strategic importance of St Domingue to France and indicating that the threat posed by L'Ouverture's constitution will be expunged by Leclerc and his military expedition. Bonaparte follows with an explicit threat as follows: "A contrary conduct would be irreconcilable with the idea we have conceived of you. It would have you lose the many rights to recognition and the benefits of the republic, and would dig beneath your feet a precipice which, in swallowing you up, could contribute to the misfortune of those brave blacks whose courage we love, and whose rebellion we would, with difficulty, be obliged to be punished." (Nesbitt 2008 Pg. 63). The threat is clearly stated in massa double speak, any resistance to his will expressed with Leclerc and his military force will be punished by destroying L'Ouverture and his order of power over the colony through military conquest that reimposes enslavement, which is the chosen alternative to L'Ouverture's order of power. Bonaparte, in this letter using white supremacist double speak and double think makes the agenda clear, only those burdened with hallucinatory whiteness could not grasp the threats made. L'Ouverture with the arrival of the French fleet in February 1802 resisted then vacillated, reporting to Leclerc, walking away from battle, making himself a soft target to rendition from the colony to France, refusing to embrace guerrilla warfare biding his time until the yellow fever hit with a vengeance. The L'Ouverture apologists infer all sorts of glorious intent by L'Ouverture in their incessant bid to create myths of massa lackeys as our heroes to constitute successive generations of us as massa lackeys.

18. Proclamation 25 November 1801

At the end of his rule as the dictator of St Domingue L'Ouverture unleashes a discourse of all that is wrong with the newly emancipated non-white masses of St Domingue straight out of massa white supremacist discourse of the nigger, thereby giving a potent lesson of the nature of the discourse and worldview of non-whites plagued with hallucinatory whiteness. Responding to the labor rebellions in October 1801 which signaled the collapse of his hegemony over the masses, L'Ouverture now berates them as a white supremacist to justify his forced labor and hard-line suppression of dissent. L'Ouverture states as follows: "Since the revolution, I have done all that depended upon me to return happiness to my country and to ensure liberty for my fellow citizens." Nesbitt 2008 Pg. 65). L'Ouverture's governance is then exemplary and rooted in virtue, he is then the prophet and pope of the colony and the newly emancipated, which means his rule is absolute, he will tolerate no rebellion and his brand of justice will be meted out even to his adopted nephew Moise. L'Ouverture continues as follows: "I laid out the obligations of fathers and mothers, their obligations to raise their children in the love and fear of God. Nevertheless, how diligently fathers and mothers raise their children, especially in cities." "They seem to inspire in children contempt for agriculture, the first, the most honorable, and the most useful of all occupations. Barely are they born than we see these same children with jewels and earrings, covered in rags, their clothing filthy, wounding the eyes of decency through their nudity. Thus they arise at the age of twelve, without moral principles, without a skill, and with a taste for luxury and laziness as their only education. And since bad expressions are difficult to correct, it is certain beyond any doubt that they will be bad citizens, vagabonds, thieves. And if they are girls, they are prostitutes all of them ready to follow the prompting of the first conspirator who will preach murder and pillage to them. It is upon such vile mothers and fathers, on students so dangerous, that the magistrates of the people must ceaselessly keep an open eye." (Nesbitt 2008 Pgs. 66-67). L'Ouverture is a discursive agent of white supremacy in the era of the emancipation of the enslaved in St Domingue. He formulates a Manichean duality of good and evil, the "soul" to enclose the body of the free non-white which defines the good non-white citizen from the bad, evil non-white citizen. L'Ouverture frames the evil non-white citizen as a criminal who must be constantly surveilled and punished by the state for these evil citizens are criminogenic, lazy, indolent, moral reprobates burdened with the wrong value system and worldview, making them a burden on those who work. L'Ouverture now takes the criminalization of dissent, the denial of workers' rights and the rejection of the serfdom he has instituted for them to the ultimate white supremacist level by insisting that there is something inherently wrong with non-white people which can only be remedied with the embrace of white supremacy at the level of the idea, hence the only good non-white are those burdened with hallucinatory whiteness and those unregenerated by hallucinatory whiteness are inherently evil, criminogenic and a grave threat to decent and respectable non-white people, hence they must be marginalized into marginalized spaces to better facilitate repression. L'Ouverture with his rabid hate for his own kind has made his lumpen, especially the urban lumpen, the fall guy of his repression of workers and the rebellion against his position by workers. All those who rebelled are lumpen who refused the path to discipline, to regeneration into good citizens he had established for their true emancipation hence are enemies of the state meriting arrest, trial and public execution as his adopted nephew Moise. L'Ouverture sets in train the formulation of a white supremacist discourse of the evil, lazy, indolent free non-white which is remarkably resonant with that formulated in response to emancipation in Britain in 1834 and the end of apprenticeship in 1838.

L'Ouverture now presents his discourse on the plantation workers as follows: "The same reproaches equally apply to cultivators on the plantations. Since the revolution, perverse men have told them that freedom is the right to remain idle and to only follow their whims. Such a doctrine could not help but be accepted by evil men, thieves and assassins. It is time to hit out at the hardened men who persist in such ideas." (Nesbitt 2008 Pg. 67). Those in the plantation lands who refuse to surrender to L'Ouverture's forced labor, no worker rights and wage levels set by L'Ouverture rather than bargaining between worker and management are inherently evil influenced by evil men who teach that freedom means the right to be indolent. These evil men pose a grave threat to the colony and must now be policed, marginalized and eradicated from the colony as they can infect the good non-whites and wage war on the tranquility of the social order with their criminality. L'Ouverture is putting down a hatchet job on his own race to the benefit of himself and massa that would plunge a white supremacist operative into fits of jealously. L'Ouverture indicates the potency of massa lackeys in keeping us quiet, servile and accommodating in the interest of massa, it is called neocolonial domination.

L'Ouverture now speaks to a regime of child labor on the plantations that is rooted in enslavement, not free labor, and the recognition of the state to socialize its citizens with values that ensure the sustainability of the social order, central to this is education that serves this need. L'Ouverture states as follows: "As soon as a child can walk, he should be employed on the plantation according to his strength in some useful works, instead of being sent into the cities where, under the pretext of an education he doesn't receive, he learns vice, to join the hordes of vagabonds and women of ill repute, to trouble by his existence the repose of good citizens, and to terminate it in ignominy. Military commanders and magistrates must be inexorable with this class of men. Despite this, they must be forced to be useful to society upon which, without the most severe vigilance, they will be a plague." (Nesbitt 2008 Pg. 67). Child labor, that is in fact serfdom, as they are bound to the plantation owner obligated to work on an agro based industrial unit at an age when it will do grave harm to their physical, mental and emotional development. L'Ouverture views workers of all ages as grist in the mill for the generation and accumulation of wealth of an oligarchy. The liberty and equality he uses as a propaganda tool in his interest is absent in his governance of the colony, he is simply a two bit hustler who prides himself on being a great manipulator. Children must not migrate to the city in pursuit of an education for they succumb to the grip of the urban lumpen, but there is no talk of the provision of universal education to all on the plantation. Parents who seek education for their children in order to end their illiteracy in the hope for a better life are then grave risks to L'Ouverture's order of power. This order of power polices a society that is discriminatory, stratified as a social order rooted in a caste system which relentlessly polices all attempts at upward social mobility for workers. They are to be kept servile, compliant and illiterate; enslavement is no more but the plantation lives on demanding servile labor. L'Ouverture in his rant reads as Pol Pot of the Khmer Rouge of Kampuchea/ Cambodia not as this great "black" liberator, remember Pol Pot and his comrades were all mass murderers. The masses of the colony in 1802 were then trapped between two dictators L'Ouverture and Bonaparte, both intent on exercising hegemony by any means necessary, Haiti remains trapped in this conundrum up to today. L'Ouverture continues citing the great evil as the urban lumpen, what then existed to stop him from rounding up this urban lumpen for transport to the plantation for compulsory work and the application of the Final Solution? For white supremacist discourse always views a holocaust as the preferred means to eradicate an evil that is polluting the virtue of your social order, and L'Ouverture's hallucinatory whiteness placed the holocaust of the urban lumpen on the agenda as the very epitome of what he defines as the ultimate evil in the social order.

L'Ouverture now speaks to the grave evil of female sex workers in the colony as follows: "Since the revolution, it is evident that the war has made perish many more men than women. In addition, many more of the latter, whose existence is based on libertinage, can be found in the cities. Entirely given over to concern for their attire, a result of their prostitution, they want to do absolutely nothing that is useful. It is they who harbor evil men. Who live on the products of their crimes. It would be all to the honor of magistrates, generals and commandants to not have a single one in the cities. The least negligence in this regard would render them worthy of public lack or esteem." (Nesbitt 2008 Pg. 67). Again, the cities are the haven of the moral reprobates, the inherently evil and criminogenic who refuse to obey the dictates of dictator L'Ouverture who demands that they and their children be bound to a plantation making do with wage levels set and policed by dictator L'Ouverture. Those who resist L'Ouverture's discourse of the post enslavement social order with its specific order of power are lazy, indolent, criminogenic and inherently evil, they are then the dross of the social order and must be relentlessly policed and punished. This white supremacist Manichean discourse opens the door to social cleansing as an instrument of power to ensure the well-being of the social order. Power must then purge the cities of this morally reprobate evil. L'Ouverture now pronounces on the domestic workers of the colony as follows: "As for the domestics, each citizen should only have as many as are necessary for indispensable services. The persons in whose homes they reside should be the first overseers of their conduct and should not tolerate anything in their conduct contrary to good morals, submission and order. If they are thieves they should be denounced to military commandants so they can be punished in conformity with the law. And since under the new regime all labor deserves a salary, every salary demands work. Such is the invariable and firm will of the government." (Nesbitt 2008 Pgs. 67-68). L'Ouverture has embraced white supremacist fascism, but he is non-white, which must constitute a variant of white supremacist fascism for pliant non-whites which is rooted in schizophrenia. For L'Ouverture, those who hire and pay labor are inherently superior and are charged with the task of being exemplars and overseers of the moral fortitude of their workers, their charges. The massa of enslavement was not expected to accept and carry out this task of the moral upliftment and policing of enslaved morality. The enslaved were massa property to do with what she/ he desired. Those who hire labor are then inherently superior to workers and both are inherently superior to the evil, moral reprobates of the criminogenic urban lumpen. The inherently superior are stratified internally into an order of superiority which consists of the plantation owners, the military, merchants etc. and those who hire domestic labor. Your place in the ruling elite, in the oligarchy afforded you the designation of being inherently superior, fact did not enter into this designation as the sins of the elite and oligarchy were silenced by the elite and oligarchy. This was not then a social order rooted in the conviction of the need to address the underdevelopment and trauma plaguing the newly emancipated workers and their children; it was instead a fascist social order designed to return the colony to the prosperity which existed before the rebellion of the enslaved utilizing instruments of power to render labor servile, pliable and docile. To attain this goal a disposable marginalized group was conjured up into existence to justify the need for repression and social cleansing when deemed necessary.

The moral order of L'Ouverture is rooted in Roman Catholic Christian discourse, hence he expects labor to embrace Catholicism and its moral order, thereby changing its worldview and action to enable them to embrace moral regeneration into docile, servile, contented labor. This discourse of L'Ouverture is illustrated by his position on marriage as follows: "The most holy of all institutions among men who live in society, that from which the greatest good flows, is marriage." (Nesbitt 2008 Pg. 68). The only family form that is holy, organic to constituting high moral practice is massa style marriage. The workers and the lumpen who practice alternate family forms which were constituted under enslavement, those who refuse to adopt the massa marriage form are then moral reprobates, inherently inferior and must be disciplined and punished. Again, difference is constituted by a rabid discourse of totalitarian repression of difference in order to render labor servile. L'Ouverture now reveals the practice in the military of alternate family forms and his intention to purge the military of such officers as follows: "Military commanders, and especially public functionaries, are inexcusable when they publicly give themselves over to the scandal of vice. Those who, while having legitimate wives, allow concubines into their houses, or those who, not being married live publicly with several women, are not worthy of command: they shall be dismissed." (Nesbitt 2008 Pg. 68). In the military and public administration your refusal to practice the Catholic massa family form is an adequate ground for your dismissal. The L'Ouverture instruments of power have then instruments to exert power on the inhabitants of the colony rooted solely in Catholic discourse, there is then no freedom of belief and religion,

Catholicism is hegemonic, used as an instrument to police repression of specific groups within the social order, specifically the formerly enslaved.

L'Ouverture now speaks to the abomination of idleness and how to eradicate this grievous condition as follows: "Idleness is the source of all disorders, and if it is at all tolerated, I shall hold the military commanders responsible, persuaded that those who tolerate idleness and vagabonds are secret enemies of the government. In keeping with his abilities, no one under any pretext is to be exempt from some task. Creole mothers and fathers who have children and properties should go there to live and work, to make their children work or to oversee their labor, and in moments of rest they should, either themselves or through instruction, teach them the precepts of our religion. It is through these means that useful and respectable citizens will be formed, and we will distance forever from this colony the horrible events whose memory should never be effaced from our minds." (Nesbitt 2008 Pgs. 68-69). Idleness is criminal activity which must be policed and eradicated which is the duty of the military and must be embraced by the military with unrelenting commitment and rigor. Those who refuse this duty of the military or approach this duty in a lackluster manner are enemies of the state and will be punished. L'Ouverture then presents the new duty of the whites who own and control plantations and were once slave owners born and raised in the colony. L'Ouverture unhesitatingly states the inherent superiority of this white group, recipients of his boon of forced labor and governor managed wage levels and calls upon them to proselytize the workers on the plantation to accept Catholicism. The former massa evolved into the new massa by L'Ouverture will now mold the new ideal non-white citizen of the colony through forced labor and capped wages. L'Ouverture is not delusional he is simply schizophrenic in his love for all things white, textbook hallucinatory whiteness.

At this point in the proclamation L'Ouverture now releases his decrees as follows: "Any Creole individual, man or woman, convicted of making statements tending to alter public tranquility but who shall not be worthy of death shall be sent to the fields to work with a chain on one foot for one month." (Nesbitt 2008 Pg. 70). L'Ouverture uses Creole now as one born in the colony versus a foreigner who is born abroad. The concept "tending to alter public tranquility" is as broad as it is wide, which leaves much room for abuse thereby giving the military the means to instill terror in the general population and specifically target those who are defined as enemies of the order of power. The formerly enslaved are now free and equal according to L'Ouverture, but now they are captives of a totalitarian state policed by the military.

L'Ouverture now presents his decree which establishes his national security apparatus that physically separates the lumpen from the rest of the population whilst enumerating them for easy repression and the Final Solution. L'Ouverture states as follows: "In all the communities of the colony where municipal administrations exist, all male and female citizens who live in them, whatever their quality or condition, must obtain a security card. Such card shall contain the name, family name, address, civil state, profession and quality, age and sex of the person who bears it. It shall be signed by the mayor and the police superintendent of the quarter in which lives the individual to which it shall be delivered. It shall be renewed every six months and paid at the price of one gourde for each individual, and the sums coming from this are destined for communal expenses. It is expressly ordered that municipal administrators are only to deliver security cards to persons having a known profession or state, irreproachable conduct and well-assured means of existence. All those who cannot fulfill these conditions rigorously necessary to obtain a security card will be sent to the fields if they are Creole, or sent away from the colony if they are foreigners." (Nesbitt 2008 Pg. 70). Every inhabitant of the colony is required to apply for a security card which has a life of six months and pay for it. The mayor and the police are charged with the task of policing this process and vetting all applicants to ensure that they fulfill the requirements for issuing said card. Those persons who have been refused a card or fail to apply for a card when interdicted shall be transported to the plantations and forced to work. Foreigners shall be deported from the colony. You will only be issued a security card when you exhibit the evidence of being a steadfast disciple of the L'Ouverture model of the morally upright catholic christian worker of the colony. The instrument of the security card is the front for conducting a census of the lumpen, enumerating, recognizing and plotting their locations on the landscape of the colony. The police are under the control of the military making them the enforcers of L'Ouverture's Final Solution. L'Ouverture has now returned the slave pass, but he is enabled to exceed the limits set to the slave pass because of technically free labor belonging to no one, for as juridical subjects they are now full subjects of L'Ouverture's power as governor for life. It is then compulsory upon the police and the military to police the population seeking out relentlessly those without cards, arresting and transporting them to forced labor on the plantations. L'Ouverture states as follows: "Two weeks after the presentation of the present act, any person found without a security card shall be sent to the fields if they are Creole and if they are foreigners deported from the colony without any form of trial if they don't prefer to serve in the troops of the line." (Nesbitt 2008 Pg. 70). A foreigner without a security card, either because they don't qualify or did not apply, can stay in the colony by joining the military, this is the L'Ouverture press gang.

L'Ouverture now reveals his final instrument of power in his quest to create a surveillance state rooted in discipline and punish, which as the slave state which preceded the Caribbean laboratory of massa has led the way in formulating the concept of massa democratic state in the nineteenth century. L'Ouverture states as follows: "Dating from one month after publication of the present act, all managers and drivers on plantations are to send to the commanders of their quarter the exact list of all the cultivators on their plantations of every age and sex, under penalty of one week in prison. Every manager and driver is the first overseer of his plantation. He is declared personally responsible for any kind of disorder that shall be committed, and for the laziness and vagabondage of the cultivators." (Nesbitt 2008 Pg. 71). L'Ouverture now establishes his instrument of surveillance over the plantations by naming the managers and drivers as the tip of the surveillance spear of the state on all plantations. The managers and drivers, not the owners, are charged with ensuring order on the plantations and disciplining the labor force, which means reporting all infringements of L'Ouverture's code of behaviour to the military. To erect the data base of the surveillance state, the managers and drivers must complete and pass lists of all workers on the plantation, both legal and illegal, to the military who must act on these lists. Failure to comply means that managers and drivers will be imprisoned. L'Ouverture now reveals the end use of these lists from all plantations forwarded to the military as follows: "dating from one month after publication of the present act, all commanders of quarters are to send lists of the cultivators of all the plantations of their quarter to their *arrondissement* commanders under penalty of discharge." (Nesbitt 2008 Pg. 71). These lists are to be sent to the governor promptly via the military chain of command. The strategic importance of these lists in the hands of the governor for life is as follows: "Said lists, deposited in the archives of the government, shall serve in the future as the immutable bases for the fixing of cultivators on the plantations." (Nesbitt 2008 Pg. 71). The surveillance state has to find, enumerate and surveil the urban lumpen, round them up for not having a security card, deport them to the plantations and ensure that they are present on the plantations they were dispatched to. Plantations must be monitored so as to ensure that they are not hiring card less labor without reporting this illicit labor to the state, thereby breaking the blockade against giving work to labor without a security card. L'Ouverture's intent is to starve them into submission by marginalizing them as the outlaws, outcaste, the Dalits of the colony for their own good. L'Ouverture has now socialized labor in keeping with the discourse of the transition of mercantile capitalism into early industrial capitalism, refusing to pass the cost of the reproduction of socialized labor to the state nor the employers of labor hence no labor rights, child labor and no provision of universal education, health care, housing etc. The burden of the reproduction of labor is that of a worker who is forced to work for wage levels stipulated by the dictator for life without any legal provision for a living wage. L'Ouverture insists that it is your duty to your country to work under these conditions without rebellion for the good of your country. No worker is exempt from surveillance from L'Ouverture's national security apparatus as the position on domestic workers as follows: "Any domestic who has not been judged worthy of obtaining a certificate of good conduct upon leaving a house in which he or she served shall be declared incapable of receiving a security card. Any people who, in order to favor them shall have delivered one shall be punished with one month in prison." (Nesbitt 2008 Pg. 71). The dictator for life relentlessly affords the employer the right to coerce workers to their benefit without the protection of law for the worker. There is no equality before the law for a worker in conflict with the employer as with the state. The state mediates worker/ employer conflict relentlessly in the interest of the employer, thus sending the message that the employer is central to the prosperity of the colony whilst the worker is in constant need for discipline and punishment, massa reborn in an era of free labor. L'Ouverture ends the proclamation document by describing the centrality of the military to his order of power, his dictatorship for life as follows: "All generals, military commanders and all civil authorities in all departments are enjoined to maintain a firm hand in ensuring the full and complete execution of all these dispositions on their personal responsibility and under penalty of disobedience." (Nesbitt 2008 Pg. 72). The military is the national security apparatus expected to suppress all forms of rebellion and rejected behavior exhibited by the masses. There is no conceptualization of the rule of law over all citizens of the colony, there are only provisions for policing and suppressing labor and the lumpen, which is the reality of Haiti to this day.

The French military force came ashore on 4 February 1802. L'Ouverture wrote to Dessalines commanding him to wage guerrilla war on the French in a letter dated 8 February 1802. L'Ouverture states as follows: "Do not forget, while waiting for the rainy season which will rid us of our foes, that we have no other resource than destruction and flames. Bear in mind that the soil bathed with our sweat must not furnish our enemies with the smallest aliment. Tear up the roads with shot; throw horses and corpses into all the fountains; burn and annihilate everything, in order that those who have come to reduce us to slavery may have before their eyes the image of that hell which they deserve." (Nesbitt 2008 Pg. 76). The dictator for life has ordered Dessalines in writing to undertake a scorched earth policy of resistance until the onset of the rainy season. Following his capture by Leclerc, L'Ouverture writes to Bonaparte as follows: "I alone ought to be responsible for my conduct to the government I have served. I have too high an idea of the greatness and the justice of the First Magistrate of the French people, to doubt a moment of its impartiality. I indulge the feeling that the balance in its hands will not incline to one side more. I claim its generosity." (Nesbitt 2008 Pg. 78). In July 1802 you wrote Bonaparte whilst being renditioned to France. L'Ouverture's discursive line is the inherent superiority of the French, therefore you expect justice from this inherently superior French. To invade to remove the dictator for life, destroy the non-white military of the colony and reimpose enslavement shall be easily overpowered by the inherent love the French have for justice, justice is organic to the French genome, race. You ordered Dessalines to wage war against the invaders and instructed him on the methodology of this war until the onset of the rainy season. But you never embraced the order you gave Dessalines. You willingly made yourself vulnerable, always available, unprotected in plain sight of the French military. When picked up and rendition via ship to France you are now writing Bonaparte shucking and jiving holding on to the slimmest hope of a reprieve from Bonaparte. Your final words are then devoid of the discourse of liberty, freedom and incessant war against those who would seek to reimpose enslavement. Finally, L'Ouverture's letter to Bonaparte of 17 September 1802 from his place of captivity in France states as follows: "I have had the misfortune to incur your wrath, but as to fidelity and probity, I am strong in my conscience, and I dare affirm that among all the servants of the state no one is more honest than myself. I was one of your soldiers. And the first servant of the French in St Domingue; but now I am wretched, ruined, dishonored, a victim of my own services; let your sensibility be moved at my position. You are too great in feeling and too just not to produce a judgment as to my destiny." (Nesbitt 2008 Pg. 79). L'Ouverture was simply renditioned from St Domingue to imprisonment with no charges leading to a trial laid in St Domingue and France, he died in April 1803 imprisoned, but never charged. In September 1802 L'Ouverture is writing to Bonaparte begging him to act upon this injustice meted out to L'Ouverture as he does not deserve it. You made yourself a soft target for the French, you refused to abide by the orders you gave Dessalines, the French exploited the opportunities you presented to them for a soft rendition, now from your dungeon in France you are begging Bonaparte to make a decision. The decision of the French is obvious, death by exposure for you in the cold dungeon, and so it was. You are begging the enslaver in chief for his intervention in your favor with death tightening its grip around your throat, shucking and jiving rather than embracing death as a non-white warrior. Schizophrenia constituted by hallucinatory whiteness cannot be the basis of strategic action in the face of the assault of a unified massa. By September 1802 the writing on the wall was there for the French conquest of the colony which finally collapsed in 1803 with Haitian independence declared. This victory was attained with no input from L'Ouverture as he chose to pursue life granted by the French, rather than death on the battlefield at the hands of the French. A decision constituted by schizophrenia driven by hallucinatory whiteness; a fundamental, driving desire to be white but you cannot be genetically, the essence of being bi-polar, multi-polar, hence schizophrenic in summation.

The African Revolution of Amerikkka (USA) 1960s-1970s

The discourse of revolutionary practice of George Jackson deconstructed.

This is a deconstruction of the prison letters of George Jackson, an imprisoned discursive agent of the Black Panther Party in the California penal system from 1960 to August 1971 when he was killed in prison by guards at San Quentin, maximum security prison. In 1960 at eighteen years old, the African male pleaded guilty to stealing $ 70 from a gas station, and was sentenced to 1 year to life in prison. In 1970 at twenty-eight years old he was charged with the murder of a corrections officer at Soledad prison and moved to San Quentin prison where he was killed. Jackson had extensive contact with the juvenile justice system in Chicago and then in California where he migrated to from Chicago. At eighteen years old with a public defender he pleaded guilty and was punitively punished with incarceration that could extend for life. Jackson's insight is then on criminality and its impact on African consciousness and the quest for liberation in Amerikkka. In his book "Soledad Brother The Prison Letters of George Jackson", Jackson writes an autobiographical section dated July 10, 1970 written and sent from San Quentin State Prison stating as follows: "I could play the criminal aspects of my life down but then it wouldn't be me. That was the pertinent part, the thing at school and home. I was constantly rejecting in process. All my life I pretended with my folks, it was the thing in the streets that was real. I was certainly just pretending with the nuns and priests." (Jackson 1976 Pg. 27). Jackson the adolescent, the teenager was simply not interested in the conventional path he was exposed to by his parents. He willingly embraced the call of the street and the criminality found on the streets, not at his family home. Criminality controls the street, granted space and impunity by the security apparatus of the state, which then justifies the level of policing of spaces dominated by Africans in Amerikkka. Jackson continues as follows: "Black men born in the US and fortunate enough to live past the age of eighteen are conditioned to accept the inevitability of prison. For most of us, it simply looms as the next phase in a sequence of humiliations. Being born a slave in a captive society and never experiencing any objective basis for expectation had the effect of preparing me for the progressively traumatic misfortunes that lead so many black men to the prison gate. I was prepared for prison. It required only minor psychic adjustment." (Jackson 1976 Pg. 27). Prison is the next given stage in the life of the African male in Amerikkka, it is inevitable for your skin is your sin, which constitutes African nihilism where you do the crime to do the time not to appropriate wealth from others emphasizing the quest for impunity, in perfecting the methodology of committing the perfect crime. There is no need to pursue criminal impunity, to perfect the methodology of the perfect crime as an inherently inferior being cannot commit the perfect crime against the inherently superior being. You commit the crime to do the crime and the time for all you deserve is jail time nothing else in life, you are then immersed in self-hate generated nihilism. Can you then make African revolution in Amerikkka plagued with mind numbing nihilism against the master race? No. As the drug trade in the spaces occupied by Africans expanded and deepened its presence in these areas with successive waves of addiction by new products, especially synthetic drugs, from crack to meth to fentanyl. The violence especially the gun violence has become endemic, graphic, mindless and devoid of artifice. Graphically violent crime is then the means to be rewarded with lengthy sentences or the death penalty in jail, to further intensify the trauma of the inhabitants of these marginalized spaces, to repeatedly confirm with your action the white supremacist discourse of the criminogenic nature of the nigger and the need for this race and its race spaces to be constantly policed to ensure social control of this dangerous minority race in Amerikkka. The African urban lumpen in Amerikkka is then a fetter dragging down the body politic of the African race, a stumbling block tripping up those in search of the revolutionary solution realized.

Jackson continues with the concept of being an African captive in Amerikkka as follows: "The conflicts and contradictions that will follow me to the tomb started right there in the womb. The feeling of being captured... this slave can never adjust to it, it's a thing I just don't favor, then, now, never." (Jackson 1976 Pg. 28). Jackson the African male is alienated from Amerikkka to the point where he insists he is a captive of Amerikkka, of its white supremacist order of power targeting him as an African male. He is then a captive. Jackson continues as follows: "I was captured and brought to prison when I was 18 years old because I couldn't adjust. The record that the state has compiled on my activities reads like the record of ten men. It labels me the brigand, thief, burglar, gambler, hobo, drug addict, gunman, escape artist, Communist revolutionary, and murderer." (Jackson 1976 Pg. 28). At age 18 he was then the ideal nigger criminal now incarcerated in the California prison system having victimized his race through his criminality, making him a statistic of the incarcerated African male in Amerikkka whose race is over represented in the Amerikkka prison population to this day. They victimize their race and their community, then waste away their lives in prison, occupying the prison in numbers that insist they are a criminogenic race always deserving of prison. But Jackson transcends this racist category as he now evolves in prison into a discursive agent of the African Revolution in Amerikkka, marking him for death within the prison walls.

Jackson now speaks to his experience of school days in the Chicago ghetto, first up was his contact with white boys in kindergarten for the first time in his life as follows: "Seeing the white boys up close in kindergarten was a traumatic event. I *must* have seen some before in magazines or books but never in the flesh. I approached one, felt for his hair, scratched at his chest, he hit me in the head with a baseball bat. They found me crumpled in a heap just outside the school yard fence." (Jackson 1976 Pg. 28). The white body evokes curiosity simply because you need to determine what constitutes it inherently superior to your non-white body. You are driven to seek this white body out when you are already immersed in hallucinatory whiteness, driven to plot the difference that renders this body inherently superior and you soon learn that it is genetic difference visually apparent that demarcate the difference. Jackson learnt by force that you don't touch massa, that is a grave breach of the protocol of separation between the bodies, the apartheid between the bodies. Jackson's mother in response to his beating by the white boys moved him to the catholic mission school in the ghetto. Jackson spent nine years at St Malachy catholic mission school at Washington and Oakley streets in the heart of the Chicago ghetto. Jackson states: "Holy ghost, confessions and racism. St Malachy's was really two schools. There was another school across the street that was more private than ours. 'We' played and fought on the corner sidewalks bordering the school. 'They' had a large grass-and-tree-studded garden with an eight-foot wrought-iron fence bordering it (to keep us out since it never seemed to keep any of them in when they chose to leave). "They' were all white. "They' were driven to and from school in large private buses or in their parents' cars. "We' on the black side walked, or when we could afford it use the public buses or streetcars. The white students' yard was equipped with picnic tables for spring lunches, swings, slides, and other more sophisticated gadgets intended to please older children. For years we had only the very crowded sidewalk and alley behind the school. Years later a small gym was built but it just stood there, locked. It was only allowed to be used for an occasional basketball game between our school and one of the others like it from across the city's various ghetto areas." (Jackson 1976 Pg. 30). Jackson is now experiencing inequality expressed as racial inequality, an apartheid system where white working class families are segregated from African working class persons by segregated housing which rewards the white working class for being white and punishes the African working class for being non-white. The two segregated schools are the living expression of this racist inequality and enforced segregation which locks up non-whites in urban ghettos, whilst moving the white working class to the suburbs. Segregated housing supported by the federal state gave expression to an order of power of white supremacy and in so doing condemned the urban African to a structure of power designed to house urban non-whites where their underdevelopment, their position on the spectrum of trauma combined with the criminality of the urban spaces to constitute the nihilism of the urban non-white ghetto dweller. Jackson comments on his catholic schooling as follow: "I know now that the most damaging thing a people in a colonial situation can do is to allow their children to attend any education facility organized by the dominant enemy culture." (Jackson 1976 Pg. 30). The Africans are a minority race in an order of power constituted by the discourse of white supremacy which insists that the African minority is an inherently inferior race that poses a grave threat to the white order of power for they are no longer enslaved. The discourse of white supremacy has to relentlessly constitute new discursive concepts and instruments of power to ensure the servility of this most dangerous minority race at the level of the idea. This minority race has to be systematically attacked at the level of the idea problematizing, inferiorizing all expressions of their race utilizing the white ideal as perfection expressed. This minority has to be denied opportunity, be forever underdeveloped and have their leaders servile to massa and most of all criminalized which drives a condition of apolitical being forsaking the quest for liberation and self-determination. The end result of this is that you the African must cast aside all non-white culture, values, mores, discourses and worldviews, insisting that only what is white is right and fit for purpose. But white supremacist discourse negates the specificity of the non-white self, through relentless assault. Immersing your non-white self in it which negates and problematises your non-white self, erecting a structure of dual, antagonistic discourses and worldviews that constitutes self, with hallucinatory whiteness policing its hegemony over this structure, which is a state of non-being that renders the individual a problematic social actor.

Jackson now deals with his motivation to embrace criminality in his ghetto neighborhood as follows: "We almost put the block's businessmen into bankruptcy. My mother and father will never admit it now, I'm sure, but I was hungry so were we all. Our activities went from stolen food to other things I wanted, gloves for my hands (which were always cold), which I was always wearing out, marbles for the slingshots, games and gadgets for outdoorsmen from the dime store. Downtown, we plundered at will." (Jackson 1976 Pg. 32). Life on the streets was then the embrace of criminality as a mode of survival for young developing African males in the Chicago ghetto at this time. The ever-evolving drug trade in the African ghetto has changed the order of power of the street mode of survival through criminal action. The cash that flows through this illicit trade in need of washing and injection into the legal economy and the value of the stock in trade constitutes a nexus of gun violence that emanates from all levels of the trade in the African ghettos. The ideal target for young males seeking to create a reputation that demands respect on the street is to rob with force aspects of the drug economy: those slanging dope on the street, those with product in storage, cash couriers, stash houses and transporters. In this illicit ecosystem graphic violence is the preferred means to take what is not yours and to defend what is yours.

Jackson now speaks of his grandfather George 'Papa' Davis and the impact Papa had on his development as an adult. Jackson states as follows: "My grandfather George 'Papa' Davis stands out of those early years more than any other figure in my total environment. He was separated from his wife by the system...he was living and working in Chicago-sending the wage back to the people downstate. He was an extremely aggressive man, and since aggression on the part of the slave means crime, he was in jail now and then. I loved him. He tried to direct my great energy into the proper form of protest. He invented long simple allegories that always pictured the white politicians as animals (jackasses, toads, goats, vermin in general). He scorned the police with special enmity. He and my mother went to great pains to impress upon me that it was the worst form of niggerism to hook and jab, cut and jab at other blacks." (Jackson 1976 Pg. 33). There was resistance that rejected a mode of behavior, with its driving discourse and worldview that rejects white supremacy and its constituted 'soul' draped over the African, the instrument of power to convert to, to render the African a nigger exhibiting her/ his niggerism, literally non-white peoples at war with self and with each other to the benefit of massa and white supremacy. The operational culture of the drug trade in the ghetto is niggerism incarnate as they slaughter each other with their penchant for non-white on non-white crime, they victimize and traumatize their communities into inaction whilst rejecting any and all forms of political action, even education. Criminality in the ghetto is then niggerism and it has evolved into a mindless nihilist dance of futility in a social order premised on white supremacy and the suppression of all non-white races to white hegemony and entitlement, choosing as a vocation to die, live crippled in or out of jail or to serve long sentences in prison for violence against members of your own family, community and race. In Chicago Jackson and his family moved into the projects and his criminal activities explode in scale, intensity and expanse reaching to the point where his father moves the family to California. In California Jackson will appear on the police radar ultimately leading to his first stay in the juvenile justice system of Paso Robles. Jackson's rapid escalation of his criminality on moving into the Chicago projects is indicative of the impact of segregated housing in the USA and its impact on the economy of crime in urban African ghettos. These high-rise buildings erected in underdeveloped urban areas for African tenants were erected without due care and attention to the policing difficulties they pose, failing to allocate the manpower and the funds to render them safe for the tenants across time/ space.

Jackson now speaks about his experience in the Paso Robles system of California as follows: "The very first time, it was like dying. Just to exist at all in the cage calls for some heavy psychic readjustments. Being captured was the first of my fears. It may have been inborn. It may have been an acquired characteristic built up over the centuries of black bondage. It is the thing I've been running from all my life. When it caught up to me in 1957 I was fifteen years old and not very well-equipped to deal with sudden changes. The Youth Authority joints are places that demand complete capitulation; one must cease to resist altogether or else." (Jackson 1978 Pgs. 36-37). From Chicago to California Jackson's embrace of criminality could not prepare him for his experience in Paso Robles. After various periods of time served in Paso Robles you can and will develop the discipline to survive prison but not to disengage from criminality, especially during periods of life external of the prison. The niggerism that is criminality ensures the inability to live free, devoid of criminality on the outside of prison, that will send you back to the prison. This then is a niggerism of criminality that embraces, glorifies doing the time for niggers are only relevant when they do the crime, then the time, come out of prison do the crime again to do time again. Criminality and serving time is then an expression of total freedom in action devoid of the political recognition that this discourse is designed to police a race into servility by any means necessary, including the Final Solution. To embrace this discourse of self-hate condemns one to action driven by nihilistic schizophrenia. Jackson now reflects on why he does hard time in prison from the Paso Robles juvenile detention system to adult prison, including a maximum security prison, as follows; "All my life I have done exactly what I wanted to do just when I wanted, no more, perhaps less sometimes, but never any more, which explains why I had to be jailed. 'Man was born free, but everywhere he is in chains.' I never adjusted. I haven't adjusted even yet, with half my life already spent in prison. I can't truthfully say prison is any less painful now than during my first experience." (Jackson 1976 Pg. 37). Jackson's race condemned him to be subject to an order of power where a personality as his is expected to embrace criminality, be killed or incarcerated for extensive periods of time. No opportunity was forthcoming to enable Jackson to embrace his personality matching it to a range of possible and probable outcomes which would have kept him out of the embrace of criminality. Fields as academia, politics, entrepreneurship, performing arts, a combination of all and more were simply not real, available, real for Jackson as it was for white children in the suburbs. His skin is his sin in white supremacist Amerikkka and he is constituted by hegemonic white supremacist discourse to so prove. Every non-white person in Amerikkka is then a self-fulfilling prophecy which proves the inherent superiority of massa and his right, entitlement to manifest destiny. Jackson now reveals the years it took whilst in prison to finally remove the white soul in control of his mind enabling himself to finally unmask his real, true mortal enemy in this order of power of Amerikkka. Jackson now reveals that in the Paso Roble system his quest for knowledge exploded, commencing his journey to death in San Quentin, for to pursue knowledge in jail in the service of the Black Panther party and the African Revolution of Amerikkka marked him for death, as others before and after him. Massa is a jealous massa, you can only depart the space he exerts hegemony over foot first. Jackson continues on the experience of being imprisoned as follows: "Capture, imprisonment, is the closest thing to being dead that one is likely to experience in this life. There were no beatings (for me at least) in the youth joint and the food wasn't that bad. I came through it. When told to do something I simply played the idiot, and spent my time reading. The absentminded bookworm, I was in full revolt by the time seven months were up." (Jackson 1976 Pg. 38). The pursuit of African criminality was no revolt against the hegemony of massa, it was simply playing according to massa rules for ghetto African males in acceptance of prison time as being normal, designating rank amongst African ghetto males, a pecking order, a desirable mark of courage for all young ghetto African males to emulate. In Jackson's case this stint in Paso Robles was not business as usual, but a wake up call where his personality now found the means within Paso Robles to pursue knowledge in liberation of self, for one can be liberated at the level of the idea but physically incarcerated for life. Jackson's full revolt will continue after leaving Paso Robles but the terrain he returns to places criminality as a daily survival choice. He is accused of stealing 70 USD from a gas station and does a plea deal with the prosecution where he pleads guilty and he expects to be sentenced to a short sentence in county jail. At 18 years old he is before the judge, complies with his end of the deal but is sentenced to one year to life in adult prison, which means his only way out is via the parole board, but he is dead before any parole hearing as he is charged in Soledad prison with the murder of a guard and transferred to San Quentin where he is killed. Jackson comments on his pursuit of knowledge in adult prison as follows: "That was in 1960. I was 18 years old. I've been here ever since. I met Marx, Lenin, Trotsky, Engels and Mao when I entered prison and they redeemed me." "I met black guerrillas, George 'Big Jake Lewis, and James Carr, W. L. Nolen, Bill Christmas, Torry Gibson, and many, many others. We attempted to transform the black criminal mentality into a black revolutionary mentality. As a result, each of us has been subjected to years of the most vicious reactionary violence by the state. Our mortality rate is almost what you would expect to find in a history of Dachau. I am being tried in court right now with two other brothers, John Clutchette and Fleeta Drumgo, for the alleged slaying of a prison guard. This charge carries an automatic death penality for me, I can't get life, I already have it." (Jackson 1976 Pgs. 39- 40). There was an automatic death penalty for Jackson by any means necessary via lawfare or extrajudicial killing which was preferable for liberation at the level of the idea marks you for death in Amerikkka. The fundamental question is if Jackson would have ever attained liberation roaming the wastelands of the ghetto in pursuit of African criminality? Highly unlikely and if he did this will mark him as an enemy of the criminals and African criminality. In today's African ghetto those liberated must bear arms for protection from the state, dark ops and African criminality for they are the enemy of all of the above. African revolutionaries of the ghetto today are in an even more precarious position than Jackson in the 1960s and 1970s. The lesson is then potently obvious: African criminality in the African ghetto was invented by massa to serve massa in his unrelenting drive to police the African minority and render it servile in Amerikkka to white power, the white world order.

Jackson presents a salient lesson from his experience for the reader, one which illustrates the impact of white supremacy on the survival ability of white people as follows: "I've learned one very significant thing for our struggle here in the US : all blacks do look alike to certain types of white people. White people tend to grossly underestimate all blacks, out of habit. Blacks have been overestimating whites in a conditioned reflex." (Jackson 1976 Pg. 39). The members of the state apparatus charged with policing and suppressing movements of political change in the African ghetto are adept at knowing the power games, the order of power and their vulnerabilities in the ghetto and manipulating them to ensure white supremacist hegemony. The problem is the abiding ignorance of the inhabitants of the ghetto of the order of white power that impacts their daily lives. The enemy is the ever-visible police, but the potent deadly enemy is invisible and part of the order of power of the ghetto working in conjunction with the brokers of power in the ghetto. The entire structure of the illicit trades in the ghetto is compromised by these invisibles who wield covert and overt state power, white power. There is then an African comprador class in the ghetto that aids, abets, benefits from and bolsters white supremacist hegemony over the ghetto. Any nascent political movement in the African ghetto will be assailed by a joint assault of the African ghetto comprador class and their white overlords, whilst the masses of the ghetto do not command the level of consciousness necessary to protect and nurture this revolutionary vanguard. Centuries of white supremacist assault in Amerikkka has today rendered nihilistic behavior as normality.

Prison Letter dated April 1970 from Soledad state prison

Jackson is presenting in writing his discourse of racism and fascism as follows: "After one concedes that *racism* is stamped unalterably into the present nature of Amerikan sociopolitical and economic life in general (the definition of fascism is: a police state wherein the political ascendancy is tied into and protects the interests of the upper class – characterized by militarism, racism, and imperialism), and concedes further that criminals and crime arise from material, economic and sociopolitical causes, we can then burn *all* of the criminology and penology libraries and direct our attention where it will do some good." (Jackson 1976 Pg. 42). The Amerikan social order is dominated by the oligarchy who has captured the state with the full compliance of its elected politicians. This national oligarchy is dominated by white folks which means there is economic and social domination premised on a hegemonic discourse of white supremacy. The white oligarchy dominates the order of power, has captured the state and uses the state to ensure its hegemony over the social order. The primary aim of politics in Amerikkka is to motivate the voter to embrace the order of politics that prevails as being the epitome of democracy. Racism, and a stream of discursive concepts as manifest destiny, white entitlement and inherent superiority, imperialism, militarism and neo-colonial domination are designed to keep the voter servile and accommodating of the political process. Any form of rebellion of the masses invokes the heavy hand of the state to silence this discontent. The economic order is then defined by racism and the organic needs of a race oligarchy for hegemony over the social order constituted. Inequality then has a race order of power to it as all other aspects of this specific order of power, including geopolitics. Inequality and race relations then within Amerikkka are expressed as a racist order of power of internal colonialism, whilst geopolitics is constituted by a neo-colonial imperial racist order of power which relentlessly seeks world hegemony of the white world order of power. This white supremacist order of power must constantly produce discourses of power by which to seduce the members of the social order to embrace servility. Science is a discourse of truth that serves power, not our need to understand in order to attain liberation from this order. You cannot use the knowledge of the ruling white oligarchy as the instrument of your liberation from white hegemony, you must create your own. All the libraries of the white discourses of truth cannot afford a dose of reality on the ground and the path to liberation, of exiting this racist worldview. Jackson continues to address the nature of institutions in this racist order of power as follows: "To determine how men will behave once they enter the prison it is of first importance to know that prison. Men are brutalized by their environment – not the reverse." (Jackson 1976 Pg. 43). "I was saying that the great majority of the people who live in this area of the state and seek their employment from the institution have overt racism as a *traditional* aspect of their characters. The only stops that will regulate how far they will carry this thing comes from the fear of losing employment here as a result of the outside pressures to control the violence. That is O Wing, Max Row, Soledad – in part anyway." (Jackson 1876 Pg. 44). The order of power of prison brutalizes the inmate who reacts to this attempt to re-socialize the inmate into the order of prison power with a variety of possible responses, one of which is self-brutality and brutality expressed against other inmates. Racism in the order of power of prison then further assaults the African inmate, brutalizing her/ him even further and evoking brutality which subjects her/ him to even more brutality in the special wing for dissidents as O Wing. Jackson continues as follows: "It destroys the logical processes of the mind, a man's thoughts become completely disorganized. The noise, madness streaming from every throat, frustrated sounds from the bars, metallic sounds from the walls, the steel trays, the iron beds bolted in the wall, the hollow sounds from a cast-iron sink or toilet. The smells, the human waste thrown at us, unwashed bodies, the rotten food. When a white con leaves here he's ruined for life. No black leaves Max Row walking. Either he leaves on the meat wagon or he leaves scrawling licking at the pig's feet. Ironic, because one cannot get a parole to the outside prison directly from O Wing, Max Row. It's positively not done. The parole board won't even consider the Max Row case." (Jackson 1976 Pg. 45). The order of power of prison then constitutes a daily living environment that assaults the sanity of the inmate as it de-socializes her/ him and re-socializes her/ him as a prison inmate, which means they depart prison socialized as an inmate to now return to the external world of prison which they are alienated from. The white inmate is ruined but a special regime of power, a racist regime awaits the African inmate where the intent is to eradicate the inmate, drive insane or have them cower, shuck and jive to white power. Uppity niggers are afforded the full brunt of the assault in special spaces designed and wielded as weapons of white power to eliminate the non-white threat. White supremacy insists that as daily life is a specifically designed order of power for the African in the ghetto, prison has to be even more impactful on the mind and body of the errant African in a destructive manner than daily life in the ghetto. African criminality as a daily survival strategy is the foundation of the policing of the race in the ghetto and the order of power of the prison they are incarcerated in. A case where the race aids and abets its oppression and repression by massa.

Jackson continues his analysis of the impact of Max Row on the mind of the inmate as follows: "One can understand the depression felt by an inmate on Max Row. He's fallen as far as he can into the social trap, relief is so distant that it is very easy for him to lose his holds. In two weeks that little average man who may have ended on Max Row for *suspicion of attempted* escape is so brutalized, so completely without holds, that he will never heal again. It's worse than Vietnam." "If he doesn't sound and act more zealous than everyone else he will be challenged for not being loyal to his race and its politics, fascism. Some of these cons support the pigs' racism without shame, the others support it inadvertently by their own racism. The former are white, the latter black. But in here as on the street black racism is a forced *reaction*. A survival adaptation." (Jackson 1976 Pg. 46). Max Row is designed to de-socialize the inmate placed there, it is then the chosen factory to churn out deconstructed inmates who are then consumed by the prison system rooted in terror to place the inmate on the spectrum of trauma for life. There is a division premised on race and racism in which white solidarity is promoted across the divide of inmate versus prison staff for whites in the system, and one of total war against Africans whilst they war against themselves and each other due to hallucinatory whiteness. An African racist first hates herself/ himself then others simultaneously, relentlessly seeking to win the recognition of massa by attacking his own race. Racism constituted by white supremacist discourse and embraced by an African is an instrument of white power to subject that non-white body to power, it cannot build the solidarity of racists amongst Africans, the Volk of massa. Jackson continues to show in his writings with the use of the white supremacist concept of "black" rather than non-white or African the need for purging his mind and worldview of massa white supremacist discourse, which is very much a key part of the discourse of Marx, Engels, Lenin and their historical and dialectical materialism.

Jackson now speaks to the terror that is the basis of the order of power of the prison, which is replicated in the power relations between inmates and groups of inmates as follows: "The picture that I have painted of Soledad's general population facility may have made it sound not too bad at all. That mistaken impression would result from the absence in my description of one very important feature of the main line – terrorism. A frightening, petrifying diffusion of violence is emitted from the offices of the warden and the captain. How else could a small group of armed men be expected to hold and rule another much larger group except through *fear*?" (Jackson 1976 Pg. 46). The order of power of the prison is designed to unleash terror on a daily basis by the officials of the prison on the inmates. In turn, the inmates unleash terror on each other and are always on the prowl for the space to unleash terror on the screws and the screws are perpetually paranoid of this reality, possibility and probability which merits terrorism unleashed to preempt this much feared probability. The product of this order of power is an African nihilist terrorist spawned by the white prison order of power to return to the African ghetto and victimize members of his own race with graphic violence, to either die in the ghetto or return to his source, the prison, hopefully. A cycle which justifies the policing of the African ghetto, but is never used to justify investment in the ghetto to break the cycle, power gets what it wants and the African ghetto with its cycle of graphic violence is organic to Amerikkka.

Jackson now deals with the fact that Africans are overrepresented in the prison population of Amerikkka as follows: "In Soledad's TV rooms there has been murder, mayhem, and destruction of many TV sets. The blacks occupy one side of the room and the whites and Mexicans the other, (Isn't it significant in some way that our members in prison are sufficient to justify the claiming of half of all these facilities." (Jackson 1976 Pg. 47). The African inmate population is of the required size to take and hold against re-conquest by non-African races significant proportions of the specific spaces in the prison defined for the general population, such as half of the mess hall and rec rooms. This is a national minority race so overrepresented in the inmate population thus wielding the requisite mass to conquer and hold space in the prison. The African in the heavily policed African ghetto is then a core strategy of white supremacist social control in Amerikkka. The spawning of African nihilist terrorists in the prisons and letting them loose on the African ghetto is the nitrous oxide that boosts African ghetto criminality to massa desired levels.

Jackson is now trying to wrap his mind around the fact that the prison is broken but no one in authority sees the need to reform and repair it. Jackson is here showing the weakness emanating from his grounding in the discourse and worldview of historical and dialectical materialism for it simply cannot zoom in on power, power relations, the order of power and the discourse of white supremacy in Amerikkka. Nothing has changed for the better since the death of Jackson in 1971, in fact they have worsened with the neo-liberal discourse of imprisonment and incarceration and the private prison industry which is a factory to exploit cheap incarcerated labor at minimal cost in a heavily under-secured environment with a propensity for inmate violence, drug use, rape, murder and theft. The remand and the prisons are overflowing as the discourse of the zero tolerance approach to crime fills the remand, constipates the court system and fills the prison to overcapacity. The system is not designed to rehabilitate period, but it is designed for much more than is expected of it in reference to white inmates in the case of the African in the African ghetto. For this is the enemy race par excellence. Jackson states as follows: "When people walk on each other, when disharmony is the norm, when organisms start falling apart it is the fault of those whose responsibility it is to govern. They're doing something wrong. They shouldn't have been trusted with the responsibility." (Jackson 1976 Pg. 48). "Penologists regard prisons as asylums. Most policy is formulated in a bureau that operates under the heading Department of Corrections. But what can we say about these asylums since *none* of the inmates are ever cured. Since in every instance they are sent out of the prison more damaged physically and mentally than when they entered. Because that is the reality." (Jackson 1976 Pg. 49). The prison serves power, is an instrument of power and penology is a discourse of power. Power rooted in a white supremacist discourse must establish holding pens, concentration camps for the race enemy as it established holding pens for the physically and mentally inferior, termed asylums. Now under the hegemony of white supremacist neo-liberal discourse the asylums have closed and those who would have been inmates previously now roam the streets homeless and with no access to care. Whilst the holding pens for the race enemy continue to expand in spite of budget cuts and the African ghetto is alive well, and kicking even if squeezed by gentrification, it reappears in extensive urban skid rows and for rent trailer parks owned by the massive hedge, wealth and income funds. This is not a democracy, white power accepts no limitations set by the rule of law in this Amerikkka, as Amerikkkan law was always white, for the protection of massa, for shoring up the white order of power locally and internationally. The grave limitations of the discourse Jackson embraced by which to prosecute the African Revolution of Amerika is now revealing its grave and deadly limitations when used by an enemy race to engage with massa which gives massa an unearned advantage at the level of the idea, which results in death of the revolutionaries and failure of the revolution.

December 1964 Letter to his Father

Jackson in this letter to his father is expressing openly his position on the strategy that drove the discourse and methodology of raising him in the African ghetto of Chicago and California of his parents. Jackson states as follows: "If she chooses to occupy the corner set aside for us in this society and be happy with such then let it be. I merely speak of better and different things in a society greater (in my humble opinion) and more conducive to advancement for people of my kind." (Jackson 1976 Pg. 56). Jackson is insisting that his mother is an active agent of massa promoting servility to massa as the only viable path for Africans of the ghetto in Amerikkka. Jackson's mother not only accepts the allocated role of Africans by massa but insists that it is the only viable path for Africans. George and his mother are then at odds with each other as she sees no need for the path George has adopted of the necessity for a revolutionary path for the liberation of the African in Amerikkka. George tells his father in his letter that he, George, is unleashing discourse assaulting the competence of his parents not offering advice to his parents. Jackson continues as follows: "You see I understand you people clearly. You are afflicted by the same set of principles that has always governed black people's ideas and habits here in the US. I know also how we arrived at this appalling state of decadence. You see, my father, we have been 'educated' into an acceptance of our position as national scapegoats. Our acceptance of the lie is consciously based on the supposition that peace can and must be preserved at any price. Blacks here in the US apparently do not care how well they live, but are only concerned with how long they are able to live. This is odd indeed when considering that it is possible for all of us to live well, but within the reach of no man to live long!" (Jackson 1976 Pgs. 57-58). The African for Jackson is servile to massa, accepted his lot in life allotted to her/ him by massa thereby playing the role of the scapegoats of Amerikkka. The servile African is cowed by a deep-seated fear of white power, of the impunity white power wields over the life and death of the African. The servile African fixates on survival, not quality of life where the driving existential concern is keeping alive not how well you live in your servility. The strategy then is to be recklessly pliant, the quintessential African victim of massa who refuses to oppose massa choosing instead to beg massa to save her/ his life from the impunity of white power in exchange for being pliant, subordinate servants of massa. The African in expressing that quest to live long not well continues to shuck and jive massa to this day. The fear of death is the product of the application of systematic, strategic terror against the body of Africans from enslavement to the present to purchase their servility through fear of the terror of death at the hands of massa. This morbid fear of death preempts the capacity to embrace self-sacrifice towards effecting the African revolution in Amerikkka. You cannot make revolution, you cannot liberate yourself from massa without embracing your death as being necessary for the cause. Until this countermeasure develops and engulfs the African population of Amerikkka there will be no revolution. Until then Africans will continue to expect immediate benefits from resisting massa to then use this absence of benefits to voice the need for a return to servility. Jackson now describes this condition of the African as "illusionment" which is in fact delusion spawned by hallucinatory whiteness that is rooted in schizophrenia as follows: "My deepest and most sincerely felt sympathies go out to all of you who are not able to resolve your fundamental problems because of this fundamental lack of spirit. The morass of illusionment has claimed your souls completely." (Jackson 1976 Pg. 58). In keeping with his historical materialist bias Jackson must use disillusionment insisting that you can be taught historical materialist methodology which will remove the cataracts from both eyes enabling the African to "see" objective reality clearly and act on it. The power relation between servile African and massa is much more complex than illusion for it involves delusion arising from the schizophrenia constituted by hallucinatory whiteness, a condition impervious to intervention by historical materialist methodology. A new methodology rooted in the study of power and power relations in Amerikkka is necessary to deconstruct the power relations of the African condition. Jackson says his race so plagued has no soul, no spirit as they are incapable as is to be the vanguard of the African revolution in Amerikkka. Jackson now insists that their soulless, spiritless servility to massa means that before they act to liberate themselves they have to be handed booty from the war with massa arrived at by the actions of others, not them. They are nihilistic to the core unwilling to strive for an ideal, for personal gain and that of their progeny, self-centered gazing on living long to the point of servile paralysis to massa. Jackson states: "but because you and the others of our family have always been close to me whatever successes I wring from the eternal foe you will share. Until I do this I know it is expecting too much for you to be impressed with the ideals I put forward. It's always been this way I imagine. One has to be shown the fruits and feel the rewards of a new or different thing before perceiving its merits." (Jackson 1976 Pg. 58). The African vanguard is not organic to the African masses of the African ghetto, where then is this revolution coming from? Without being organic to the masses this vanguard will then be seduced by the adventurist, nihilist discourse of those who embrace terror as the path to revolution and be chewed up by massa national security apparatus, which they were. Jackson makes it clear that his family exerts no revolutionary consciousness, in fact they exhibit a lumpen worldview where they must first taste the benefits of revolution before they embrace revolution; which is simply an excuse to mask their chronic mortal fear of massa machine to grind them into dust. To have any expectation that George will win booty from engaging with massa in prison on a life sentence and facing a capital murder charge is then George rebuking them, for death was on the cards for George, a gift from massa they continuously hope to evade by being servile.

Jackson now speaks to the action of the member of his family to give him up to the police as follows: "but let me state that I have a singular incapability, which is my strongest point, my first principle. I could never in this existence betray my kind. Love of self and kind is the first law of nature, What N. did to me in 1958 I can never forgive. I can understand why she betrayed me to the whites and can even explain why she thought herself right in doing so, but I can't forgive her because she has not made any effort to change her completely backward sympathies. It is the same thing today with her as it was yesterday. She would betray me a second time if I allowed it." (Jackson 1976 Pgs. 58-59). Will this same said family member of Jackson give him up if he was a notorious gang banger on the run with the proven capacity for multiple graphic killings? Not at all, in fact out of raw, naked fear she will aid George to escape the law and depart from her company. In 1958 George is a soft target which establishes her creds with massa, in the era of the African ghetto organically transformed by the ever-evolving illicit trades George's family member will learn to shut up the hard way. The circularity of the existence as you cannot expect to live long without the income generated to ensure to so do, especially in financial markets neo-liberal capitalism Amerikkka. To live long in this Amerikkka you must have the income to live well to cover the rising cost of housing, medical care etc. Jackson now deals with his mother's practice as follows: "but she failed me bitterly in matters of the mind and spirit. My education she put in the hands of the arch-foes of my kind. This is a betrayal of the worst kind, because of this I've had to learn everything I now know on my own by trial and error. I have almost arrived but look at the cost. I would not be in prison now if she hadn't been reading life through those rose-colored glasses of hers, or if you would have had time and the wisdom to tell me of my enemies, and how to get the things I needed without falling into these traps. She kept telling me how wrong I was and making me feel guilty. All of this I now understand, but again cannot forgive, because she is still doing this same sort of thing!!" (Jackson 1976 Pg. 59). The survival strategy with its discourse and worldview taught to George by his mother and father prepared him for jail, prison, hard time mixed with periods of pursuing the straight life, until death, life/ death in prison or life on skid row. George then was in dire need of a multifaceted socialization system where he was taught the way of organized crime, exposed to an education that exposed him to the knowledge to understand who are his friends and his enemies, and the nature of the order of power of Amerikkka. Since George learnt these realities the hard way he ended up a lifer and died in prison, but what George wanted from his parents they could not give and there was no legacy alive and active in the African ghetto to recruit George and expose him to the knowledges he sought. Just getting by on a daily basis could not outfit the parents George needed to enable him to evolve into a revolutionary of the African revolution within the African ghetto. Resistance will beget resistance and without consistent inter-generational resistance there can be no production of revolutionaries free of prison sentences. When you insist that you must live long but will not emphasize living well out of fear of losing your life you have constituted a nihilist culture predicated on paralysis at the level of the idea for fear that action will only earn you death, whilst you pursue long life in a living hell rooted in chronic deprivation and endemic violence, which naturally is anathema to long life. To embrace this as normality is in fact schizophrenia.

December 1964 Letter to his Father

George, again brings up his relationship with his mother as follows: "Mama sent me a card with a picture of some white people on the front of it. I guess she just can't perceive that I don't want anything to do with her white god." (Jackson 1976 Pg. 59). Does George reject the white massa god or theism in all its forms of expression? Jackson now presents his discourse of the white man and his civilization as follows: "The commotion, the violence, the struggles in all these areas and many more spring from one source, the evil and malign, possessive and greedy Europeans. Their abstract theories, developed over centuries of long usage, concerning economics and sociology takes the form that they do because they suffer under the mistaken belief that a man can secure himself in this insecure world by ownership of great personal, private wealth. They attempt to impose their theories on the world for obvious reasons of self-gain. Their philosophy concerning government and economics has an underlying tone of selfishness, possessiveness, and greediness because their character is made up of these things. They cannot see the merit in socialism and communism because they do not possess the qualities of rational thought, generosity, and magnanimity necessary to be part of the human race, part of a social order, part of a system." (Jackson 1976 Pg. 60). Jackson has deconstructed massa and is insisting that what separates massa from the other races of the world is their embrace of the discourse of capitalism, which has constituted a worldview and a human value system which is self-centered, narcissist, individualistic in its desire for personal wealth, power, influence etc. Jackson's embrace of historical materialist methodology does not and cannot afford him the necessary tools to deconstruct the massa condition in its complexity. For capitalism is itself subordinate to the overarching discourse of white supremacy, manifest destiny and white entitlement. The hegemonic discourse of white supremacy constitutes the racist agenda of exercising race hegemony over the non-white races of Amerikkka and the world, not capitalism per se. The organic demands of capitalism are in fact in the daily exercise of power in Amerikkka and the world are routinely sacrificed to the demands of exercising the hegemony of white supremacy. The daily power relations between the discourses of white supremacy and capitalism have to be continually deconstructed in order to plot the terrain of their interaction thereby exposing the fault lines, conjunctures which enable the assault of sustained human action. Jackson did not develop this box of tools in his evolution as a revolutionary being much too orthodox in his approach to historical materialism, an approach that drove worship not critical assessment necessary to framing the relevant, critical discursive approach to the African Revolution in Amerikkka. Demonizing massa is simply not fit for purpose, what is necessary is a penetrating deconstruction of her/ his discourse and worldview of white supremacist capitalist world hegemony which is necessary to formulating and unleashing our countervailing discourse with its worldview that liberates us at the level of the idea whilst dismantling the white world order of power.

February 1965 Letter to his Mother

In this February 1965 letter to his mother George Jackson continues his assault on his mother's values as an African woman of the African ghetto of Amerikkka. In this ongoing assault George accepts no blame for his role in being a lifer after pleading guilty to stealing 70 USD from a gas station. Massa played him for his reckless approach to daily life on massa plantation of California. Jackson states as follows: "It is clear that you don't love me when you refuse to aid me in the only way you can, the only way I expect! By telling me I am right and that I have your blessings." "There are things brewing now that could ruin you completely if, when they break, you are in sympathy with wrong. Robert is the same way, he pretends or he may earnestly not feel the effects of the circumstances I expect to explain. He is sympathetic to wrong. But I can overlook him more readily because of his almost complete lack of mental training." (Jackson 1976 Pg. 62). Jackson writes to his mother informing her that she does not love him as she gives him no support he needs in prison which she can afford to give. Jackson wants her affirmation of his revolutionary credentials and she refuses to give it. Jackson insists that both his mother and father sympathize with wrong which is why they cannot support his position in prison. Jackson is insisting that his both parents are servile to massa not committed to African revolution, hence he has no support from them which he wants. Jackson now states that it is a question of betrayal as follows: "When I consider my own experiences bought at the cost of these terrible years, supplemented in love and concern by your own experience and learning, what am I to think that something is radically wrong, that I am being betrayed. The question in one grave proportions to me. I cannot stress this too clearly." (Jackson 1976 Pg. 62). Jackson is on his own, without the support and affirmation of both parents which speaks to betrayal, selling him down the river to massa. The probability of betrayal by both parents arises from their sympathy for wrong, their servility to massa at the level of the idea. Jackson continues as follows: "I feel that you have failed me Mama. I know that you have failed me. I also know that Robert has never held an opinion of his own. You have influenced his every thought ever since you have known him. You have always have had the running of things. You have done him a disservice. You are doing Jon a disservice now. You are a woman, you think like a bourgeois woman." (Jackson 1976 Pg. 62). Jackson reduces a complex issue of individual consciousness of self in the context of a racist, segregated capitalist social order to a Marxist label of bourgeois woman. His mother is woman, African, has no direct relation to capital and she is poor and according to Jackson is the dominant force in the power relations of the nuclear family unit of married parents with their children in a residence. How can Jackson's mother think like a bourgeois woman when she is unemployed, poor and African? What she can be is servile to the white order of power by making choices from a menu of choices that his mother is convinced is strategically necessary to her survival and that of her family. This is not thinking as a bourgeois woman, this is thinking as a non-white, poor, unemployed woman in a white supremacist capitalist social order with its order of power which relentlessly exhibits instances of white power for you to police your non-white poor self into servility. Jackson's mother and father are servile to massa, they are incapable of thinking as bourgeois women and men, and this failure to distinguish the gulf that separates both positions arises from a devotion to Marxist orthodoxy and a problem with a strong African woman dominating a household where males are in the majority. Jackson is now insinuating that a dominant African woman who thinks as a bourgeois woman socialized him and his brother Jonathan to be servile as her. This grave failing of his mother then set him on his path to life in prison for stealing 70 USD in a gas station. Jackson now continues with his position on his mother insisting that a woman cannot socialize men to deal with the male order of power of the social order as follows: "This is a predatory man's world. The real world calls for a predatory man's brand of thinking. Your way of viewing the world is necessarily bourgeois and feminine. How could I, Roberts, Jon, or any of the men of our kind accomplish what we must as men if we think like bourgeois women, or let our women think for us. This is what's happening all over this part of the world. Robert should have been stronger, should have had more time and freedom of movement. So should Grandfather and Great Grandfather." (Jackson 1976 Pg. 62). No woman can socialize a male child to be effective in the social order dominated by predatory males, women can never be predatory males exerting power, hence incapable of socializing predatory males. But women socialize men, interact, procreate, live with, and are victims of predatory males, they are therefore engaged in power relations with predatory males all their lives. Their knowledge of men is then vitally necessary to the daily survival of women and a necessary input to socializing men from serial killers to African revolutionaries in Amerikkka. Jackson is riding his personal hobbyhorse seeking to turn it into revolutionary maxims for his flawed discourse and worldview of historical materialism. Why blame your mother for your father's weakness as a male rather than praising your mother for filling the breach created by the reluctance of your father to be the central power in the family unit? What is obvious from this tirade addressed to your mother is the weakness of your knowledge base that drives your discourse and worldview of the African revolution in Amerikkka. You are working towards an African revolution against massa but you are using white discourse that cannot see, nor gaze upon the white supremacist capitalist order of power of Amerikkka. A white discourse that cannot see, nor gaze upon the nexus between idea, discourse, worldview and the order of power of a social order which subsumes production. Jackson can only see production and you are what you are because of your relation to production, refusing to recognize that production can never be absolute of the realm of the idea hence the order of power. The idea of the centrality of production is incapable of articulating the order of power which seduces and convinces the individual to comply, to be servile, to obey; that seduces the African in Amerikkka to embrace hallucinatory whiteness as normality, order and progress. Jackson was incapable of such analyses given his devotion to his flawed historical materialist discourse, and therefore not much different from his mother and father qualitatively. Jackson insists that his mother and father sympathize with wrong, but he is mouthing revolutionary maxims as absolute constituted by a discourse and worldview that cannot gaze upon the white supremacy within its discourse and the grave inability to discern what is power and the terrain of power and power relations in this context. Jackson then shows sympathy for what is unable to constitute an African revolution in Amerikkka at the level of the idea.

August 1965 Letter to his Father

Jackson is engaging with his condition of life in prison where awareness, knowledge and revolutionary consciousness have brought no relief from the weight of his existence as follows: "Why can't I rid myself of the sorrow and emotion that awareness has brought me. I get rid of the self-destructive force of error and ignorance only to be torn and miserable by what I discover. It happened that I knew all along that some imbalance did exist, or I'll say a few imbalances existed, that disallowed me from progressing further in my development." "The struggle is almost over, my friend, complete and harmonious development can be mine, everyone's. Only one fourth of the sorrow in each man's life is caused by outside uncontrollable elements, the rest is self-imposed by failing to analyze and act with calmness." (Jackson 1976 Pgs. 84-85). Jackson's experience was one in which awareness did not emancipate him from sorrow, emotion and rage for understanding is not revolutionary change, that is a praxis that reflects the nature of the individual physically, mentally and emotionally. Jackson learned through affixing the gaze on his self, he realized that he was plagued with imbalances of the mind, imbalances at the level of the idea that only he could rectify. Jackson has now embraced the necessary methodology to remove these imbalances: rigorous self-analysis and the implementation of the requisite praxis with calm, surety of purpose, conviction and action. This methodology of Jackson, which he insists erases personality imbalances and unleashes the necessary calm in which the revolutionary must analyze and act, cannot master a grave core problem he faces in the process of analysis and action with calmness. This is the inability of the discourse of historical materialism, which he accepts as absolute, to unravel the order of power and the power relations that impact on a daily basis the African in Amerikkka. With his absolute in train he has no working idea of white supremacy and the specific order of power it constitutes in Amerikkka to render servile the African minority at the level of the idea. With this persistent ignorance how then can Jackson free himself from hallucinatory whiteness using the absolute of historical materialism? His beloved absolute kept him until his death in prison servile to massa at the level of the idea for his revolutionary maxims were incapable of constituting the African revolution of Amerikkka.

February 23, 1966 Letter to his Mother

Jackson now presents his embrace of the reality that he is engaged in a war with the order of power of massa prison which is waging an intense war on him to either render him servile or dead, or both for its power is not limited by law. Jackson states as follows: "I have learned something by the experience: never again to look for mercy, never again to expect or hope for justice, never to look for quarter without strings being attached. The last illusion has been shattered; I know the way from here; ask no quarter of fate and give none." (Jackson 1976 Pg. 94). Jackson reveals that he did embrace massa sleight of hand distraction that is democracy. He actually believes that he is a juridic subject endowed with rights by a supreme Constitution, he actually believed and expected to be a recipient of bourgeois democracy, which is the product of his hallucinatory whiteness. He, as all non-whites seeking the affirmation of massa ,actually believes that he is human with rights in massa democracy refusing to accept and embrace massa white supremacist rejection of the humanity of all non-white peoples. This is delusion as you cannot speak of African revolution in Amerikkka and hold on to expectations that are not forthcoming from massa. But your historical materialist discourse does speak of the progressive nature of the bourgeois as they set in train developments which will inevitably end in the proletarian revolution. Bourgeois democracy is then a necessary, compulsory step in the path to proletarian revolution, which ensures that those believers in the absolute embrace bourgeois democracy. This discourse cannot deconstruct the order of power of white supremacist colonial, imperial capitalism, especially in Amerikkka. Jackson's admission of his embrace of bourgeois democracy in

Amerikkka reveals the depth of hallucinatory whiteness that pervades the psyche of the non-whites in Amerikkka.

Jackson now presents a telling analysis of the African condition in the ghetto as follows: "Right here at this juncture of time we as a people have nothing, absolutely nothing but each other, some fresh air, the blue and gold of day and silver at night, a clean conscience, and the promise of cloudless days to come. But some do not enjoy these things enough, don't understand the nature of our circumstances and commit unpardonable crimes, unnatural crimes that must in the end bar them from partaking in the benefits that is planned for tomorrow. In the end a requiem will be sung over the whole vast complex of disorder." (Jackson 1976 Pg. 94). African criminality in the ghetto has no consciousness of the white supremacist order of power that relentlessly wields arrested development, deliberate underdevelopment, poverty and ignorance to render Africans servile to massa and his Amerikkka. African criminality simply cannot evaluate the position of its race in this white order of power and determine a methodology of its emancipation. African criminality victimizes its own race as if it is the majority race of Amerikkka exercising hegemony over the other races, it kills, mobs and robs its own kind as if they are the ruling oligarchy of Amerikka. The strategy of African criminality does not reflect the position of the African in the white supremacist order of power of Amerikkka. African criminality is then intensifying the arrested development, underdevelopment and ignorance that plagues the African of the ghetto in the white supremacist order of power of Amerikkka. This has worsened with the rise of the illicit trades and Gangland of the illicit trades where African criminality has heightened the level of graphic violence unleashed on its fellow Africans, whilst intensifying the extraction of value from the already poor and underdeveloped inmates of the African ghetto of Amerikkka, which ultimately benefits massa order of power and wealth accumulation processes worsening the underdevelopment of the African of the ghetto in the 21st century. African criminality is then a potent fetter, hindrance and roadblock against all attempts at self-liberation by the African from massa order of white supremacist power.

March 3, 1966 Letter to his Mother

Jackson now gives an analysis of the existential condition of the African marginalized to the ghetto in Amerikkka with specific reference to the gender roles adopted by the marginalized Africans as follows: "You are right of course in what you contend. The black woman in the past few hundred years has been the only force holding us together and holding us up. She has absorbed the biggest part of the many shocks and strains of existence under a slave order. The men can think of nothing more effective than pimping, gambling, or petty theft. I've heard men brag about being pimps of black women and taking money from black women who are on relief. Things like this I find odious, disgusting you are right, the black men have proven themselves to be utterly detestable and repulsive in the past. Before I would succumb to such subterfuge I would scratch my living from the ground on hands and knees, or die in a hail of bullets." (Jackson 1976 Pgs.94-95). Under the slave order of white power in Amerikkka the enslaved African and Mixed-race woman was conceptualized as: labor power, reproductive power/ womb, and an object of desire, massa sexual entity who existed to satiate desire of all white males on the plantation and other males with the permission of massa. The African drivers serving massa on the plantation were given permission by massa to rape at will as white men enslaved women on the plantation, rape was then cultivated as an instrument of massa/ white power over the body of the non-white woman. Under the order of power of enslavement and emancipation the non-white woman was the only constant, the foundation upon which survival strategies were built in the face of the assault of white power. The non-white males developed a slate of survival strategies, one of which is African criminality, which has expanded its dominance of daily life in the ghetto with the rise of the ever evolving drug trade and its dependent gangland in the ghetto. From the 1990s to the present the ever evolving drug trade and its gangland have mounted the most potent assault on the structure of non-white female survival strategies with female addiction, dislocation, underdevelopment, and violence all emanating from the ever strengthening call of the streets with gangland in charge and its impact on female headed family units and households. These female headed households of non-white women in the ghetto are now faced with: the impact the neo-liberal economy has on their ability to earn the level of income needed to fund the necessities of life as shelter, medical care, food and clothing on a daily and long term basis. The impact of the illicit trades and gangland on the family units seen in the violence within the family, male members of the family incarcerated or killed at a young age, some leaving dependent children who must now be responsibility of the family unit, the involvement of females of the unit embracing the game which impacts the family as is the case with its males but the death or imprisonment of these female members with children, a greater burden is placed on the unit than in the case of its males, as females are the prime caregivers of the children they and their female relatives bring into the world. The African woman as the foundation of the survival strategies of the race marginalized in the urban ghetto has been under attack since the 1980s by ever evolving African criminality in the ghetto and the assault on the African female headed household is ripping apart this family form rendering it incapable of responding effectively to the assault of massa and his drivers using the instrument of massa power of African criminality in the ghetto. It is now strategically necessary for African women and men in Amerikkka to now formulate and unleash a new survival strategy to deflect the assault of African criminality on the African family forms of the ghetto.

Jackson continues as follows: "My hat goes off to every one of you, you have my profoundest respect. I have surrendered all hope of happiness in this life to the prospect of effecting some improvement in our circumstances as a whole. I have a plan, I will give, and give of myself until it proves our making or my end." (Jackson 1976 Pg. 95). How can you be an agent of change in your community, in your race in Amerikkka when you are a lifer in prison, the target of massa whose only path out depends on convincing the parole board of your fitness for freedom? Jackson then paid with his life whilst incarcerated which presents the potent dichotomy between the gnawing need for African liberation and embracing African criminality as a sustainable survival strategy. African criminality can only heighten the underdevelopment of the marginalized African in Amerikkka, not their liberation. Jackson continues by speaking to the issue of the men of the race once again as follows: "The men of our group have developed as a result of living under a ruthless system a set of mannerisms that numb their soul. We have been made the floor mat of the world, but the world has yet to see what can be done by men of our nature, by men who have walked the path of disparity, of regression, of abortion and yet come out whole. There will be a special page in the book of life for the men who have crawled back from the grave. This page will tell of utter defeat, ruin, passivity, and subjection in one breath, and in the next, overwhelming victory and fulfillment." (Jackson 1976 Pg. 95). In this Manichean duality Jackson describes as the personality of the African male in Amerikkka there can be no wholeness, no liberation and as long as the race is trapped in the inter-generational underdevelopment of the ghetto and is placed on the spectrum of trauma what Jackson is seeing as wholeness is in fact schizophrenia. Therapeutic healing is only possible with the liberation of the African race from the ghetto, from the white supremacist order of power in Amerikkka. Trapped in this white order of power there can be consciousness of liberation, what is to be done at the level of the individual, but joint action is demanded in order to liberate the race, which leaves the conscious individual a castaway within the space inhabited by his race. Jackson will remain liberated at the level of the idea in prison, in hostile territory under the control of massa on his plantation: prison. Jackson is then internally and externally alienated from his race locked away in massa plantation at his mercy. This raises the pressing question of Jackson's relevance to the African revolution seen in the tendency in his writings to forsake revolutionary realism for revolutionary posturing, postulation and adventurism. One can say that his life history, his guilt, regrets and blame he ascribes to his parents' socialization of him coupled with his incarceration which is a daily threat to his life whilst simultaneously he is absent from the struggle on the ground on a daily basis, drives this tendency to embrace desire as reality on the ground. Daily life in this grinding reality leaves Jackson one viable option: to die in prison at the hands of the guards, a martyr for the African revolution. Jackson has then to transform the legacy he bequeathed to himself with his embrace of African criminality by turning it into an opportunity for revolutionary heroism, martyrdom. In this action there is healing, consciousness, liberation at the level of the idea, but wholeness is lacking which is only attainable in a social order driven by a new order of power, a non-elitist, non-discriminatory socialist order of power.

March 20, 1966 Letter to his Mother

In this letter the contradiction between a christian mother preaching to an imprisoned revolutionary son who has made it clear repeatedly to his mother his rejection of her faith is manifest. Jackson presents his position to his mother as follows: "I have explained my feelings to you many, many times, so I won't go any further with this. If children being blown out of this existence while attending church services, men being lynched for a gesture, colonialism, the inquisition, and H-bombs haven't affected you, nothing I say here can help you. If you could live my life one week and see the things I see, feel the pain I feel, and die a little bit each day as I do, all your illusions and apparitions would vanish." (Jackson 1976 Pg. 96). In March 1966 there is no evidence of a truce between Jackson and his mother on the contentious issue of his mother's embrace of Christianity coupled with her unyielding conviction to proselytize him. Jackson insists that if his mother had to live every day in massa prison her servility to Christianity at the level of the idea shall be destroyed, such is the nature of barbarism unleashed by Christians on inmates. Jackson is in fact being a doctrinaire historical materialist triumphalist, not a revolutionary realist. Jackson believes that the objective material conditions of his daily life shall falsify christian discourse, thereby contributing to a liberationary environment; whereas the christian will bolster their faith by insisting that their criminality must be punished in this life, which is an opportunity to repent and attain salvation. This is a wasted exchange of discourse which speaks to the potency of hallucinatory whiteness plaguing both sides of the debate. Jackson continues the debate with his mother as follows: "All my life now you have told me about European gods and European Christians who were supposed to be knowledgeable. When do you plan to say something that will help me? You may not know any better, if not, I am wrong in saying what I have, but find it hard to admit that my mother could be so insensitive to the truth?" "You do not have eyes to see, ears to hear, and a brain to interpret, so I'll tell you and kind of outrageous story." (Jackson 1976 Pg. 96). Both Jackson and his mother are then investing in conversion of the other to their personal worldview, both refusing to work out terms of engagement premised on mutual respect of each other's worldview. This state of continued warfare now prompts Jackson to state as follows: "Ordinary people, the mediocre, need to feel or believe in something greater than themselves. It gives them false security and it makes them feel that help may be forthcoming. This is self-delusion in the extreme. I cannot partake in any foolishness." "When I need strength, Mama, I reach down within myself. I draw out of the reserves I've built – the necessary endurance to face down my opposition, I call on myself, I have faith in myself." "I place no one and nothing above myself." "If there is a god, Mama, he hates me and I'll have to resist what he is doing to us." (Jackson 1976 Pgs. 96-97). For Jackson, persons who embrace Christianity are ordinary, foolish and mediocre, servile at the level of the idea to massa white god, dependent and incapable of self-reliance, hence of being part of the African revolutionary vanguard. Jackson is speaking as an arrogant historical materialist atheist, a triumphalist, for self-reliance does not make a revolution, it is revolutionary realism and he shows very little in this continuing sterile debate with his parents. Jackson now returns to his favorite whipping boy in his ongoing war of words with his mother as follows: "All my life, Mama, I've had to work things out for myself. I've had help from no quarter. I've been alone now for a long time. This is why I have had so much pain and trouble. Robert gave me nothing. You gave me god and that horrible church. Even god managed to take something away from me. I have nothing left but myself." (Jackson 1976 Pg. 97). Jackson insists that he is the victim excoriating the manner he was socialized by his parents, but he refuses to practice self-criticism for he did everything in his power to pursue his career in African ghetto criminality and pay the price thereof in massa prison system. His parents made the wrong choice of their survival strategies in life especially after becoming parents in the ghetto, which he exacerbated by following suit by immersing himself in criminality in both Chicago and California, which heightened rather than diminished the worldview and the survival strategy he adopted and practiced. It was incarceration that triggered the embrace of the new path of the African revolutionary, a member of the African revolutionary vanguard but incarcerated where he will die. The choices he made and pursued in the past affects his impact as an African revolutionary as he is a lifer incarcerated and his repeated attempts to blame his parents for his choices are not credible. He insists that he is now self-reliant, self-focused but he wages this internecine war with no illustrated penchant to practice self-criticism.

January 23, 1967 Letter to his Father

Jackson is now expressing his realization that he must now work the system in order to win parole to exit the California prison system and in so doing he expresses the realization that the parents he berates were never imprisoned, never had to deal with the system hoping for parole. An African revolutionary of the African vanguard without freedom of movement because of his embrace of criminality in massa social order. Jackson's life in 1967 is then a contradiction in terms which demands on a daily basis that he chooses between death at the hands of massa instruments of prison power liberated at the level of the idea or death whilst being servile to massa, his death being the only constant, given. Jackson states as follows: "Although I would very much like to get out of here in order to develop a few ideas that occurred to me – although I would not like to leave my bones here on the hill. If it is a choice between that and surrendering things that make me a man, the things that allow me to hold my head erect and unbowed, then the hill can have my bones. Many times in the history of our past – I speak of the African here in the US – many times we were presented with this choice, too many times, too many of us choose to live the crippled existence of the near-man, the half-man. Well, I don't care how long I live. Over this I have no control, but I do care about what kind of life I live, and I can control this. I may not live but another five minutes, but it will be five minutes definitely on my terms." (Jackson 1976 Pg. 106). Jackson refuses to surrender for the sake of living, to be the living hollow man, the nigger, the less than man for the quality of one's life trumps living as a servile nigger to/ for massa. He would now like to play the system with the hope of departing prison on parole, but he will not trample on his liberated state to pursue parole, he would rather die in prison. Jackson's choice is made easier by the signals being sent by massa that within the California prison system, Jackson is in fact marked for death by any means necessary. Even before playing the win a parole game from the parole board Jackson is already faced with the likelihood of being charged for the death of a prison guard at Soledad prison. Jackson is charged with murder of the prison guard along with two other inmates, transferred to San Quentin prison where he was killed in a supposed escape attempt. Massa made it clear to Jackson that his servility is of no importance as there was no realistic hope of parole for him, what is on the agenda is his death in prison by any means necessary, judicial and extra-judicial. This was the message sent by the white supremacist national security apparatus to the entire structure of the African revolution in Amerikkka. Jackson's embrace at a tender age of African ghetto criminality as a viable alternate lifestyle placed him on the path to lengthy incarceration in the California prison order of power with all its attendant risks to life and limb and its impact on the race trapped in the ghetto. What changed Jackson's course of his prison life was his epiphany during incarceration where he embraced Marxist methodology as the means to the African revolution in Amerikkka. The nature of this epiphany and his association with the Black Panther Party whilst incarcerated was in fact his death wish and it was fulfilled by massa. Jackson was then testing his commitment to personal and social revolution using massa order of power with its certainty of death in prison as the catalyst for revolutionary change, stasis or regression on a personal level. Jackson's commitment to revolutionary change at a personal, race and social level then assured his death in prison, his was then personal success rewarded with death which ensured that he was spared a long life in prison having to bear the assault every single day of life until death in prison, which includes the quest for parole and the politics of parole denied repeatedly by either the parole board or the ruling politicians when the parole board grants parole.

January 31, 1967 Letter to Frances

Jackson is writing his sister and presenting his plan to now engage with the prison system in an attempt to gain parole as follows: "I must now start doing all that is humanly possible to get out of prison. I can see great ill forecast for me if I don't find some way to extract myself from these people's control." "I don't mind dying but I'd like to have the opportunity to fight back." (Jackson 1976 Pg. 107). Jackson knows and accepts his inevitable demise in prison, but he is seeking parole to engage with the white order of power external of prison which encompasses death by cop or by black ops. Jackson wants then the freedom of movement to wage war on the white order of power and die in the course of this urban guerrilla engagement. Jackson desires death attained in battle where he is armed and waging war, not as powerless meat in prison which is his fitting way to die as a revolutionary rather than a cornered, a caged animal in prison. Massa had no intention for Jackson to exit the prison system via a parole granted, with his capital murder charge for the death of the guard at Soledad prison and his transfer to San Quentin prison his death in prison was now assured.

March 1967 Letter to his Mother

In this letter to his mother Jackson is now expressing his position on the discourse of non-violence of King as follows: "You know I have grown very, very tired of talking, and listening to talk. King and his kind have betrayed our bosom interests with their demagogic delirium. The poor fool knows nothing of the antagonist's nature and has not the perception to read and learn by history and past events. In a nonviolent movement there must be a latent threat of eruption, a dormant possibility of sudden and violent action if concessions are to be won, respect gained, and the established order altered. That nonviolent theory is applicable in civilized lands among civilized people, the Asians and the Africans, but a look at European history shows that anything of great value that ever changed hands was taken by force of arms." (Jackson 1976 Pg. 110). A leader of the African revolution in the west who is mindful of what massa is cannot seriously expect an instrument of non-violence to engage successfully with massa. Massa has no practice of dealing with non-white races non-violently, without colonial and neo-colonial imperialist domination. Jackson then insists that King is plagued with "demagogic delirium" where he is a demagogue in his leadership of the movement plagued with delirium for he is not strategically engaging with massa, he is engaging with a massa that he created as real, the massa of King's desire not what massa is in action. This delirium is expecting massa to respect your non-violent resistance in a democracy whilst denying yourself the right to self-defense against the state. You kill the demagogue, the movement collapses, it was already out of steam with its demagogue in search of a new rallying cry, leaving its followers unshaken in their servility, hallucinatory whiteness and trapped in the ghetto. Jackson's position is then the choice of a non-violent strategy is viable when you are dealing with civilized non-white races, but pure lunacy when dealing with massa in your quest for liberation from massa hegemony.

Jackson ends this letter by providing another instance of his belief that revolution is an absolute, hence inevitable, in a social order dominated by capitalist relations of production. This is the product of his embrace of historical materialism which drives the desire for change into blind revolutionary adventurism rooted in revolutionary denial, not revolutionary realism. Jackson states as follows: "You know the world. The depressed peoples of the world are very shortly going to grow tired of being wooed and lulled into passivity and quiet endurance by chromium and neon lights." "They'll come out of their coma with a blood lust and justified indignation for social injustice that will sweep the asphalt right from under the empire builders. This is the only reason I hang on. I want to be in the vanguard." (Jackson 1976 Pg. 110). Jackson's expected mass action that indicates their rejection of their daily existential reality did not happen under capitalism, there was then no African mass action in Amerikkka to constitute the African revolution with the vanguard in Amerikkka. The failure of the mass action to materialize empowered the white supremacist national security apparatus to identify, surveil and silence the vanguard of the African revolution in Amerikkka.

March 26, 1967 Letter to his Mother

Jackson continues his internecine warfare with his mother as it is plainly apparent that they are both uncompromising and unrelenting in their positions. Jackson states as follows: "Why did you think me insane for wanting a new bicycle instead of the old one I stole piece by piece and put together? Why did you allow us to worship at a white altar? Why even now, following tragedy after tragedy, crisis after crisis, do you still send Jon to that school where he is taught to feel inferior, and why do you continue to send me Easter cards? This is the height of disrespect you show me. You never wanted me to be a man nor Jon either. You don't want us to resist and defeat our enemies. What is wrong with you, Mama? No other mama in history has acted the way you act under stress situations. I won't be a good *boy* ever." (Jackson 1976 Pg. 112). Jackson is insisting that his mother is massa driver for the family refusing to learn from the mistakes made with George she is now willingly repeating with Jon his younger brother. Jackson is charging his mother with hypocrisy as she had no trouble with him stealing a bicycle piece and piece but had one with Jackson wanting a new bicycle which must be purchased legally. For Jackson his mother is so deeply socialized by and servile to massa she unquestionably follows the pathway of massa, without reflection on its efficacy and applicability to African life in the ghetto. In so doing his mother's intention willingly or unwillingly is to castrate the African males of the family, relentlessly assaulting their rebellion against massa demanding their servility. Jackson states that she punished her father, his maternal grandfather, his father Robert, his brother Jon and himself with her disrespect for George's position and beliefs being readily apparent. For George her undying embrace of Catholicism and her unfailing attempt to socialize her sons into Catholicism regardless of how Catholicism dealt with the non-white in Amerikkka. For George his mother is the living embodiment of the castrating African woman plagued with hallucinatory whiteness that has rendered her servile to and in the service of massa, she is then massa driver for the family. George again repeats to his mother that there is no surrender for him and according to him his mother is deaf, unchanging. The lesson afforded by the Jackson family is then potent for revolution is not an absolute, a given, as consciousness it has to be built from the ground up and massa is in every space of the African ghetto as he resides in the mind, worldview and discourse of every African in the ghetto relentlessly seducing them to police themselves into good, servile niggers.

March 27, 1967 Letter to his Mother

George Jackson is now playing the game of hard/ soft with his mother or both mother and son are exhibiting signs of schizophrenia triggered by hallucinatory whiteness. George Jackson states as follows: "Please don't take what I expressed in my last letter too seriously. I was feeling extremely bad. Try to relax; the mental depression you are presently gripped by comes from a very common cause, particularly amongst us blacks here in the US. As a defense, we look at life through our rose-colored glasses, rationalizing and pretending that things are not so bad after all, but then day after day – tragedy after tragedy strikes and confuses us, and our pretense fails to aid or dispel the nagging feeling that we cannot have security in an insecure society, especially when one belongs to an insecure caste within this larger society. I believe sincerely that you will be very unhappy and perplexed woman for as long as you try to pretend that you have anything in common with this culture, or better, that this culture has anything in common with you, and as long as you pretend that there is no difference between men, and as long as you try to be more English than the English, while the English ignore your attempts and use our humility to their advantage." (Jackson 1976 Pgs. 113-114). Jackson has re-launched his assault on his mother utilizing a therapeutic approach to his mother's report of her depression. Jackson is insisting to his mother that her depression is the product of her hallucinatory whiteness as she relentlessly pursues the unattainable quest of being white at the level of the idea, discourse and worldview but trapped in a non-white body which can never be white in spite of chemical bleaching of the skin, straightening of the hair and cosmetic surgery, for your genome is your destiny. The core, central driving reality of Jackson's mother is her desire to be white, which results in her use of white supremacist discourse to affirm her humanity and to demand recognition and affirmation from massa. She is servile at the level of the idea to a discourse that cannot recognize her humanity, it must relentlessly deny her humanity, render her servile because she is inherently inferior belonging to an inherently inferior race. Trapped in her non-white self she must relentlessly denigrate herself in order to be white, acutely hate herself in order to save herself by being white at the level of the idea. The rational outcome of this process of self-abuse and hate is schizophrenia, depression, bipolarity driven by self-hate expressed as nihilism as a survival strategy in Amerikkka. Jackson posits that the white supremacist order of power in Amerikkka has now constituted groups within the social order by combining class with race where non-whites occupy a common position to capital which has evolved into a caste position as your physical features are an indication of your relation to capital, hence the African, Hispanic and Native ghettos of Amerikkka. You walk with your inferior soul attached to your non-white body nourished by the self-hate that drives the non-white nihilism.

Jackson continues by dealing with the appropriation of blame in his life as follows: "Do you know who I blame for what has happened to me the last 25 years, and before to my ancestors? I would be narrow-minded indeed if I blamed any of you, my folks. I do not blame you for not teaching me how to get what I wanted *without getting put in jail*, nor do I blame myself. I was born knowing nothing and am a product of my total surroundings. I blame the capitalistic dog, the imperialistic, cave-dwelling brute that kidnapped us, pulled the rug from under us, made us a caste within his society with no vertical economic mobility. As soon as all this became clear to me and I developed the nerve to admit it to myself, that we were defeated in war and are now captives, slaves or actually that we inherited a neo-slave existence, I immediately became relaxed, always expecting the worst, and started working on the remedy." (Jackson 1976 Pg. 114). The grave question is if Jackson's remedy is in fact efficacious to the task of liberation of the African in Amerikkka? Jackson speaks of the capitalist imperialist cave dwelling brute but there is nothing forthcoming on the specific white supremacist nature of the discourse of this imperialist, capitalist cave dwelling brute. There is no explanation of how in a capitalist democracy a slave, a captive is emancipated and turned into a neo-slave, a race based, defined and expressed caste in a caste system that constitutes the social order which contains all non-whites in Amerikkka. Jackson does not speak to the discourse of white supremacy, the order of power and its instruments of power utilized to maintain nonwhite race inferiority, underdevelopment, arrested development and placement on the spectrum of trauma that plagues the non-white races in the social order of Amerikkka across time/ space. The limitations of Jackson's discourse of liberation in Amerikkka is the product of his embrace of the discourse of historical materialism as an absolute, as truth that transcends space/ time meant that he was unable to embrace the alternate discourse of Frantz Fanon, only playing lip service to it. Jackson's discourse of liberation of the African in Amerikka is then unfinished, flawed and unable to deconstruct the nexus between power, race and capital in Amerikkka.

May 9, 1967 Letter to his Father

In writing to his father Jackson now presents his strategy of making the best of his imprisonment by using its routine of daily life incarcerated to develop his remedy for the liberation of the African in Amerikkka. But what is his relevance to daily life in the ghetto when Jackson has no freedom of movement nor speech in prison and what is the applicability of this remedy formulated in prison to conditions in the ghetto? Jackson states as follows: "With the pursuit of food and shelter relegated to the state, I have been able to channel all my thoughts to important things, significant things. So I attempt to bend this experience to our benefit rather than let them weaken and destroy me, as they would like. You are aware, that these places, this one in particular, will either bring out the best in an individual or ruin him entirely." "But I can promise nothing, the future holds no surprises for me. I expect anything, including trouble, especially trouble, considering the times. I have adopted, these last several months, a new attitude, however, that will limit the scope of my troubles." (Jackson 1976 Pg. 115). Faced with the reality of life in prison without parole Jackson concludes that it is now strategically necessary for him to exploit his jail time in order to work on and perfect his remedy for his race in the Amerikkkan ghetto. But he remains cognizant of the prison reality of endemic violence and he, Jackson being hunted by forces within the prison seeking his demise, which given the order of power of the prison presents a grave threat to his life. His quest for the remedy and his propagation of that remedy within and without the prison will merit action against him in prison, judicial and extrajudicial political action.

May 21,1967 Letter to his Father

Jackson in this letter to his father reveals the extent of the deterioration of his eyesight in prison and the tension that is present in the marriage of his parents. Jackson states as follows: "I am holding off the ill effects of the concentration camp as best I can. It seems a losing battle, however, I've had to take to wearing glasses of considerable strength due to failure of my eyesight. Living in this constant half-light, I guess." (Jackson 1976 Pg. 117). The progressive deterioration of Jackson's eyesight in prison has increased his vulnerability to attack as an inmate thereby heightening his trauma. Jackson now deals with the marriage problems of his parents as follows: "I am sorry that you and Mama don't make each other happy. European-Anglo-American brainwashing is at the bottom of this. Those empty pseudo-middle class ideas that we have adopted from the opposition make us unhappy in the same way the middle class itself is unhappy. Then too when poverty comes through the door, love leaves by the window. We all know who has caused our poverty. I have experienced the same thing with women and men. All the women I've had tried to use me, tried to secure through me a soft spot in this cutthroat system for themselves. All they ever wanted was clothes and money and to be taken out to flash these things. I no longer have time for such small ideas and small people. Blacks that I have met here who exhibit such characteristics I disdain and ignore. The same with any woman I may have when I get out. She must let me retrain her mind or no deal." (Jackson 1976 Pg. 118). Jackson is again trapped by his embrace of the discourse of historical materialism as an absolute where he is now incapable of gazing upon the specificities of African life in the ghetto that makes it distinct, separate and apart from the daily life of the white American middle class, especially of the suburbs; given the blindness of the discourse of historical materialism to a white supremacist order of power with its instruments of power in a capitalist social order. Jackson is then denying the specificity of daily life of the African in the ghetto which separates the race from the daily life of the white middle class in the suburbs and in so doing denying that a specific white supremacist order of power with its instruments of power impact all non-whites in Amerikkka simply because there is an organic need to ensure white power over non-whites as they pose a threat to white entitlement, power. Jackson with his servility to massa discourse of historical materialism cannot gaze upon and accept as real this white supremacist order of power in a "rational" capitalist order that is Amerikkka, he has then to insist that what has the African in the ghetto unhappy also has the white middle class in the suburbs unhappy also but these white folks are not niggers, devoid of entitlement and subject to only white social control as niggers. Niggers are the living embodiment of white supremacy expressed as a soul enveloping an inherently inferior human rendering them docile because of their inherent inferiority. The white middle class of the suburbs is inherently superior to the nigger, they exert control over the nigger and the entitlement they enjoy vis-a-vis the deprivation of the African in the ghetto obligates them, white folks, to police themselves into obedient white citizens of Amerikkka. The refusal of the white citizens to exert social control over the African and to police themselves relentlessly to ensure they are the white citizens Amerikkka demands, will collapse the white order of power of Amerikkka giving rise to the power of the non-white races in Amerikkka. Fear of a black planet. Jackson's discourse of the predatory, castrating African woman with reference to gender relations with African males which springs from his position that he is a victim of such African women is in fact setting up the African women as the villain of the piece, as he is yet to excoriate the action of African males in the ghetto with regards to gender and family relations, especially their approach to their duty as fathers. Jackson's strategic position is that the nature of his relations with Africans is determined by the value system they espouse, which means his gender relation is premised on his dominance and her servility at the level of the idea. Is his revolution then a male dominated affair, male demagogy? Jackson does not explain the refusal of the African male to abide by male gender roles assigned according to white middle class values; whilst insisting that all is wrong with the African in the ghetto and middle class whites especially in the suburbs arises from white middle class values. Jackson is then taking complex social realities and reducing them to the simplistic economism of the discourse of historical materialism. Jackson is then seduced by a white discourse which cannot grapple with and deconstruct the specificities of African daily existential reality in Amerikkka. He remains a captive of massa at the level of the idea.

May 28, 1967 Letter to his Father

In this letter to his father Jackson betrays the grave strategic fault, weakness, blindness of historical materialism which has now influenced Jackson's methodology of dealing with persons he considers inferior. Jackson has no concept of power and power relations at its micro level, the personal and interpersonal, hence he interacts without a long term strategic goal, without guile to attain that goal. This is so as he continues to view reality in terms of Manichean dualities which means he is still thinking in keeping with massa model of the idea, discourse and worldview, in spite of his proclaimed remedy he is still afflicted with hallucinatory whiteness. Jackson states as follows: "I really cannot imagine how anyone can stay detached and complacent for any period and maintain social contacts on any level. It no longer surprises me, but I still find the general acceptance and widespread practice of the more deranged products of Western culture disturbing. Prying, nosy, schizophrenic, domineering, psychoneurotic people press you from all sides. They remain in a continual state of agitation always on the basis of doing something maniacal!" (Jackson 1976 Pg. 119). Jackson is insisting that with consciousness there comes the inclination to separate oneself from the masses as western capitalism constitutes mentally disturbed populations. What is the then the possibility of revolution, of personal liberation at the level of the idea in the west? The vanguard of the revolution has then to be adept therapists but what happens in the cases of social orders that evolved from colonial to neo-colonial domination by western imperial capitalism? Why then the only surviving anti-capitalist revolutions occurred and survived in these countries, the paramount example being the People's Republic of China? This problematic arises from Jackson's uncritical embrace of the discourse of historical materialism and its absolute of revolution. As long as revolution is an absolute for Jackson, he can continue to hold on to massa discourse and still expect revolution. But history has shown that revolution is not an absolute, never inevitable, it instead has to be purchased with a relevant practice whose success is never assured. But Jackson cannot personally deal with such uncertainty hence his embrace of the myth of the absolute.

For Jackson capitalism is the dynamo that makes revolution inevitable in spite of constituting persons with mental health issues, which means that capitalism is in fact the absolute. Jackson states as follows: "Capitalism, I believe, the capitalizing on the next man's labor, on the next man's weakness, has contributed greatly to the development of the anomalous 'Western man' ; capitalism, competitive enterprise, man competing against man for the necessary things, for status symbols, for power to repress his competition and secure his personal well being to exercise his ego, his fancy." (Jackson 1976 Pg. 119). Jackson cannot discern from history the nature of pre-capitalist social orders which indicates what is the product of discourse that is common to all human civilization, and the specificities of the western capitalist social order that ensures it is unique, inherently different. There was exploitation before capitalism, as there was power and power relations before capitalism, as there was the discourse of white supremacy before capitalism. Jackson is then propagating myth when he insists that capitalism is the root of all evil in the history of humankind which demands the second absolute to erase capitalism and the mental illness it constitutes: revolution, but Jackson's revolution failed. He has then formulated a remedy that is myth as he is addicted to historical materialism, and has to save it from itself, just another white idea internalized by a non-white seeking wholeness, but instead rewarded with the schizophrenia of hallucinatory whiteness. Jackson now speaks to massa agenda critically but failing to admit that he is still subservient to massa at the level of the idea as follows: "the odd man is trying to convey to us that we must adjust ourselves to his warp, that we must learn to be more like him, that because we're not we're backward, underdeveloped, unsophisticated! This is strange and contradictory." (Jackson 1976 Pg. 119). Jackson purports that his remedy will liberate us from massa oppression, from the inferiority complex, the mental illness constituted by domination by capitalist massa. But it cannot liberate us from hallucinatory whiteness as Jackson's remedy is rooted in massa Manichean duality of ideas, which includes white supremacy. Jackson cannot gaze upon the existential condition that plagues dominated non-whites and formulate an idea that liberates us from it as Jackson never liberated himself from the hegemony of historical materialism at the level of the idea. Jackson, in spite of his remedy, is still plagued with hallucinatory whiteness arising from reading Frantz Fanon to discover historical materialism affirmed rather than its critique.

Jackson now states as follows on his criminality: "I am deeply sorry that I ever told a lie, stole anything, robbed and cheated at everything - mainly because it is so much like conforming in Western ways." (Jackson 1976 Pg. 119). Jackson now takes white supremacy and retools it as non-white supremacy to defeat and replace white supremacy and its order of power, this is his remedy. Jackson is insisting that evil, criminality is the preserve of massa and his capitalism, which means that all non-white non-capitalist social orders were noted for their value systems that drove human behavior that was exemplary, evil is then white and capitalist and good non-white. Jackson has then taken the white Manichean duality and reversed it to constitute his remedy, but that cannot be the remedy as the core discourse remains white supremacy, but you are now using it as justification for non-white triumphal racism again focused on the inferior non-white self. This is lunacy for you are servile at the level of the idea whilst Jackson is insisting that this is the remedy, personal liberation. In his embrace of historical materialism Jackson cannot deconstruct the very nature of his hallucinatory whiteness, all he can do is strive to be as massa.

July 13, 1967 Letter to his Father

In this letter Jackson writes on his historical destiny which he will not walk away from as follows: "I'm sorry that I won't be able to conduct my relations with the world as you would have me conduct them. I see the big picture where you may never have. I think I see the larger historical concept in its full detail. The obligation you felt toward us, I feel toward history. I must follow my call. It is of great importance to me that you understand this and give your blessing. I don't care about anyone else." (Jackson 1976 Pg. 121). Jackson has a historic destiny to attain, one which he alone understands in its entirety as all adherents of historical materialism should, for it is only utilizing historical materialism can you understand the dynamics of history in Amerikkka and act upon this understanding to attain history. George is not interested in seeking the blessing of his mother, only that of his father thereby continuing his assault on his mother at the time of conflict in the marriage of his parents. This is yet another indication of Jackson's uncritical orthodox embrace of historical materialism as a cult belief system with all its frailty.

July 15, 1967 Letter to his Father

In this letter Jackson is writing about his daily existential condition in prison which raises the question of how can he attain his historical destiny when he is incarcerated in prison? Revolution is a game of mobility in specific sections of a population who affords the revolutionary space to build revolutionary momentum in conjunction with the masses. How can you execute this praxis in prison and embrace criminality as a survival strategy that leads to long episodes of imprisonment. Jackson states as follows: "I'm just locked down and forgotten." "the officials have preconceived notions about my behavioral patterns and consequently look for the worse in me." "Control over the circumstances that surround my existence is of the first importance to me. Without this control, or control in someone else's hands. I am forever insecure, subject at all times to the whim and caprice of the man in control, and you and I know how whimsical some men can be." (Jackson 1976 Pgs. 122-123). How can you expect to exert self-determination, to be a sovereign individual under the rule of law when you are a lifer in prison after being found guilty of a criminal charge? Your means of exit are: win a victory in a court of appeal, die in prison or "earn" a parole from massa. You now have the prison reputation of an enraged African ghetto male and will be defined as a grave threat to prison staff given your propensity to inmate violence. Your revolutionary practice in prison has now earned massa agenda to silence you in prison by any means necessary and in prison this is done with impunity. Your desire does not match the power relations of prison to which you have been consigned by your actions until death. You are not in prison as punishment for revolutionary practice, you are there because of your embrace of criminality by African ghetto males in Amerikkka.

July 23, 1967 Letter to his Father

George is writing to his father and once again he returns to the issue of the quality of relationship he has with his mother. In writing on this topic to his father George makes statements on the African woman of the ghetto in Amerikkka that again illustrate his concept of the problematic African woman in Amerikkka as follows: "I understand her and all black women over here. Women like to be dominated, love being strong-armed, need an overseer to supplement their weakness. So how could she really understand my feelings for self-determination. For this reason we should never allow women to express any opinion on the subject, but just to sit, listen to us, and attempt to understand. It is for them to obey us, and not to attempt to think." (Jackson 1976 Pg. 125). In Jackson's revolution there is a sexual division of labor, it is led by men and women follow, women are commanded to keep silent in this church of revolution for men are the head of the woman. George has apparently swallowed massa science of the second sex uncritically as we pick up the trail of Freud's discourse of female sexuality, penis envy and their relationship with the male. George is insisting that the unregenerated African female and the embrace of African criminality by the male are the grave threats to the African revolution and they both interact in a power relation constituting the African male as a career criminal rather than a career revolutionary. The unregenerated African female is then an instrument of massa oppression who is central to the embrace of the African male of criminality. The African female is then George's fall girl within the African ghetto communities.

July 28, 1967 Letter to his Mother

In this letter to his mother George now engages with his mother on the issue of his atheism versus her catholic beliefs, Jackson states as follows: "The theory of an existing and benevolent god simply doesn't make sense to anybody who is rational. A benevolent and omnipotent god would never allow such imbalances I see to exist for one second." (Jackson 1976 Pg.

125). One who believes in the existence of god is then irrational as the discourse of massa theocracy makes no sense. An omnipotent, benevolent god will exert direct rule, exercise power over the world thereby obviating the chaos that is daily life in the world. Jackson's problem with massa theocracy is an omnipotent benevolent god who does not exert hegemony on a daily basis over his creation, having abdicated hegemony to man which has unleashed imbalance across time/ space which drives the history of humankind on this earth, not god's power. An African of Amerikkka, especially an African woman who has embraced this god, is worshiping a weak, ineffective powerless god who has effectively handed hegemony to massa over the world, you are therefore worshiping massa, denying the African revolution in Amerikkka. An African woman who worships this massa god is unleashing harm on the African race as she is especially constituting male children to embrace African criminality, deny the revolution, thereby maintaining massa hegemony over the African in Amerikkka. George the criminal reflects the socialization of his mother, George the African revolutionary is his rebellion against his mother and massa, his creation of self-determination.

Jackson now presents his position on what are his needs as follows: "I seriously fail to understand when someone speaks of my soul, but I do know what my body needs. I know what my body incessantly craves. Gratification of these is what I must pursue. As a woman I can understand your being naturally disposed to servitude. I can understand *your* feelings but what I can't understand is why you would have me feel the same, considering that I am a man. Why you have always attempted to implant womanly ideas into my character?" (Jackson 1976 Pg. 125). Jackson insists that since a woman is constituted to be dominated by men which means that women cannot socialize real men, revolutionary men, and women are incapable of revolutionary action for the liberation of women unless instructed and led by revolutionary men. Since Jackson is an ultra-orthodox historical materialist then production has defined roles for the two genders that subjugates the woman to the man, from hunting and gathering to capitalism. Jackson is then proposing functionalist historical materialism where revolution is organic, functional to production where it takes on a unique dimension with the rise and evolution of capitalism. Jackson is intent on building a discourse of women, especially African women in Amerikkka, which blames them for the existential condition of the race in the ghetto. This is simply an assault on his mother blaming her for his active embrace of African criminality in Amerikkka postulating that his revolutionary practice is his liberation from her enslaving action that impacted his mind in Amerikkka to embrace criminality. In his agenda against his mother Jackson is fundamentally racist, immersed in self-hate which he expresses as the inferiority of the African woman, to mask his hallucinatory whiteness. Jackson now addresses the issue of christian love insisting that the African cannot love what under-develops the race and it is not an effective instrument to protect the race from the assault of massa as follows: "Love has never turned aside the boot, blade, or bullet. Neither has it satisfied any hunger of body and mind." "What I do feel is the urge to resist, resist, and never stop resisting or even think of stopping my resistance until victory falls to me. Extreme, perhaps, but involved is my self-determination, and control of the environment upon which my existence extends, and the existence of my father, mother, Debra's and Penny's sons, and all that I feel tied to. We are in an extreme situation. (Jackson 1976 Pg. 126). Love is not the basis of resistance to massa, hence it cannot be the basis of African liberation in Amerikkka. Those who insist to Africans that they must be immersed in love, that love is liberating are in fact instruments of massa endlessly seeking the servility of the African in Amerikkka. African women, as his mother, must then be relieved of the task of socializing African males into the revolutionary tradition. Given the propensity for African males in the ghetto to evade the duty of raising and supporting their children with a single or multiple women, which male will then embrace this strategic task? How can Jackson attain and exert resistance, self-determination, and enjoy victory whilst imprisoned for life making him a charge of massa, institutionalized by massa subjugating his body to both legal and extra-judicial assaults? George Jackson is in an extreme situation which finally abrogates his life, his brother also loses his life through revolutionary adventurism, resistance is not necessarily liberationary in the majority of instances in Amerikkka as it only affords the liberation of death, the release from this life under the hegemony of massa. Jackson brought then no liberation to his family in this life or to himself, but given his embrace of criminality death in prison was his legacy to himself. Jackson continues on being a victim of massa as follows: "I am his victim, born innocent, a *total* product of my surroundings. Everything that I am, developed into because of circumstances and situational pressures. I was born knowing nothing; necessity and environment formed me, and everyone like me." "I can never delude myself into thinking that I love my enemies. I can hardly do any worse than I was doing now; if worst comes to worst that's all right." (Jackson 1976 Pg. 126). Jackson is then not the product of love in action which demands that he adopt the discourse of love in turn. Jackson is the product of massa ghetto not his mother's socialization, it is relation to production in the ghetto which seduces him to embrace criminality in the ghetto. To end the embrace of criminality in the ghetto you must then remove massa from power and dismantle his ghetto. Jackson in this text makes this statement: "Did I colonize, kidnap, make war on myself, and neglect myself, steal my identity and then being reduced to nothing, invented a competitive economy knowing that I cannot compete? Sounds very foolish, but this is what you propose when you place the blame on me or on 'us,'" (Jackson 1976 Pg. 126). Jackson is positing that the very existence and potency of the African ghetto as an instrument of massa power is that it socializes an inmate, the African, who is alienated from modern and post-modern capitalism by massa order of power which means she/ he cannot compete in an evolving intensely competitive capitalist economy of Amerikkka, thereby posing to inmates of the ghetto criminality as a viable survival strategy across time/ space. The African has then to be burdened with arrested development in order to sustainably underdevelop the race across space/ time which demands the use of white supremacy, its discourse, worldview and its instruments of power to justify an order of discrimination that sustainably under-develops the race. Capitalism does not need this, this is not organic to capitalism but it is organic to white supremacist capitalism. This is the distinction Jackson was incapable of discerning and its unique dynamic, for capitalism must have a hegemonic discourse of the social order and its order of power as this discourse is not organic to capitalism but the product of the power relations of the social order. Jackson is then hinting at the African ghetto in Amerikkka being an internal colony of Amerikkka, the African ghetto is then demanded by white supremacist capitalism not capitalism per se, but was there ever capitalism per se? No, there is white supremacist North Atlantic capitalism which demands an order of power to render non-white races servile and there is socialism with Chinese characteristics rooted in a capitalist economy which has no racist order of power. In both instances the social order framed by an idea, a discourse and its worldview that enables capitalist relations of production are mutually exclusive, even contradictory but yet capitalism is facilitated.

September 12, 1967 Letter to his Father

In this letter to his father Jackson critiques the strategy of non-violent protest, protest of the mouth, of his era which resonates to the reality of the 21st century in Amerikkka. Jackson states as follows: "You should know about protesting with the mouth. It never avails us anything but grief. I no longer do so in any form, but it indicates naivete. It means that subconsciously one may still be looking for justice or humanity from places that we have ample proof of it not existing." (Jackson 1976 Pg. 129). The embrace of protest of the mouth divorced from protest of the hands means that there is no strategy dictated by the discourse of the idea of change, protest, action, of revolution in Amerikkka. The African in Amerikkka engaging in only protest of the mouth is delusional as they actually believe that they are citizens of the republic and are entitled by law to enjoy the entitlement of massa guaranteed in the constitution. There is then a minority of white folks who are preventing them from enjoying their entitlement as African citizens of the republic. The disenfranchised African simply has to protest only with the mouth, tie their hands behind their back and the inherently good, christian white majority will embrace and affirm the African by removing the obstacles in their path to enjoy what is theirs according to the constitution, deadly delusion driven by self-hate. Delusion triggered by the grave fear of massa and the white power wielded on the body and mind of the African in specially designated African spaces of underdevelopment, marginalization and violence, the internal colonies for all non-white races of Amerikkka.

November 1967 Letter to his Father

In this letter to his father Jackson now expresses in detail the nature of his alienation from his father as follows: "This last word from you in Jon's presence convinces me that that we can never reconcile our differences. I never realized that I was a source of embarrassment to you, I thought most blacks, especially those of our economic level, understand vaguely at least, that these places were built with us in mind, just as were the project houses, unemployment offices, and bible schools." (Jackson 1976 Pgs. 138-139). George has experienced, in the presence of his brother Jon, the embarrassment of his father over his imprisonment, George has now recognized that there is no hope for reconciliation and peace with his parents during the duration of his imprisonment, he is doing hard time assailed without and within. Jackson's parents are exhibiting and holding on to their servile worldview of hallucinatory whiteness for dear life as all what they define themselves by are under assault by the family ties to imprisoned George, which George is holding on to at all costs. Is Jackson's father embarrassed by his incarceration for criminality or his evolving revolutionary position since imprisonment? George keeps relentlessly insisting that it is because of his revolutionary credentials which exposes the servility to massa of his parents. Jackson continues as follows: "Life has failed me. People I have had a right to expect something of, in the past, have failed me. And I fail myself almost every day." "Your inability to understand and support me puts me at a loss, but I cannot allow this to influence my course. I must follow my mind. There is no turning back from awareness. If I were to alter my step now I would always hate myself." "I would die as most of us blacks have died over the last few centuries, without having lived." (Jackson 1976 Pg. 139). Having attained awareness, George is now, finally an African alive and aware in Amerikkka, he is finally living even though imprisoned. Jackson's parents are then applying pressure on George for him to walk away from living and return to being a dead nigger though alive, whereas George is insisting that he will seek death in prison though alive for the first time in his life father than surrender again, return to being an nigger, banish awareness and be of the walking dead of his race. George's parents are then adept at socializing criminals, niggers who live but are never alive as they are simply not human having embraced massa discourse of the nigger. George has now had his epiphany and has made his final choice: awareness, life and death by the hands of massa openly rejecting the servitude of his parents to massa, refusing to work out terms of endearment with their son George.

January 1, 1968 Letter to His Father

George speaks to confinement in this letter and his strategic response devised to cope with it as follows: "Confinement in this small area all day causes a buildup of tension. The unavoidable consequence is stupidity, a return to childish behavior, overreaction. I refuse to let myself be punished with stuff like this. Locked in jail, within a jail, my mind is still free. I refuse ever to allow myself to be forced by living conditions into a response that is not commensurate with intelligence and the final objective." (Jackson 1976 Pg. 144). George is a lifer in prison because of the specific manner he responded to his living conditions by embracing criminality as his survival strategy. In prison he has now learnt that he once again is faced with the challenge of his living conditions and how he responds to these conditions. To respond to imprisonment as he responded to his living condition in Chicago and California is not feasible and is not in keeping with his new life strategy of self-determination, liberation and the African revolution in Amerikkka. George the lifer in prison now has intelligence, strategic direction and consciousness. George continues as follows: "This will apply even more on the other side of the wall, out there where you are. What if there was nothing on earth that could be taken from me which would result in my discomfort. What if a person was so oriented that the loss of no material thing could cause him mental disorganization? This is the free agent. He is nameless, faceless, emotionless, loveless. He is without habit, without the weakness of the flesh. He travels light and only in the company of those who like himself prize self-determination above baseball and beer. Only the free agent can win for us the necessary control over the direction of our unrewarding lives. You should know that I only do what I think is best, and most appropriate. I'm a man with few alternatives." (Jackson 1976 Pg. 144). George is using daily life in prison in order to perfect himself as the living embodiment of the free agent which is the foundation and building block of the revolutionary vanguard of the African revolution in Amerikkka. George has no choice in this matter as he lives a daily life with few alternatives present, namely: die in prison, be killed in prison or win parole from the board of parole. George has to either now walk his talk and die in defiance or surrender in servility and die a servile captive African of massa. George is presenting his model, himself as consummate free agent of the African revolution but George is imprisoned, this free agent has no practice in the ghetto, external of prison walls. Jackson affords no evidence that his praxis is in fact replicable on the ground external of prison walls. Jackson is positing an individual with a practice rooted in a moral order of revolutionary behavior constituted by a revolutionary moral order of power. Jackson has then a revolutionary discourse, its worldview, order of power with its instruments of power which constitutes a revolutionary moral being with its hegemonic value system. Jackson's free agent is detached having rejected desire conditioned by massa, replacing it with revolutionary desire which places self-determination in this life above living life for living sake. Death in the pursuit of self-determination, revolution is a given expected and sought as this is the means to break the back of race servility in the quest to simply live, survive not to enjoy life and generate wealth in your lifetime. How does detachment as a practice dismantle the discourse of hallucinatory whiteness? It cannot! George is proposing detachment as the instrument with which to build revolutionary practice but the discourse he embraces cannot deconstruct and dismantle white supremacist Amerikkkan capitalist discourse as it sees only relations of production as the motive force of history, of social orders. White supremacy exists only because it serves capitalism, not the other way around, ideas exist then, only when they serve production. But the discourse of white supremacy has evolved in the North Atlantic from pre-capitalism to capitalism and through the various evolutionary stages of capitalism which raises the question of ideas being independent of production whilst being specific to civilizations, epochs of a civilization independent of production. The formulation of ideas, discourse and worldview in any civilization rooted in a social order must be grappled with in the context of power and power relations in a social order where the order of power must be deconstructed in order to articulate the nexus between idea formulation, power, power relations and hegemony of an idea over the social order. Power must be rooted in a discourse in pursuit of hegemony or exerting hegemony, by which members of the social order are seduced by it to police their action in keeping with the idea. The need to seduce Africans to police themselves in keeping with the discourse of the nigger is an issue of power and power relations, with production being an excuse forwarded by the materialists which keeps power masked, hidden from scrutiny vital to a revolutionary process.

June 29 1968 Letter to Georgia

George is writing to his mother and he is optimistic of winning a parole from prison from the board, failing to understand that massa has no intent to release him from prison until dead. George states as follows: "I'll be out of here soon, perhaps in eight or nine months. I'll have eighteen months clean when I go to the board in December. You know that I have my time in. That's what they want, time and clean conduct." (Jackson 1976 Pg. 162). Massa wants from George Jackson much more than time spent in prison without charges laid by the prison administration, he wants him leaving prison feet first only, which was accomplished in August 1971 at San Quentin prison.

Jackson now deals with the nature of persons constituted by the social order of the USA as follows: "those that we meet in the US are generally of a single type. By and large they are all fools, intellectual non-persons, emotional half-wits. Status symbols, supervisory positions, and petty power motivate their every act. Personal, individual, financial success at any price is their social ethic, the only real standard upon which their conduct is built." (Jackson 1976 Pg. 163). Jackson is once again presenting his analysis of the Amerikkkan social order and the nature of the persons constituted by it, indicating the folly of embracing production as the absolute of North Atlantic capitalist social orders. The value system Jackson describes is rooted in white supremacist humanism, which insists that the white race is the master race thereby entitled to dominate nature and all non-whites to the material and ideational benefit of the white race. White supremacist humanism demands an order of power with its instruments of power that exalts the white race whilst it abases and dominates all non-white races of the world. The inherent superiority of the white race has to be made manifest in the material differences between the white race and non-white races in the daily life of the social order. White superiority has to be relentlessly indicated by white entitlement, white power in every single instance of the daily operation of the social order. This system of apartheid has to be erected and maintained in a democracy under the rule of law which demands relentless investment in an order of power that will render the non-white races of Amerikkka servile and the whites forever content. Any changes to the white and non-white sides of the equation throw Amerikkka into anarchy that beckons civil war, as Amerikkka is today in an undeclared state of civil war.

Jackson now deals with the case of the African in Amerikkka as follows: "For us blacks in particular this is a nightmare proposition. When this standard, this criterion for the measurement of individual merit and worth in this society is applied to us, measure against our standing or holdings, we cannot help but come out with a very low opinion of ourselves. From the womb to the tomb this plays in our minds. *We are not worth more than the amount of capital we can raise.* That is why you see blacks pretending to be doing all right." (Jackson 1976 Pg. 163). Jackson is describing the impact of the white supremacist humanist apartheid order of power which must punish the African for being non-white in a white Amerikkka relentlessly to ensure the sustainability of white entitlement across time/ space in Amerikkka from 1776 to 2023 and thereafter. Endemic deprivation within the non-white races of Amerikkka is simply an indication of the nature and potency of white entitlement in Amerikkka. This has nothing to do with production as an absolute, this is racism applied to a multi racial social order that must be policed and managed according to white supremacist humanist discourse. Jackson now deals with the nature of the white supremacist assault on the African and its effects on the African in Amerikkka as follows: "And again with blacks this whole thing goes even deeper. No man or group of men have been more denuded of their self-respect, none in history has been more terrorized, suppressed, repressed, and denied male expression than the US black." (Jackson 1976 Pg. 163). In Amerikkka, the nigger is central to the white supremacist humanist project as the nigger is constituted by white supremacist discourse as the living embodiment of the grave threat posed by the non-white races to massa. The nigger is massa bogey man, the very personification of black evil in the heartland of white Amerikkka. With emancipation in 1865 a multiplicity of strategies emerged to deal with this black threat. Those from the ex-slave owners insisted on denying the African the rights of a free person, which were all summed up with the system of segregated living. The conquering states of the union would provide the potent lesson to the old slave owners of the confederacy on the necessity of ensuring a free servile African limited to urban spaces reserved for them in which segregation will be expressed by the quality of daily life, its housing, education, wage levels, high unemployment, criminality etc. in urban spaces into which the African is crammed and languishing. This has nothing to do with production, this is deliberate design by governance to protect massa from the black peril which is heightened by the criminality of the African. From the limited menu of choices afforded the urban African, choices made to intensify the fear of the evil nigger thus justifying the continued apartheid, policing, criminalization of and the grinding poverty of these urban marginalized spaces. The victim is victimized, blamed and punished for their skin, for their skin is their sin in Amerikkka, forever placed on the spectrum of trauma.

Jackson in this letter to Georgia deals with the reality of his younger brother Jon as follows: "Jon's *real* problems can only be solved through community action: a massive, total, mutual effort. We are not surviving and cannot survive as individuals or as family units; we must get together. And then too, what can Robert give Jon in his present state of mental development? He can only benefit from contact with people he might learn from." (Jackson 1976 Pg. 164). Jon is free from prison, on the outside and pursuing the craft of revolutionary activism, with George imprisoned Jon cannot depend on George for the daily guidance and illumination he is in need of and the family cannot fill the breach as Jon has rejected the worldview of his parents. George is of the opinion that their father is particularly inadequate for the task at hand of leading Jon on his path of development with minimal hiccups. George then insists that persons as Jon must have a community containing groups of relevant individuals providing support to young searchers as Jon. But massa and the criminals of the ghetto will attack such groups relentlessly as they challenge the hegemony of massa and his lumpen over the ghetto. On August 7, 1970 Jonathan Jackson died from gunshots received in the course of breaking up a hostage situation which he precipitated via an armed invasion and hostage taking situation in a Marin County courthouse, California. This was Jon's revolutionary adventurism in action which cost him his life with no death blow to massa hegemony delivered. Jonathan then threw down the gauntlet for George who followed in August 1971.

August 17, 1968 Letter to his Mother

Jackson is this letter to his mother is once again expressing his rejection of her discourse and its worldview and stating his alternate discourse of the African woman of Amerikkka as follows: "It can all be reduced to the simple fact that we want you to be yourself, secure within your *reality*. Why should my woman have to follow someone else's criterion of right and wrong, beauty and ugliness? Please believe me, Mama, the truly ugly thing is the pretending, faking it, imitating – monkey – see, monkey – do – adoration of the repulsive." (Jackson 1976 Pg. 165). Jackson is spelling out what the servility of the African woman to massa entails. This servility means that the servile African woman is an obstacle in the path of the African revolution in Amerikkka which demands formulation of a programme of liberation of the African woman by severing their dependence on massa at the level of the idea. The servility of both African women and men at the level of the idea is rooted in their seduction to embrace a discourse which problematises their genetic condition, their human capacity and humanity and implementing ideas, action and a menu of choices including physically changing their bodies in a bid to be white in thought, words, deeds and physically. The intent is to have Africans forever problematizing themselves and forever seeking to perfect this less than adequate self into a perfect white self; but this is impossible for you can never be white. Hence you are burdened for life with hallucinatory whiteness and its nihilistic self-hate. Jackson continues his engagement with his mother as follows: "On closer examination, what you are saying is that black women standing naked and natural are ugly or less than beautiful. From this nakedness and natural posture the *only* way for her to remotely resemble anything beautiful is to bleach and straighten her hair, and hang her limbs with clothing designed in Paris, London, the US, and other parts of the barbarian world. For you there is only this one standard of beauty, the Western standard. I revolt against this absurdity." (Jackson 1976 Pg. 165). African servility at the level of the idea is built on the foundation of self-hate as the only state worthy of being desired is the white state of existence, and since non-whites can never be white genetically, we are condemned to hate our natural selves whilst desiring an existential condition that is unattainable: the outcome must be nihilism rooted in schizophrenia with self-destruction, self-flagellation, self-immolation, for what we desire is unattainable.

Jackson is focused on the African woman and the task involved in liberating themselves from subjection to massa at the level of the idea which points to his discourse of the problematic of the African woman in the African revolution of Amerikkka. Jackson states as follows: "The women's role though will go unfulfilled because you, folks don't seem to be able to change, or reestablish the values and cultural entities of our antecedents." (Jackson 1976 Pg. 165). Jackson's problematic is the supposed embrace of the African female of desire massa has prescribed for the liberation of the African from her/ his inferiority, making the woman the fall guy of the African revolution in Amerikkka. The African male has to liberate himself first, then work on the intractable resistance of the African woman he is faced with, whilst under the constant attack of massa. Blame has to be assigned to the African woman in Amerikkka with the failure of the African revolution. George is now taking his war with his mother as the model that informs the strategy to de-fang the threats posed to success. Jackson is then insisting that the African woman is massa fifth columnist in the race with no such analysis of the African male, thereby denying the reality on the ground.

Jackson now speaks to what is reality and dealing with it as follows: "Reality is the key. In order for you to be intelligent, as you state it, you must like Western music, clothes, food, architecture, Western education, religious superstition, pseudo-philosophy, and Western ideals. St Augustine!! What kind of example is that? The reality is that we are a caste at the bottom of class society, the only group that has built-in factors (physical characteristics) that prohibit any form of socioeconomic mobility. We are totally disenfranchised, the whipping boy, the scapegoat, the floor mat of the nation. (Jackson 1976 Pgs. 165-166). This reality of desire for massa prescription for wholeness and humanity applies to all non-whites under the hegemony of massa in the past and present, colonial and neocolonial imperial domination. Jackson stresses on the African woman in his war with his mother which can translate into a sexist chauvinist position on the ground. In seeking explanation Jackson creates the discursive concept of the African in the order of capitalist class society is in fact a caste by dint of their race denied upward mobility. Jackson is trying to renovate historical materialism to save it from itself and its inadequacies to grasp reality on the ground. The Africans are a caste in Amerikkkan class society because of their race, but what of the absolute of production and the African? To posit that production cannot override the impetus to place Africans in a caste because of their race and constitute all Africans as members of class society means that production is not an absolute, hence revolution is also not an absolute in Amerikkka. The absolutes of historical materialism have then to be discarded and the gaze applied to power relations and the order of power in Amerikkka and the position of the African in this order. Jackson in 1968 was then in transition in the evolution and development of his discourse of revolution in Amerikkka. He was faced with the choice of recognizing the inherent flaws of his discourse and work on rectifying it or holding on to historical materialism as an addiction. Jackson now deals with his refusal to shuck and jive to win the affirmation of massa, to be "liked" by massa as follows: "I don't want anyone to accept me. As an individual I don't worry about my future. I know my ideals will prevail, so I don't worry about that. They can't harm me, because the reality is that I have nothing to lose but my chains." (Jackson 1976 Pg. 166). The path to personal liberation commences with the first step of self love, of embracing our non-white selves and rejecting the dependent, servile need to have massa affirm our whiteness, our imitation white humanity which they promptly withdraw when faced with an uppity non-white or just for the fun, sweetness, desire of exerting power over us. Walking the path of liberation heightens the need for distance to be placed between you and massa, distance which is created by exposing the falsity of massa discourse, purging it and replacing it with non-white revolutionary discourse as personal liberation is the basis of national liberation, emancipating yourself, mind and body from servility to massa at the level of the idea must precede and be the basis of national liberation. Jackson writes of reality in this letter to his mother and in ending he faces up to the driving reality of his life: massa will not give him the means to leave prison legally and alive as follows: "It is clear they are not going to give me a chance. You were right, that is exactly what they fear. Just because I want to be my black self, mentally healthy, and because I look everyone who addresses me in the eye, they feel that I may start a riot anytime." (Jackson 1976 Pg. 166). Massa cannot and will not give space to an African who is indicating personal liberation, emancipation from the hegemony of massa at the level of the idea. This person presents a grave threat which must be neutralized for the good of the white order of power. Jackson cannot leave jail alive nor can he continue to live in prison as he has the power and influence to precipitate unrest amongst the African prison population wherever he is housed. Jackson is then a non-white who is no longer fit for purpose in Amerikkka, he has then to be erased for the good of the white order of power.

December 3, 1968 Letter to his Mother

In this letter to his mother Jackson ventilates on all that is wrong with his race as illustrated by their discourse, worldview, values and behavior as follows: "I can't say just what the problem is. We all seem to be in the grip of some terrible quandary. Our enemies have so confused us that we seem to have been rendered incapable of the smallest responsibility. I see this same irresponsibility in every exchange with my kinsmen here, irresponsibility, or mediocrity at best, disloyalty, self-hatred, cowardice, competition between themselves, resentment of any who may have excelled in anything, heads bowed, knees bent to some man or some stupid idea of a god." (Jackson 1976 Pg. 167). Jackson insists that his race in Amerikkka exhibits irresponsible behavior patterns which are the product of the history of Africans in Amerikkka as a caste marginalized in a class society to deny its members upward mobility. This behavioral irresponsibility is the product of a personal quandary, personal confusion, personal mediocrity, disloyalty, cowardice, self-hatred, competition between members of the race impacted by being jealous of those of the race who have excelled leaving the rest behind and being servile to massa at the level of the idea, shucking and jiving to earn the affirmation of and favors from massa. Graphic gun violence amongst race members where you are literally killing members of your race as the enemy which places you on the radar of massa prison system where African males are overrepresented in the national prison population of Amerikkka. Jackson is pointing to but cannot deconstruct, an existential condition that is applying a discourse with its worldview of African nihilism in Amerikkka which constitutes a menu of choices of action to those who wield this discourse and its worldview which can only be irresponsible, of no strategic value to African survival in Amerikkka as it is nihilistic, thereby ensuring the sustainable servility of the African in Amerikkka to massa. African liberation in Amerikkka will only be realized when this African narcissist culture is destroyed and replaced by a revolutionary action culture of African liberation in Amerikkka. To formulate this discourse of liberation with its worldview there must be a deconstruction of hallucinatory whiteness which drives the creation of African liberationary discourse. George Jackson is then pointing to sign posts along the way, but the exit point of the singularity is yet to be attained. This is a singularity at the level of the idea, the mind, which must be exited by those trapped in it at the level of the idea. Whilst George has constituted another singularity with his knee-jerk discursive concept by which he seeks to make his beloved historical materialism relevant to his task at hand. To do this he creates an African caste system within Amerikkkan class society, a contradiction in terms which generates a non-liberationary concept incapable of generating ideational rigor. Ideational workers are then charged with engaging with, deconstructing massa hegemonic discourse towards falsifying it with our counter liberationary discourse, thereafter comes the revolutionary practice which is rooted in rejuvenation of the mind and behavior modification to remove nihilist practices.

June 12 ,1969 Letter to his Mother

George is writing to his mother giving her the news that his application for parole was denied by the board, but he has the opportunity to re-apply in June 1970.

September 9, 1969 Letter to Jon

George is writing to his brother Jon and has raised the issue of the practice of their father, and by extension the race and all that is wrong with it as follows: "He pretends that he is proud of his self-control. I believe he has actually twisted his thinking to consider himself a better man, 'Now that he can take it'. A lot of us colored folks are like that, in fact he is the majority. That is why we are the floor mat of the world, because we can take it." (Jackson 1976 Pg. 171). George is insisting that his father's daily survival strategy is to live, not die no matter what the price he has to pay and this is his self-respect, self-determination as a human in a social order. Their father then shucks and jive, surrenders, is servile relentlessly in daily life while he deludes himself into believing that he is in fact a free African endowed with rights by the constitution in Amerikkka. This is formulated as a self-defense, survival strategy in the face of white supremacist power exercised in Amerikkka on non-white races. This is then a response to racist terror which heightens the spectrum of trauma the non-white is trapped in. There is no liberation from this spectrum of trauma possible with the coping mechanism formulated and embraced by Africans in Amerikkka. Liberation only commences with the admission that the coping mechanism is heightening traumatization, it is not a liberationary discursive concept. George continues as follows: "Robert is a good brother on an individual, personal, brother-to-brother basis, but you must reject his philosophy: the credo of the slave, the self-destructive, self-perpetuating doctrine of the menial, the woodcutter, the water-boy, the groom, the employee, the flunky's flunky, the abased." (Jackson 1976 Pg. 171). To live long you don't challenge massa order of power, you never seek development to the limits of personal ability as this will challenge massa order of power. You then police yourself to live long by not seeking personal achievement, growth and development, upward mobility in the social order as this will mark you for elimination. You never challenge massa order of power whilst you police yourself insisting that you understand fully massa order of power, which you do not. To police yourself, to embrace underachievement and poverty in order to live long under the hegemony of massa power means that you never challenge massa order of power, especially when it is at its weakest, whilst you grant it power over you which it should not have. The servile African willingly heightens and worsens her/ his position in the social order by depriving themselves of power they should wield passing it to massa. Action in this power relation between African and massa consists of action by massa to render Africans servile and the counter action of Africans which willingly give power over themselves to massa for free. From this power relation nihilism arises to define and explain the logic of the African action to gift power over themselves freely to massa. African criminality is then one product of this nihilist condition in which Africans subject themselves to the power of massa willingly in order to live long in the ghetto.

George now deals with the inability of the African to contemplate and embrace self-determination when immersed in the power relation with massa as follows: "There is no chance of changing Robert," "There are those among us, we must admit, who cannot take any sizable amount of freedom. They are in the majority! You cannot relate to them with ideals. They have fallen beyond caring about ideals. The only thing that will make them move is a push, no explanation, just a shove." (Jackson 1876 Pg. 171). The Africans in Amerikkka who have bought into massa discourse constantly convince themselves that they're in charge of their lives, their destiny hence they are free decision-making subjects of power. They are then policing themselves, transferring power they should exert over massa they first exert over themselves which heightens the power massa wields over them as they pass this power to massa. Convinced that they are in charge of their destiny they then see no need to question the nature of the power relation with massa, there is no need for ideals as this power relation is to ensure that they live long not better, which is all they must desire. The majority of Africans then rationalize that living long is the best they can do, all they can do, hence African nihilism is the rational product of this delusion rooted in self-hate.

October 17, 1969 Letter to his Mother

George now returns to the dire need for the African to embrace the concept of self-determination as follows: "Relay to Penny that no effort toward self-determination is futile. It is one of the things that men just cannot do without. Without it life loses its value." (Jackson 1976 Pg. 175). Life without self-determination is doing everything you perceive you need to do in order to live long under the hegemony of massa order of power. Life without self-determination is only living on a daily basis to police oneself into a practice which you believe will place you off massa radar screen which allows you to live long but poor. It also justifies to you the embrace of criminality and the victimizing of your own race in your pursuit of criminality as the means for you to live long and well, but on massa radar screen. The strategic choices made every instant then in pursuit of living long operate in a nihilist context, can only constitute nihilism as a rational context for action in this power relation. One so immersed in this strategic action and is convinced it is working for them will then see no need to embrace self-determination, in fact will view it as a threat to the core survival strategy in which they have complete confidence. The core issue is then hallucinatory whiteness and the manner in which it seduces the African to embrace sustainable servility to massa at the level of the idea.

November 27, 1969 Letter to Jon/ Jonathan

George is writing to his brother reporting on massa games in prison to have him surrender to massa order of power as follows: "They called me up to classification last week. Said they were considering sending me back to San Quentin. They are supposed to need the space here for something, and I wasn't doing well enough. They said if I improved a great deal, it

is possible that in four or five years I might be considered for Chino –
the prison for honor inmates." (Jackson 1976 Pg. 176). Massa expects that
George, like all niggers, will seek to live long in prison rather than to
die in prison shortly. Massa then applies the test to George to determine
if he is ready to rock n roll with massa by applying the hard and soft
simultaneously. The hard: George will be transferred back to San Quentin,
which is where he was killed in August 1971, to do hard time. At Soledad
prison he has not changed his behavior pattern to deserve parole or to
remain at Soledad prison hence the decision to return him to San Quentin
prison. Massa has delivered the message to George that he continues to be
recalcitrant, refuses to be servile which means he is now marked for death
in San Quentin prison. In August 1971 this promise was made manifest
at San Quentin. Massa gives George hope for a reprieve at this stage if
he is willing to give to massa four to five years of servility, shucking and
jiving, with extra doses of non-white nihilism. With this he might well
qualify for a transfer to Chino where he will be a lifer of renown, an
inmate of honor within the prison system. Can massa be trusted? For massa
lying is compulsory, strategic in the subjugation of the non-white races.
George was transferred to San Quentin where he died in August 1971
with his self-determination intact. George chose a short life, dying with
his self-determination intact rather than seeking a long life in servility to
massa. George chose what was certain, his death rather than to surrender,
to embrace servility in the hope that massa will grant you a long life, for
with or without surrender there is no certainty that massa will respond
as indicated as this power over the non-white is unchallenged by the
non-whites of America, massa then enjoys impunity thanks to the servility
of the non-whites.

December 28, 1969 Letter to Jon

George now writes to Jon on his atheist worldview as follows: "Forget
that Western backward stuff about god. I curse god, the whole idea of a
benevolent supreme being is the product of a tortured, demented mind.
It is a labored, mindless attempt to explain away ignorance, a tool to keep
people of low mentality and no means of production in line. How there

could be a benevolent superman controlling a world like this. He would have to be malevolent, not benevolent. Look around you, evil rules supreme. God would be my enemy. The theory of a good, just god is a false idea, a thing for imbeciles and old women and, of course, Negroes. It's a relic of the past when men made words and mindless defenses for such things as sea serpents, magic and flat earths." (Jackson 1976 Pgs. 179-180). Jackson is ridiculing the African in Amerikkka for embracing massa discourse of god and Christianity insisting that only a race with mental inadequacies can embrace massa discourse of god for so long uncritically. Rather than attacking the mental capacity of his race what is necessary is deconstructing massa discourse to unearth how god and Christianity is an instrument of massa order of power. The nihilism constituted by policing oneself into servility demands self-medication ,where the human develops a menu of choices in the relentless need to self-medicate hallucinatory whiteness, schizophrenia, self-hate, one instrument of self-medication is massa religion, as massa illicit drugs, alcohol, and criminality. As long as Africans are convinced christianity heals what they feel incessantly in their lucid moments, they will seek out, embrace and police themselves with massa discourse of the christian god. The issue is not that massa discourse of the christian god is falsified, just superstition and those Africans who embrace it are feeble minded. The salient issue is the unraveling of the order of power of massa that makes the discourse of the christian god still attractive after all these years of oppression by massa. Attacks as this one by Jackson cannot effectively assault massa order of power and his discourse of the christian god. What it does is find reasons for further dividing the race into those conscious, those seeking self-determination and the majority imbeciles. Jackson now gives Jon the strategic imperative of strength in the path to liberation as follows: "Strength comes from knowledge, knowing who you are, where you want to go, what you want, knowing and accepting that you are alone on this spinning, rumbling world. No one can crawl into your mind and help you out." "Strength is being able to control oneself and your total environment – yourself first however." (Jackson 1976 Pg. 180). Personal liberation is the task of the individual seeking self-determination, but what is this strength that is the foundation of liberation and the discourse of power that defines and operationalizes liberation, self-determination? There must be detailed presentation of this discourse of liberation in order to have persons study it, gain knowledge, evolve knowledge and instruments of power in the compulsory quest for hegemony at the level of the idea. With George Jackson imprisoned his contribution to this strategy is limited by massa order of power which Jackson made himself a victim of with his embrace of criminality. But when he embraced criminality as a viable life strategy he had no consciousness, no strength, no desire for self-determination, what he desired was defined and constituted by massa order of power. With imprisonment, finding Jesus was then one viable outcome for the old George but not self-determination for liberation, African revolution. George then walked away from massa discourse in prison, hence the reason for his death in prison.

George Jackson received from Mrs Fay Stender, Attorney-at-Law his first letter from her dated 11 February 1970 on the matter of his charge for murder of the prison guard at Soledad prison. By way of letter dated 13 February 1970 George replied to Stender indicating his interest in reading the transcript of the meeting of the grand jury which voted to prosecute the three inmates for murder.

March 2, 1970 Letter to Fay Stender

George has now established his lawyer/ client relationship with Stender which he is using to bounce his ideas off, a new voice in his life as follows: "Either way, it denotes the effects that trauma has on people, especially people who are affected by little else. I am convinced that black people can never be influenced by ideology alone. The men have been too conditioned against it by violence and they are afraid, The women think of themselves as too practical, they can be moved by one thing only: 'Money honey.' However, I love them all just the same. I reason that with a continuous stream of shocks and the promise of spoils they can eventually be induced to reach beyond their immediate surroundings." (Jackson 1976 Pgs. 182-183). The African in Amerikkka has then been reduced to a lumpen proletariat by massa order of white supremacist power, where they are incapable of responding to the drive and call of the absolutes of production/ revolution. The instrument of white power used is white supremacist terror from enslavement to the present but with different impacts on males and females arising from different strategies employed. George Jackson with this discursive concept is potently illustrating the inherent problematic of his embrace of historical materialism and its applicability to the African and the African revolution in Amerikkka. White supremacy in Amerikkka has divorced, alienated the African from the absolutes of production and revolution using white supremacist terror thereby traumatizing the African male into servility expressed via nihilism and criminality combined. Racism then trumps production in constituting the African male in Amerikkka, which falsifies historical materialism. This non-white creature constituted by white supremacist terror has been rendered incapable of being motivated by ideology, discourse to liberate themselves from white supremacist hegemony, to embrace the quest for self-determination. The African male has to be then motivated by factors that they can identify with, of relevance from their milieu: trauma, fear and the spoils of criminal exertion. In this position Jackson is underrating the resolve of the white supremacist order of power to exert hegemony by any means necessary and its resilience faced with gravely flawed opponents. How can non-whites plagued with hallucinatory whiteness and trauma mount an effective onslaught against massa order of white power devoid of an alternate discourse of liberation with its attendant worldview, order and instruments of power? They cannot do so successfully, hence the failure of Jackson's African revolution in his lifetime which continues to today. Jackson in this letter continues his assault on the African woman as the villain of the piece, failing to grasp the specificity of the white supremacist assault on the African woman from enslavement to today. White supremacist discourse defined the African woman as: labor power, reproductive power and sexualised object of desire/ pleasure for all white men, as the African woman was the well spring of white male pleasure, which he could not expect and demand from his white wife as this would be proof of his marriage to a white whore. Non-white men in the service of massa, as the driver, were given limited, defined ability to so exploit African women on the plantation. With emancipation in 1865 in Amerikkka these power relations continued where the African woman was the target of all men, whilst having to deal with men with whom she bore children but refused to execute their duty as father to raise those children. Add to this the continuous assault of hallucinatory whiteness on the African woman, especially its ability to intensify the spectrum of trauma plaguing non-white women in Amerikkka. On a daily basis the salient issue facing African women and their children is survival by any means necessary, which has dire blow back on themselves and their children. Especially so is the internecine warfare of the ghetto where Africans kill each other with impunity further traumatizing the race, heightening hallucinatory whiteness and intensifying its deprivation.

March 5, 1970 Letter to Fay

George in his letters to his attorney Fay is now revealing details of his discourse and its worldview not revealed in his letters to members of his family. In this letter George is expressing the impact of white power across time/ space in Amerikkka and its impact upon his perceptions of his self, his place in the world so constituted and his alienation from massa order of white power as follows: "You see, someone failed before me, trembled and failed, my father, his father, leaving Campbell in a position to leave me out. I have very bad moments when I think of that, and of course it follows that I must think of my own failings. - can you understand that being a helpless type affects me deeply." "Why should I have to relate and exchange from such a position of weakness. It comes down on me at times. I am tortured by the vision of someone like myself standing at the bars of his cell two hundred years from now cursing *me* – dereliction.!!? (Jackson 1976 Pg. 184). The driving issue for Jackson is the weakness of his position as an African incarcerated in prison for life. His willing embrace of African criminality which placed him on the radar of the white order of power resulted in Jackson literally walking himself into prison for life. Ancestral race weakness derived from the choice of strategy made across time/ space by his race to engage with the white supremacist order of power of Amerikkka. His parents were the living expressions of these failed African survival strategies who then socialized a man child who did everything possible with his agency to contribute to the hegemony of the white order of power. George imprisoned has then to live his weakness every second of his imprisonment, which with his revolutionary mind set is in fact torture designed to further traumatize George into nigger servility. The race and George have then failed in their response to massa order of power to break the back of African underdevelopment, trauma and oppression in Amerikkka. The first judge assigned to his trial for the murder of the prison guard at Soledad prison recused himself in response to his defense's claim of the racist bias of judge Campbell is but another life lesson for George. For George the lesson is the fact that such persons are still appointed as judges to police the Africans caught in the justice system. The continued appointment of white racist judges for George is again a potent indicator of the failure of the race and George. This grave weakness of the race in the face of white power frightens George that two hundred years after 1970 the model of the weak, nihilist African lifer continues in Amerikkka because of the failure of the African race to liberate themselves from white hegemony. This means that George has also failed, but can you succeed imprisoned in massa meat grinder?

March 23,1970 Letters to Fay

George now writes about the nature of endemic violence in the prison as follows: "And things just keep escalating from one desperate situation to a situation more desperate, and I seize the bull by the horns. I'll ride him till his neck breaks or until he pins me to the wall – conflict, struggle, and preparation for more struggle. You can't understand how it is to have to watch everyone who get within arm's reach, or when under the gun to have to stay close to something to crawl under." (Jackson 1976 Pgs. 188-189). The violence is interpersonal and interracial simultaneously with the violence from the minority who wield power in the prison being the hegemonic constant. George is then engaged in daily power relations within the prison that demand his servility to power, but as expected George is intent on establishing his own power bases where he earns his reputation as an inmate player, connected, a survivor. This is then Jackson's daily struggle that hones his skills under fire and drives the formulation of a constant stream of survival strategies in response to an ever-changing landscape of power, especially that involving the minority prison authorities. This is then George's revolutionary terrain on a daily basis which is certainly not the wider, more potent terrain of power of the African revolution. George, is then dealing with on a daily basis an extreme form of the white order of power of Amerikkka, which has learnt well from massa order of plantation power under enslavement.

March 24, 1970 Letter to Fay

George now continues his detailed description of the power relations of prison by now reporting on the qualities exhibited by those in the prison system, inmates and, employees, as follows: "I'll here admit that most of the persons who come through these places are genuinely sick in one way or the other, monsters, totally disorganized, twisted, disgusted epitomes of the parent monster. Those who aren't so upon their arrival will surely be so when they leave. No one escapes unscathed, An individual leave his individuality and any pride he may have had behind these walls." (Jackson 1976 Pg. 190). The white order of power of prison operates to socialize all humans within the system by first de-socializing them upon entry and re-socializing them into a creature of the prison. Inmates are surveilled and re-socialized to be pliable and competent to live on a daily basis only in prison culture whilst their morbidities are enhanced, heightened, thereby spurring the evolution of career criminals who are alienated from the wider society, but one with prison culture. In the case of the African male the prison process of de-socialization, re-socialization creates a male with a criminal record burdened with grave morbidities alienated from the social order of the ghetto, capable only of functioning within prison culture. These males released from prison return to their community and find meaning only in acts that challenge massa order of power to once again charge, convict and return them to mass prison for lengthy sentences. This revolving door movement indicates the reality of the order of power of prison, which is charged with social control by exclusion and marginalization, not rehabilitation and development. Jackson is insisting that those Africans who enter prison already monsters are the products of monster parents, failed parents and the grave shortcomings of individuals, parents and children, are all constituted by hegemonic white discourse. Jackson retained and built upon his pride and individuality in prison resisting the assault of hegemonic white discourse because of his revolutionary praxis and paid the price set by the prison order of power for that.

George now deals with observed African behavior in prison that he considers a quandary as follows: "Then it seems that blacks are much more concerned in establishing records that will lead to parole than whites or browns. I can't understand this, since they have so much less to go home to." (Jackson 1976 Pg. 191). Why do you embrace criminality which puts you on massa radar screen for a stint in his prison order of power and when you fulfill the prophesy of your action with incarceration you do everything in your power to shuck and jive to win massa affirmation as a model prisoner worthy of a parole? Then with parole a noteworthy percentage of you on the outside re-embrace criminality and return to the re-embrace of prison? Your actions send the message that the African in Amerikkka is constituted for prison, made for prison, has an organic need for prison given the grave threat the race poses to massa in Amerikkka. This African in Amerikkka behavior pattern reeks of and is driven by a nihilist worldview rooted in self-hate which has since the evolution of the illicit trades in the ghetto evolved into the quest for inter-African genocide in the ghetto, which is now amongst the prison population, further evolving the inter-African genocide in the face of the continued evolution of the inter-racial wars of massa order of prison power. In this prison reality, African inmates are now under great pressure to join for self-preservation prison gangs which command their allegiance when they leave prison, which places them in the vortex of the inter-African genocide when they return to life in the ghetto outside massa prison.

March 24, 1970 Letter to Fay

George writes about his rage as an African male of the ghetto who embraced criminality and as a result ended up in massa order of prison power as follows: "I'm going to charge them for this, twenty-eight years without gratification, I'm going to charge them reparations in blood, I'm going to charge them like a maddened, wounded, rogue male elephant, ears flared, trunk raised, trumpet flaring. I'll do my dance in his chest, and the only thing he will ever see in my eyes is a dagger to pierce his cruel heart. This is one nigger that is positively displeased. I'll never forgive, I'll never forget, and if I'm guilty of anything at all it's not leaning on them hard enough. War without terms." (Jackson 1976 Pg. 195). George is now an African male of the ghetto who liberated himself in massa prison order of power whilst imprisoned and is asking no quarter from massa. Liberated George Jackson in prison is now aggressively hunting his death at the hands of massa order of prison power for he has accepted that his death is the way he will be freed from the exercise of massa power over his living being, his death is his only path to liberation. By the choices he made and acted upon George found liberation, but no hope of freedom except with his death, which he embraced in order to be free.

March 25, 1970 Letter to Fay

George continues revealing the discursive concepts of his discourse of African revolution to his lawyer in this letter. He first presents his critique of non-violence as a revolutionary methodology in Amerikkka as follows: "The concept of non-violent protest, whatever political forms it may take, presumes two things about the imperialist establishment that are so obviously historically unreliable, so logically unsound, that the espousal of any purely non-violent anti-establishment policy reduces one automatically to a corpse." (Jackson 1976 Pg. 195). Jackson is writing this in March 1970 with Martin Luther King assassinated in April 1968 which is the evidence Jackson cites of the futility of utilizing non-violence in the African engagement with massa over civil rights in Amerikkka. King and other African leaders and their followers paid with their lives for embracing non-violence as the preferred methodology to deal with massa order of power. For Jackson the choice is then clear for massa will kill you whilst you are non-violent why then your aversion to revolution? Hallucinatory whiteness expressed as self-hate and nihilism only wants massa affirmation and revolution is not the preferred means to attain massa affirmation for massa has to continue wielding power in order to affirm Africans, whilst revolution seeks liberation and the end of massa order of power which means that Africans will have to now affirm themselves. That is why with the murder of King the choice was to riot, loot and burn the ghetto where they are marginalized to rather than say Wall Street.

In his analysis of the potency of the concept of non-violence utilized in the civil rights movement of Amerikkka, Jackson now insists that the social order of Amerikkka under the hegemony of massa order of power is in fact an expression of internal colonialism as follows: "The people of the US are held in the throes of a form of colonialism. Control of their subsistence and nearly every aspect of the circumstances surrounding their existence has passed into the hands of a clearly distinct and alienated oligarchy. If today's young revolutionary vanguard are not merely entertaining themselves with a new kind of 'chicken', a political form of bumper tag, if they seriously intend to step out front and take the monster to task, they should understand from the outset that the monster is merciless." (Jackson 1976 Pg. 196). The massa of Amerikkka is merciless, a monster which exerts hegemony over a specific social order which is rooted in and riven by contradictions expressed by discordant discourses that describe the power relations of Amerikkka. Amerikkka is a sovereign entity, nation housed within a demarcated geographic space. In this designated space the nation is a democracy under the rule of law as defined by a constitution, but in the structure of the social order there is a structure of discrimination that underdevelops non-white races and the spaces they inhabit in this democracy whilst the spaces occupied by whites are qualitatively superior to that of non-whites and an oligarchy which is dominated by white persons dominates this democracy. An analysis of this social order reveals a structure of racial differentiation between hegemonic whites and subservient non-whites in a democracy very much like that of a classic imperial colonial colony of massa in the global South. In Amerikkkan democracy there are then a number of metropoles dominated by the white oligarchy across the landscape outnumbered by the marginalized spaces reserved for the marginalized non-white races. These are the colonies, the ghettos of Amerikkka. Whites also inhabit marginalized spaces, but white expectation of white entitlement insists that these spaces for marginalized whites be differentiated from that of non-whites. The marginalized whites must be always exposed to instruments that enable them to grasp upward mobility which must be denied to non-whites to maintain the expectation of white privilege in the face of non-white underdevelopment. In this social order they relentlessly insist to non-whites they are free, endowed with rights that enables them to access upward mobility if they work hard, pull yourself up by your bootstraps. Generations of non-whites have been seduced by this massa discourse, have policed themselves into good, servile niggers and are yet to grasp the upward social mobility they sought. In the ghetto there is an overwhelming bias to seek this upward mobility in the illicit trades rather than in conventional channels which has now spread external of the ghetto to those non-white families who escaped the ghetto for whatever reason. How then can non-whites who are engaging with massa to change this colonial order of racist power choose and expect non-violence methodology to work on this massa of Amerikkka? They so believe because they are docile, servile niggers bearing their delusional burden of Amerikkkan democracy, where all non-white citizens have rights. Yes, massa confirmed that they have the right to die, nothing else, which soon crippled the movement. On this Jackson states as follows: "The danger derives from the very realistic fact that the statement and pursuit of non-violent tactics will always be mistaken for *weakness*, as these tactics stand alone. The contradiction is then revealed, in that power is expected to surrender to weakness." (Jackson 1976 Pg. 197). Massa of Amerikkkan democracy is a merciless colonial massa who will defend his race hegemony over Amerikkka by any means necessary including extermination of leader and led, this is a merciless colonial massa. There can then only be wars of liberation for non-whites in Amerikkka, anti-colonial wars against a massa who shall never envisage, much less act on replacing the hegemony of a white oligarchy with a multi-racial democracy. This colonial massa faced with non-whites shouting and practicing non-violent methodology will earn no respect from nor generate fear in the mind of massa of Amerikkka, this movement will be subverted and the violence applied to remove its leadership and incarcerate its followers unleashing massa instruments of terror to further traumatize the non-whites of Amerikkka. In fact, the question arises of the effectiveness of an anti-colonial liberation movement in Amerikkka if it is not ongoing for decades in an Amerikkka where the whites are now the minority race exerting hegemony as the case of the colonies of the global South. In this strategic scenario a besieged minority race under effective non-white guerrilla assault will force compromise as those resolved amongst the whites during the war for independence, the civil war and the great depression.

March 25, 1970 Letter to Fay

George is in this letter writing about the process of revolution in the global South and the need of the African revolution of Amerikkka to learn salient lessons from the global South as follows: "The successes of China, Cuba, Vietnam, and parts of Africa cannot be attributed to an innate, singular quality in the character of their people. Men are social creatures, herd animals. We follow leaders. The success or failure of mass movements depends on their leadership and the method of their leaders. We must take our lessons from these people, reorganize our values, decide whether it is our personal desire to live long or to chance living right." (Jackson 1976 Pg. 198). The African revolution in Amerikkka will only succeed when it constitutes the leadership it organically needs to overthrow massa. This organic leadership has to formulate the knowledge base that informs the creation of an effective strategy to dismantle massa Amerikkka. This leadership must lead from in front, by example and its most important task in building the revolution is in personifying and articulating the discourse of African liberation, emancipation from hallucinatory whiteness. To drive the revolution there must then be a cultural revolution first that purges the hegemonic discourse of massa which dominates the African at the level of the idea insisting on relentless black/ nigger servility. The leaders must then neverendingly exhibit their determination to reject and to refuse action influenced by the desire for long life, never refusing to take action in the quest for living right, to respond to the idea and ideology regardless of its personal cost. To forbid and abandon nihilism by embracing African self-determination. Without this cultural revolution, this change of discourse and worldview, of practice and action brought about by African leadership there will be no African revolution in Amerikkka. In keeping with the discourse of George Jackson from 1970 to 2023 this organic leadership of the African revolution in Amerikkka has yet to appear, whilst hallucinatory whiteness has not remained discursively static, it has evolved and intensified its impact on the mind of the non-whites of Amerikkka.

In this letter Jackson states the grave price that will be paid for revolt that fails to terminate in revolutions as follows: "Class struggle means the suppression of the opposing class, and the suppression of the American General Staff, and the Corporate Elite. The moment this three-headed monster detects the danger contained in our ideas and ideals, he will react violently against us. Just the whisper of revolt excites in him a swift and terrible reflex, so swift we won't even know how we died." (Jackson 1976 Pg. 199). Jackson's uncritical embrace of historical materialism impacts his production of quality revolutionary analysis vitally necessary to formulating an effective revolutionary practice. There is no class solidarity, consciousness amongst workers across race lines in Amerikkka, that rejects the white order of power in Amerikkka. Jackson cannot then speak of the African revolution with class conflict as its engine. There is an order of white power which assures the hegemony of the politicians and the oligarchs they serve. These politicians animate a structure of race power which relentlessly moves to bind the white working class in servility to the white oligarchy through the white politicians. Race solidarity is then the instrument to defuse class conflict by posing non-whites as the common enemy of all whites in Amerikkka. For this solidarity of race, the white working class has an expectation of rewards that will differentiate them from the non-white masses. This white order of power is dominated by white males in Amerikkka which means it compresses race, gender and class characteristics into a structure of differentiation, difference, unequal distribution and underdevelopment; where race difference presents assumptions of superiority/ inferiority, manifest destiny/ subservience, entitlement/ discrimination. The discourse of white supremacy then defines the power relations of the order of power of Amerikkka. The discourse of white supremacy then defines race, class and gender distinctions which is the basis of the white order of power in Amerikkka. This order of power shall be defended from assault by non-whites, especially by any extrajudicial means necessary, which will heighten to a civil war as the white majority shrinks into a race minority in Amerikkka. The African revolution is then built upon an assault on hallucinatory whiteness that evolves into a preventative assault on reinfection with revolutionary success. Issues of gender and class relations and discrimination have to be defined by its nexus with hallucinatory whiteness which defines both of them at the level of the idea. There is then no emancipation from gender and class discrimination without the assault, deconstruction and dismantling of hallucinatory whiteness at the level of its white supremacist idea. Those who insist that you can defuse gender and class discrimination whilst in a rolling embrace of white supremacy are the agents of massa agenda to preserve the hegemony of the white order of power.

May 4, 1970 Letter to Fay

This is a lengthy letter George writes to Fay which in its expanse George reveals the complexities of his discourse of the African revolution in Amerikkka in May 1970 which with time he did not have, George was destined to be the premier discursive agent of the African revolution in Amerikkka. George states as follows on Amerikkkan capitalism, fascism and the African as follows: "The fascists, it seems have a standard MO for dealing with the lower classes. Actually oppressive power throughout power has used it. They turn a man against himself – think of all the unusual things that make us feel good, but that makes some of us feel guilty. Think of how the people of the lower classes weigh themselves against those who rule." (Jackson 1976 Pg. 206). George is explaining why there are lower classes in the Amerikkkan social order and he comes up with a generic explanation that explains class society where man is alienated from himself, from the human essence which is classic historical materialist discourse, but it has grave limitations of applicability to specific orders of power, especially those rooted in the discourse of white supremacy. The specificity of a non-white being alienated from a non-white self that is defined by white supremacy as being inferior cannot be articulated by this historical materialist concept of "alienation". New concepts with the necessary efficacy have to be formulated external of and liberated from the discourse of historical materialism with all its limitations in dealing with idea and constituting power exerted on humans. In Amerikkka there is no class solidarity, no class conflict and the possibility of revolution premised on class conflict and solidarity. Much more important is the specificity of non-white oppression in Amerikkka which cannot be articulated and solved by the discourse of historical materialism. George then is hunting for new ideas, seeking to formulate concepts that fill the need for explaining the specificity of the African in Amerikkka.

George presents his new concepts as follows: "Blacks embrace capitalism, the most unnatural and outstanding example of man against himself that history can offer. After, the Civil War, the form of slavery changed from chattel to economic slavery, and we were thrown on the labor market to compete at a disadvantage with poor whites. Ever since that time, our principal enemy must be isolated and identifies as capitalism. The slaver was and is the factory owner, the businessman of capitalist Amerika, the man responsible for employment, wages, prices, control of the nation's institutions and culture." "Black capitalism, black against itself. The silliest contradiction in a long train of spineless, mindless contradictions. Another painless, ultimate remedy: be a better fascist than the fascist." (Jackson 1976 Pgs. 206-207). Jackson's discursive concept is the threat capitalism poses to the African in Amerikkka from enslavement and thereafter, but it cannot address the specific realities of the power relations that render the African servile to the white supremacist order of power in Amerikkka. Jackson fails to embrace the fact that under enslavement the enslaved produced commodities that were exported and sold on local and foreign markets which enabled the generation and accumulation of wealth in specific white hands that drove the development of industrial capitalism in Amerikkka, and especially Britain. The enslaved African in Amerikkka was chattel, the property of massa whilst tied to the production of commodities which commanded a price in money on markets within massa order of power external and internal of Amerikkka. The groups of whites who commanded the wealth generated by enslaved labor were then gifted with the capital to rapidly evolve this slave mode of capitalist production to capitalist production rooted in free servile labor. In the aftermath of the US civil war two contending models emerged in Amerikkka on how to manage the now free African population. Signal former member states of the confederacy fought tooth and nail to restore the power relations of enslavement in order to render the free African servile. This model was expressed via a strident discourse of white supremacy and entitlement which actively sought to break the law in order to turn back the hands of time to before 1865, Jim Crow was his name-o. The other model embraced by signal members of the union demanded the removal of all fetters on the evolution of capital and capitalism in Amerikkka. In spaces of Amerikkka where the African enslavement renaissance was in fact retarding the evolution and hegemony of capitalism over these spaces such hindrances must be removed by the politicians. The Africans were then pushed out of the enslavement renaissance spaces to the open capitalism incubators to experience with their arrival massa order of power of these open capitalist hot houses, the crushing nature of a racist order of discrimination and underdevelopment different from and much more effective than that of the enslavement renaissance model. The salient issue was not then capitalism per se, but capitalism enmeshed within a white supremacist discourse of power. The civil rights movement was then the push back against the enslavement renaissance model, part of a wider movement for the open capitalist white supremacist model to now exert hegemony over these spaces with federal action and intervention. This battle continues to this day without resolution. The reality is much more complex than the picture painted by Jackson and it must be grasped fully in order to formulate a revolutionary praxis that works when the white order of power is engaged with. In Amerikkka, to embrace capitalism as the relevant non-white order of power means embracing your inherent inferiority and surrendering to the inherent superiority of massa. The idea of the social order of capitalism in Amerikkka is one under the hegemony of white supremacy expressed as massa and his order of power. Jackson now deals with the methods utilized which divide the masses into mutually exclusive races in competition with each other for hegemony over the social order as follows: "So first they turn us against ourselves, precluding all possibility of trust, then fascism takes any latent divisible forces and develops them in fact: racism, nationalism, religion." (Jackson 1976 Pg. 208). Jackson must understand that the discourse of white supremacy precluded capitalism in the North Atlantic and in no way hindered the development of pre-capitalist accumulation and wealth generation and capitalist development and evolution. Fascism was then a specific discourse of a white supremacist capitalist order of power that arose in a specific epoch of crises of capitalism with its white supremacist order of power in the North Atlantic.

Jackson now describes the African existential condition in Amerikkka as follows: "We were colonized by the white predatory fascist economy. It was from them that we evolved our freak subculture, and the attitudes that perpetuate our condition. These attitudes cause us to give each other up to the Klan pigs. We even on occasion work gun in hand with them. A black killed Fred Hampton; blacks working with the CIA killed Malcolm X; blacks are plentiful on the payroll of the many police forces that fascism must employ to protect itself from the people. These fascist subcultural attitudes have sent us to Europe, Asia (one-fourth of the fatalities in Vietnam are black fatalities), and even Africa (the Congo during the Simba attempt to establish people's government) to die for nothing. In the recent cases of Africa and Asia we have allowed the neoslaver to use us to help enslave people we love. We are so confused, so foolishly simple that we not only fail to distinguish what is generally right and what is wrong. But we also fail to appreciate what is good and not good for us in very personal matters concerning the black colony and its liberation." (Jackson 1976 Pg. 219). Jackson is critiquing the behavior pattern of the African in Amerikkka constituted by hallucinatory whiteness which is the product of the discourse of white supremacy designed to render the African servile, pliant to the white order of power. The discourse of hallucinatory whiteness preceded the discourse of fascism as it was unleashed in the era of white conquest and expansion before the hegemony of European mercantilism, evolving further from then to the present. The servile, pliant African exhibits ideas, discourses with their worldviews and menus of choices of behavior which institutionalize their servility, their pliancy even though they are not beneficial to the African. Hallucinatory whiteness drives the African to only relentlessly seek what they feel is the affirmation of massa, not their personal benefit nor that of their children, family and race. Nihilism is then their modus operandi. Africans in Amerikkka are the free but colonized, enslaved at the level of the idea and their praxis, driven by nihilist self-hate, self-abuse and self-destructiveness. Jackson having recognized Amerikkka as a practitioner of internal colonial domination of its non-white citizens had but one viable choice open to him in order to build a relevant revolutionary discourse with its practice. This was a much deeper insight of the oeuvre and the revolutionary discourse of Frantz Fanon. This he failed to do given his unwillingness to gaze upon the inherent flaws of historical materialism as a revolutionary discourse relevant to all non-whites under white supremacist hegemony. This was the grave failing of a mind in transition, marked for death, which denied the evolution of this mind during the course of daily power relations.

Jackson continues by stating his personal agenda and addressing the black mothers as follows: "I don't want to raise any more black slaves. We have a determined enemy who will accept us only on a master-slave basis. When I revolt, slavery dies with me. I refuse to pass it down again. The terms of my existence are founded on that. Black Mama, you're going to have to stop making cowards; 'Be a good *boy*;' 'You're going to worry me to death, *boy*;' 'Don't trust those niggers;' 'Stop letting those bad niggers lead you around, *boy*;' 'Make you a dollar, *boy*;' Black Mama your overriding concern with the survival of our sons is mistaken if it is survival at the cost of their manhood." (Jackson 1976 Pg. 220). Jackson has determined at this time and made the choice to cease policing himself in prison to ensure he remains a servile nigger in Amerikkka. He intends to die free, exercising self-determination which insists that he will no longer police the behavior of other non-whites, Africans for the benefit of massa order of power. Jackson will then no longer socialize slaves by being free, emancipated, self-determined. This revolutionary praxis ensures and demands that Jackson is silenced in prison with death. Jackson is by extension, insisting that the Black Mama socializes her sons to be slaves rather than to be dead revolutionaries. To determine what is good, acceptable behavior and what is not by the maxim: "does it earn a dollar." Revolutionary action, liberation and self-determination earn the death of the liberated slave, massa determined this fate, hence good dutiful sons must evade these niggers as they are bad niggers. The embrace of criminality especially the illicit trades is then a superior choice to revolutionary action amongst Africans in the ghetto. The Black Mama is then socializing her sons to serve massa as slaves in the absence of the father in the household grappling with his duty to raise those children of his. In cases where the father is present there is no appreciable difference in the strategy adopted by the household to survival under massa order of power. In fact, the threat to the security of those living in this household is heightened when a resident father uses the residential space for activities of the illicit trades. Jackson's continuing emphasis on the black mama is the product of his personal problems with his parents where he demonizes his mother and dismisses his father constituting his model of the black parents who failed their black sons. Hence his uncritical embrace of the absolutes of historical materialism: production/ revolution for revolutionary consciousness is problematic with slaves. The inevitability of capitalist production in Amerikkka, hence the inevitability of revolution solves his problem of revolutionary consciousness and the African in Amerikkka.

April 17, 1970 Letter to Fay

In this lengthy letter to his lawyer, Jackson reveals that he has, in his mind, completed his revolutionary discourse with its worldview and its praxis/ practice which now affords him the opportunity to focus on revolutionary action external of the prison in Amerikkka. Jackson at this stage is in fact in denial as he holds on to the conjoined absolutes of historical materialism, seeing it as the theoretical solution of a condition of reality that he considers daunting to overcome, for he has never deconstructed hallucinatory whiteness in Amerikkka to unearth its structural weaknesses at the level of the idea. This is the focal point at which the assault of an alternate, revolutionary discourse focuses and commences its attack towards deprogramming the constituted African. Jackson's relentless crusade against his parents and the manner in which he was socialized without the deconstruction of this socializing discourse, means that, Jackson has overdetermined the problem at hand of being socialized with slave consciousness, and its deterrence of the process of acquiring revolutionary consciousness to the point where his only escape point is the absolute of historical materialism. But this escape point exists only in the mind of Jackson for the revolution is yet to express the traction necessary to building momentum, in the face of an assault of the instruments of massa order of power intent on destroying the threat it poses by any means necessary. Jackson is then constituting luxuries and assets in his mind which are not and never will be real.

George presents his discourse which is rooted in a specific concept of slavery as follows: "Slavery is an economic condition. Today's neoslavery must be defined in terms of economics." "The new slavery, the modern variety updated to disguise itself, places the victim in a factory or in the case of most blacks in support roles inside and around the factory system (service trade) working for a wage." "If you're held in one spot on this earth because of your economic status, it is just the same as being held in one spot because you are the owner's property." "Succinctly; an economic condition which manifests itself in the total loss or absence of self-determination. Only after this is understood and accepted can we go on to the dialectic that will help us in a remedy." (Jackson 1976 Pgs. 221-222). Enslavement that is the product of a discourse of white supremacy which insists that it is the manifest destiny of the white master race to capture, sell, transport to Amerikkka from Africa where they will be sold again and placed in a slave economy to generate and maximize wealth for massa. This discourse of white manifest destiny establishes an order of power with its instruments of power which focuses on the inherent inferiority of the enslaved, to have the enslaved Africans police themselves into servile slaves. Massa is then relentlessly problematizing the African, their body, values, sexuality, culture, discourses and worldviews, rendering them inferior, unfit, uncivilized, worthy of enslavement in order to teach them white civilization; which is itself only effective when the African embraces, internalizes and police themselves with massa white supremacist discourse. This is not production, economic nor economic position, this is white supremacist assault on the African to render them servile in order to maximize the generation and accumulation of wealth for massa. With

African emancipation in 1865 in Amerikkka, massa refused to accept that the African was now a citizen endowed with constitutional rights, hence the deepening of the assault on the African by problematizing all things African by now insisting to them that they are now free with rights which obligates them to comply, be servile, to be good citizens. With freedom in 1865 the assault on all things African is heightened and further problematised in order to render the African problematically servile, servile burdened with hallucinatory whiteness accepting of structural discrimination because they present a grave threat to white society. Jackson simply cannot grasp the reality that with emancipation and the evolution of industrial capitalism where Amerikkka became the workshop of the world the free African became a throw away population massa had no need for, unlike under enslavement.

The second world war forced the African male and the white woman into the factories for war production, but with the end of this war the African was faced with a national project to return them to their marginalized status in the ghetto with a vengeance in Amerikkka. This was the process to create the suburbs filled with white male workers and their white female housewives to the exclusion of the African. The frantic erection of white only suburbs meant that Africans remained in the ghetto burdened, denied the opportunity to become homeowners. Neoslavery is not an economic position as the African in Amerikkka is not a central, core asset in the generation of wealth in America from the 1950s to the present. Enslavement and neoslavery are in fact the product of a discourse of white supremacist political power which is intent on exercising white hegemony over non-white races in the interest of massa. The idea then makes it possible for massa to exploit non-white races for **his** benefit, not that of production. Jackson's infatuation with Marx's knee-jerk economism blinds to crucial realities as: the African is a minority race in Amerikkka, how can you expect a minority race to overthrow massa order of power without even the unity of all non-white races in Amerikkka? There was no need for African neoslavery in Amerikkka after 1865 in order to supply the labor needed to evolve Amerikkka into the workshop of the world given the waves of white immigration that flooded Amerikkka from Europe in the nineteen and twentieth centuries. In 1865 the white population of Amerikkka had a non-white race in their midst they did not want and were not dependent on to generate wealth, raising the question of what to do with them? Africans refused to embrace repatriation and/ or the political movement to have their own state dominated by non-whites in Amerikkka. Massa would move to destroy segregation to end this call for non-whites having their own state in Amerikkka, as massa was not willing to hand over an inch of the territory granted them by manifest destiny to an inferior race. Whilst Africans insisted that they are Amerikkkan citizens endowed with rights by the constitution, relentlessly waiting on massa to give them these said rights. George Jackson's revolutionary praxis is just another instance of the delusion derived from hallucinatory whiteness that afflicts Africans in Amerikkka; by using massa ideas against massa to effect African liberation is delusion which offers non-whites up as cannon fodder to massa instruments of power in Amerikkka.

A different discourse of the utility of the urban ghetto to massa order of power in Amerikkka is offered by Richard Rothstein "The Color of Law A Forgotten History of how our Government Segregated America" which offers insights into the operational nature of massa order of power in Amerikkka. Rothstein states as follows: "Residential segregation is hard to undo for several reasons: Parents' economic status is replicated in the next generation, so once government prevented African Americans from participating in the mid-twentieth century free labor market, depressed incomes became for many, a multi generational trail." (Rothstein 2017 Pg. 179). The Federal state in the 1950s used the power of law to exclude Africans from the post war boom of the 1950s thereby impacting negatively the earning power of the urban African leaving them stranded in the ghetto whilst the white working class was moving on up to home ownership in the suburbs, enjoying a standard of living denied the African. This was then deliberate to ensure that the African remain stranded in the ghetto willing the poverty of the parents to successive generations. This is not an economic situation of neoslavery, this is racist apartheid unleashed on a colony created to house non-whites in massa Amerikkka.

Rothstein continues as follows: "The value of white working and middle class families' suburban housing appreciated substantially over the years, resulting in vast wealth differences between whites and blacks that helped to define permanently our racial living arrangements. Because parents can bequeath assets to their children, the racial wealth gap is even more persistent down through the generations than income differences." (Rothstein 2017 Pg. 179). Massa order of power set out to create white suburbia by excluding the Africans from it on the grounds of race. This was deliberate done to ensure that the African could not enjoy the hand out that the state gave to whites, but denied Africans. This hand out increased the wealth generating capacity of white suburbia whilst the African was left stranded in the ghetto with its projects, becoming in real terms inter generationally poorer. This was not an economic position, but the product of white supremacist strategy to punish the enemy race and reward the white working class for being steadfast in its devotion to the hegemony of white supremacy in Amerikkka.

Rothstein continues as follows: "We waited too long to try to undo it. By the time labor market discrimination abated sufficiently for substantial numbers of African Americans to reach for the middle class, homes outside urban black neighborhoods had mostly become unaffordable for working- and lower middle class families." (Rothstein 2017 Pg. 180). During the post war prosperity the state made investments in and offered incentives for investment in erecting suburban white housing excluding Africans. This decision coincided with a labor market that discriminated in favor of white labor to the detriment of nonwhite labor in Amerikkka. Jointly operationalized African labor was excluded from entry into the mainstream of the labor market and from accessing to own subsidized housing in the suburbs. These discriminatory measures negatively impacted the ability of African labor to generate the necessary levels of wealth and its accumulation to lift successive generations out of poverty. This inter generational poverty then became a self-fulfilling prophecy, for, when under political pressure generated by resistance to the white supremacist order of discrimination forced the opening up of access to upward mobility by Africans they were now faced with high cost of available housing outside of African neighborhoods. Upwardly mobile Africans were then expected to pay a nigger premium on a house in a mixed or white dominated neighborhood. This African drive for upward mobility did not elicit from the state similar intervention made in favor of white working class home ownership in the suburbs. The African demand for housing in markets where house prices were expected to appreciate on an annual basis forced Africans to pay high prices bolstered with the nigger premium. Africans were then pushed to dominate the category of owners termed sub-prime mortgagors. With the meltdown of neo-liberal financial markets capitalism in 2008 these Africans lost their homes, their jobs, and became homeless because they were too small to save, in 2008 massa ravaged those Africans who had benefited from the political assault on massa order of power launched by the masses.

Rothstein now deals with the planned resilience of segregation operationalized in Amerikkka as follows: "Once segregation was established, seemingly race-neutral policies reinforced it to make remedies even more difficult. Perhaps most pernicious has been the federal tax code's mortgage interest deduction, which increased the subsidies to higher income suburban homeowners while providing no corresponding tax benefits for renters. Because de jure policies of segregation ensured that whites would most likely be owners and African Americans more likely be renters, the tax codes contribute to making African Americans and whites less equal, despite the code's purportedly nonracial provisions." (Rothstein 2017 Pg. 180). The idea constituted the need for an order of power that institutionalized difference between the white and non-white races of Amerikkka, the white race must exert hegemony and be rewarded sustainably for its inherent superiority as a race. This inherent superiority of the race must be visible, palpable in the social order seen in the development of whites and the under-development of non-whites. Politically the wall of white superiority will be breached, but the instruments of power that ensure the operational survival and hegemony of white supremacy is assured by the body of law that is supposedly color blind, abides by the constitution which in effect work to ensure the sustainable segregation of the races across time/ space in Amerikkka.

Rothstein continues on the signal importance of law and governance policies to the sustainability of segregation in Amerikkka as follows: "Contemporary federal, state, and local programmes have reinforced residential segregation rather than diminished it. Federal subsidies for low income families' housing have been used mainly to support those families' ability to rent apartments in minority areas where economic opportunity is scarce, not in integrated neighborhoods. Likewise developers of low income housing have used tax credits mostly to construct apartments in already segregated neighborhoods. Even half a century after government ceased to promote segregation explicitly, it continues to promote it implicitly, every year making remedial action more difficult." (Rothstein 2017 Pg. 180). Politically it is today not expedient to feed segregation with federal prescriptions which bar sales to non-whites by developers who access federal funds and incentives. But it is contradictory to the idea of the necessity of segregation to liberate the African from the ghetto. Segregation with underdevelopment of the African is then maintained by building in the ghetto only to rent and to have Federal intervention target renters, not homeowners external of and internal to the ghetto. Segregation to effect African underdevelopment thrives in Amerikkka today. The Revolution never happened, it failed to happen. This is the product not of capitalism but of the discourse of white supremacy which operationalizes capitalism in the North Atlantic, gives it its worldview, its order of power with its instruments of power. In the Peoples' Republic of China, the idea that operationalizes capitalism today is Socialism with Chinese Characteristics for the New Era which potently illustrates that there is no discourse of power that is organic to capitalism, this is the product of the power/force relations of the social order of which the capitalist oligarchy is part. The oligarchy has then to contend with power /force relations which limit the power it wields over the social order hence the driving need of the capitalists to make themselves into an oligarchy by exerting hegemony over the politicians and the State. Capitalism can and does function with different orders of power being hegemonic, as it must do so in order to survive, attain and exert hegemony over the social order. Capitalism itself is not an absolute and is never the occupant of the driver's seat save and except if/ when the oligarchy formed by political action now captures the State.

Capitalism does not demand African underdevelopment in Amerikkka in order to ensure its hegemony, white supremacy demands from capitalism that it thrive sustainably across time/ space in Amerikkka in spite of segregation. Amerikkka, from its creation, determined that its capitalism will be dominated by its oligarchs and politicians to the detriment of its democracy, which demands that emphasis by the politicians on making white entitlement visible, the optics of which is intensified by non-white underdevelopment in Amerikkka.

Failed Black Nationalism in the Caribbean Today

This chapter deals with skin bleaching by non-white Caribbean women as a potent indicator of the collapse and servility of Caribbean black nationalism to massa white order of neocolonial power, in spite of being independent states having supposedly walked away from colonial imperial domination. A deconstruction of the act of bleaching one's non-white skin where it becomes **not** classic non-white skin, but it is certainly **not** white as your genome remains non-white. This unyielding reality is then the thin edge of the wedge that further problematises the self-hate of the bleacher demanding cosmetic surgery to change the body further in conjunction with chemical treatment of the skin and hair. But there is much more to this practice of self-hate in action in the Caribbean in the 21st century that must be deconstructed to expose the strategic assault of massa white supremacist order of power on the action of bleachers in the Caribbean in the 21st century. In the 21st century, bleaching is now being propagated for non-white women as part of a package of actions that are vitally necessary to break out of the massa category of black ugliness in a quest to acquire white beauty, but you are not white genetically, delusion in action. Bleaching is then a futile attempt to win the affirmation of massa, but what you present as evidence of your evolution to whiteness is a grave parody which burdens the non-white mind at the level of the idea to constitute nihilist action, nihilism rooted in delusional futility which is hallucinatory whiteness.

Bleached skin, chemically altered hair, other persons' hair and a menu of cosmetic surgical interventions are now compulsory to attain this white ideal of beauty by the non-white individual. The menu of cosmetic surgical interventions targets the buttocks, the nose, the lips, the breasts and the vagina. The African buttocks and vagina constituted by a white supremacist discourse of African body ugliness, evidence of being less than human from the 16th to the19th century has now been revised and unleashed on non-white women as desirable on the grounds that the buttocks and the vagina of the African are ugly, non-white, less than human, with those of the white woman being perfectly human and desirable for white men. But the buttocks and the vagina of the African woman holds the promise of sexual proficiency, potency and capacity and raw unlimited savage desire which a white man cannot expect from a white woman as this capacity has been meticulously erased from the white woman to ensure her inherent superiority, morally and physically, over non-white women.

The African woman is then labor power, reproductive power and a repository of animal desire long erased from the white woman. In the 21st century in the Caribbean when the bleacher embraces massa package they are signaling to massa that they are a willing repository of animal desire available for exploitation. In the 21st century we are now willingly embracing the white supremacist ideals of massa which project us as potent, extreme objects of sexual desire for exploitation, nothing else, the sexualisation of the non-white woman as sexual objects for massa to exploit, to have his desire satiated continues in the 21st century. We are then intent on making fares, turning tricks for massa in a quest to be white and successful by any means necessary, but alas we the non-whites of the Caribbean can never be white. The delusion of hallucinatory whiteness exposed, laying bare our social orders noted for nihilist action by its members, futility as normality.

The 21st century liberal massa discourse of bleaching is very instructive of the great emphasis placed on it by massa, its strategic importance as an instrument of white power over us. This discourse has no answer for why must we bleach our skin, hoping to look like whom? What it insists is that bleaching creams loaded with lye are dangerous to the health of the bleacher, but there are safe bleaching creams available and advanced formulas are on the way to make our bleaching of our skins a perfectly safe and normal acceptable practice by non-white races, especially Africans. Massa remains then unrelenting in his assault on the self-determination of non-white races under his hegemony and the ugliness of the non-white in the face of the inherent beauty of the white, inferiority/ inherent superiority remains one of his leading-edge white supremacist weapons of assault to render us servile.

Skin bleaching in the 21st century in the Caribbean is an action that utilizes a chemical agent/s that literally assaults the level of melanin present in the skin to change skin color to a desired tone which is deemed appropriate to present self to the public. This chemical assault on the DNA of non-white races of the world can and does result in horrific damage to the non-white skin including damage to the DNA chain of the applicant.

You bleach your non-white skin in pursuit of an ideal, acceptable skin color which you believe will enhance your life chances for social mobility or as the fit and proper expression of your capacity, ability and right to upward social mobility obtained. There is then a need to bleach your skin as you believe it is much too dark/ black to enable your upward social mobility as in your Caribbean island's social order the exemplars of wealth, power and impunity are dominated by non-African minority races as whites, Arabs, Jews and Chinese and in Guyana, Trinidad and Tobago (T&T) and Barbados Indians are present in the oligarchy. Whilst amongst the professional elite, politicians and those employed in the private and public sector at the managerial levels show an over representation of those considered brown, less black hence superior to black, a desirable condition worth being earned by chemical skin bleaching. The 21st century Caribbean islands' social orders continue to be structured in an order of race preference which excludes the African majority race of these populations from the rank of the economic oligarchy of the private sector. In Jamaica, Barbados, T&T and Haiti the African race is excluded from the ranks of the economic oligarchy which is dominated by non-African races whilst dominating the politics, the public sector and the professions of these states. In T&T and Barbados Indians have made it into the economic oligarchy whilst Africans have not and in the case of Guyana Indians dominate the oligarchy along with minority races whilst Africans are excluded.

In the Caribbean, African economic exclusion from upward mobility into the ranks of the oligarchy of the private sector from the era of the 1960s to the present in the case of the former British colonies indicate that the racist exclusion that targeted the African race from enslavement to independence did not end with independence commencing in the 1960s. Independence under black nationalist discourse deliberately refused to dismantle the built in system of anti-African exclusion, choosing instead to maintain the racist division of labour established under white supremacist colonial domination in an era of "freedom" and "independence."

Black nationalist discourse then willingly established the neo-colonial condition as being normal and acceptable for the African population of the Caribbean including Haiti, especially in the case of the Francois Duvalier dictatorship. This neo-colonial order is rooted in the continued racist discrimination against Africans, even though they are the majority race, and dominate the politics by effectively policing the space that restricts upward mobility and a regime of the distribution of wealth that locks the majority of the African population in grinding poverty whilst the minority non-African races of the oligarchy plunder with the impunity afforded them by the African politicians and the state agencies. In these Caribbean states the non-African race minorities of the oligarchy have then captured the state animated by the African politicians, with the complicity of these politicians to the detriment of the African majority. In no Caribbean state is this neo-colonial reality vividly portrayed in its extremism as Haiti in the 21st century where it has now collapsed. Massa constantly intervenes into Haiti to maintain this status quo which only intensifies the power relations on the ground that further punishes the majority African population of Haiti. Haiti in the 21st century is a living example of white supremacist genocide regularly unleashed against an African population to keep that race in its place with the full complicity of Haitian politicians to the benefit of the minority race dominated oligarchy, sections of which have now grown into trans Caribbean enterprises through super exploitation of the African masses of Haiti.

What we note in the Caribbean in the 21st century is the willingness to embrace skin bleaching by Africans as expressions of a survival strategy in relation to their deprived living conditions. Amongst the African working class and underclass of the Caribbean, the discourse is articulated that their poverty is linked to their black skin color which demands that they change their skin color in order to ensure their social mobility is real, realized. The bleaching creams are widely available and sacrifices are made to afford them and the person seeking upward mobility does the application themselves or with help which heightens the risk of mishap leaving them to seek help in the public health system, leaving them disfigured for life. This experience is common throughout the Caribbean including Haiti, where there is now a heightening embrace of skin bleaching as the collapse of the social order is now endemic. In the Caribbean, African insecurity/ deprivation coupled with the quest to emancipate yourself from this suffering has now embraced skin bleaching as an acceptable, proven survival strategy. The fact that it is also embraced as a survival strategy in Africa, especially in West Africa by Africans seeking to emancipate themselves from deprivation and its suffering indicates to us that skin bleaching is an instrument of power of the white supremacist neo-liberal capitalist world order of power which continues to exploit non-whites as economic objects and non-white objects/ things which white power must be exercised upon simultaneously for white supremacist power is their manifest destiny, race entitlement and gift of their white god.

There is then a discourse of science which drives the incessant formulation of means to change the non-white body in the image and likeness of the white ideal of beauty as we are ugly, less than human, hence incapable of success in this unmodified body. To succeed and more importantly now to express your success as a non-white in this white world order of power, you must modify your body, upgrade it relentlessly in keeping with the white ideal of beauty which we must ever pursue but never attain for we are not white genetically. This discourse of science exploits us economically as desiring objects and polices us to render us servile by relentlessly problematizing our selves, bodies, images of self by having us addicted to self-hate and perpetually acting upon this self-hate which renders us schizophrenic as we are plagued with hallucinatory whiteness. A condition in which we hate what we are and pursue whiteness as the ultimate solution, but we can never be white. Our pursuit of whiteness then intensifies our self- hatred to the point of schizophrenic destruction of self, for at all times we are burdened with multiple personalities rooted in multiple bodies, discourses and worldviews. This condition is potently illustrated by the African personality who is jubilant for their personal success which is then expressed via skin bleaching which finally provides the public explanation for this success: their whiteness at the level of the idea which is now expressed by their bleached skin. This is the Vybz Kartel syndrome which is now seen amongst African politicians of the Caribbean who express their success, their personal superiority over the African masses given their willingness to sacrifice and work hard to liberate themselves from the poverty they grew up in, by now bleaching their skin having earned their hallucinatory whiteness. In T&T and Guyana the Indian populations of these states also exhibit the willingness to bleach their skin driven by the discourse that a skin color that is less than black, dark is the color of success, the ideal to have, to wield and to seek. Changing your non-white body utilising chemicals and surgery is a global reality amongst the non-white races of the world such as surgery to remove the slant of the Oriental eye and the non-white nose.

Hallucinatory whiteness is an instrument of white power exercised on all non-white races of the world, but in the Caribbean context white supremacist colonial domination, with and after enslavement, unleashed on the First Peoples, the Africans, the Mixed races and the Indians; on all non-whites indigenous, transported or the product of reproduction here, created a spectrum of trauma premised on their inherent inferiority combined with the daily brutality of colonial domination. This spectrum of trauma was not addressed by independence and black nationalism, but amplified as the colonial social order was replicated as a free social order where the inequalities of a racialized colonial social order were preserved and heightened thereby driving and increasing the colonial spectrum of trauma as if on steroids during the era of independence. Politics divided the non-white masses into tribes at war with each other premised on their allegiance to two political parties, tribal war which became race war heightening the hatred of the racialized social order to the benefit of the non-African oligarchs, whilst deepening and expanding the impact of the spectrum of trauma of the African masses. In the ex-colonies where multi-non-white populations were transported by massa the black on black race tensions fostered by colonial discourse were embraced by the independence politicians to their advantage by creating the race enemy that threatens the political hegemony of your race over the independent state, binding the race differentiated masses to the politicians who represent their race granting them political impunity. For you vote to keep the enemy race out of power, never in reference to what the politicians you elected have done for you lately. In these multi-non-white races social orders the black on black racism is palpable working in concert with hallucinatory whiteness driving the evolution of the spectrum of trauma to the point where the population is now enveloped in a nihilistic worldview driven by self-centered desire. These social orders are then crippled by stasis rooted in the inability to grasp the reality of our existential condition and formulate a liberationary discourse by which we will free ourselves from this morass of hallucinatory whiteness, dependence, underdevelopment and servility at the level of the idea. Who say massa day done!

There has then been no liberation from this spectrum of trauma passed from generation to generation under independence for black nationalism was never a constructed discourse of liberation of the non-white peoples of the Caribbean. In its servility at the level of the idea to hegemonic white supremacist capitalist discourse black nationalism cannot be liberationary, all it can accomplish is the deepening of our collective spectrum of trauma perpetually linked to our servility to massa across time/ space. Black nationalism openly mocks the sacrifice of our non-white ancestors in resisting enslavement and colonial domination to the point where it was no longer viable for massa as he had lost social control over the enslaved population, perpetually condemned to living in morbid fear of the Haiti effect, hence massa's fixation with destroying Haiti as the living symbol of African self-reliance, independence and liberationary action. Black nationalism must ceaselessly mock and relentlessly seek to falsify the fact that our ancestors resisted colonial domination to the point where independence was the means adopted by massa to exit the colonial power relations, replacing it with the neo-colonial power relation rooted in independence, freedom and self-determination, even though you remain servile at the level of the idea to a hegemonic white supremacist capitalist world order of power. Free constitutionally but servile at the level of the idea, discourse and worldview from which springs eternal the present driving nihilism of Caribbean post-independence culture of the 21st century where self-hate drives desire for all things white thereby perpetually canceling our non-white selves, willfully dehumanizing consistently our non-white selves in pursuit of whiteness that cannot promote our healing and wholeness, only our self-hate and self-destructive acts hence our driving, ever heightening self-centered desire for all things white whilst we destroy willingly the solidarity of non-white cultures of resistance, the ethnicities of resistance to white racist hegemony that our ancestors bequeathed to us. We are then today only capable of self-hate and racist hate for the "Other", that servile black nationalist discourse generates to serve its massa as Steven and Uncle Tom, shucking and jiving to win the affirmation of a massa that is only capable of contempt and hatred for all non-whites. Those who have surrendered to the hegemony of black nationalism in post-independence Caribbean social orders in the 21st century are incapable at the level of the idea to grasp the reality on the ground and construct discourses with their instruments of power that are liberationary, emancipative, capable of providing the vision to enable non-white peoples to liberate ourselves from the spectrum of trauma that damages us, render us servile to massa enabling us to unleash a revolution with development that finally enables us to attain the vision our ancestors formulated for us, their progeny living in this Caribbean island space. Where the victims of enslavement and colonial domination can now find peace rather than relentlessly roaming the terrain of their struggle against the order of massa. Where the victims of the wars of gangland in which non-white slaughter each other for no benefit, whilst the oligarchs of the Caribbean and massa enjoy the power of super exploitation with impunity. In Jamaica ceaseless war rages in the zinc fenced communities of the sufferers whilst the drug trafficking families of the Jamaican oligarchy amass wealth with impunity untouched by the violence. In Trinidad and Tobago the same model applies where black nationalism has embraced the Colombian business model of trafficking cocaine through the Caribbean to the benefit of the drug trafficking families of the oligarchy, especially those of the minority races who not only utilize the impunity black nationalism affords them to amass wealth derived from illicit drug trafficking but also to capture the state enabling them to wield hegemonic power over the majority non-white races of T&T, which has expanded the expanse and depth of the racialized social order inherited from the colonial massa and embraced by black nationalism with "independence" thereby constituting black national neo-colonial dependence and arrested development of the majority races of T&T and the Caribbean in the 21st century.

Black nationalism, in its subservience to white supremacist capitalist discourse, utilizes instruments of power from white supremacist discourse to render servile the African race of the Caribbean where it is the majority race in Caribbean social orders. One assault constantly insists to Africans that they are a besieged race, a race constantly under assault by its Others, hence its need to embrace the discourse and political institutions of black nationalism. A majority race in a racialized social order is seduced to visualize themselves as a besieged minority race, but your enemies are the same as you they are never identified as the oligarchy dominated by minority races or the white world order of power of massa. Black nationalist politicians have not reversed the marginalization of specific sections of the African population inherited from colonial domination, in fact the marginalization has intensified under independence which constituted the fertile ground to now present to this marginalized African population the desirability of criminality as a survival strategy that enables exit from a marginalized existential condition in an independent social order. African criminality is then for black nationalism an instrument of social control, hence the absence of any imperative to end the marginalization of sections of the population. Black nationalism has learnt well from their white supremacist American massa. African criminality as a survival strategy exercised on the ground has not alleviated the impact of marginalization it has instead heightened it, it has increased the spectrum of trauma that plagues us all especially with its unrelenting gun violence against the poor and marginalized and it has not generated wealth to lift wide sections of the marginalized population out of poverty as the wealth generated is held by an elite who is external to the ghettos including the oligarchs. In fact, the embrace of criminality as a survival strategy has heightened the malaise of the ghettos. The embrace of criminality ensures the hegemony of black nationalism, the oligarchs local and foreign and the white supremacist world order.

Likewise black nationalism has deepened the problematisation of African and other non-white skins to the point where now in the 21st century it is fetishized, where it is now a grave burden, a handicap to all those condemned by their DNA to have it. A menu of solutions dating back to enslavement and massa colonial domination is still in operation, to which is added skin bleaching. Skin bleaching is then a symptom of a punishing malaise fabricated under white colonial domination which was embraced by black nationalism with independence and grown and honed to a potent instrument to render us servile, which was not possible under colonial domination given the unyielding resistance of our ancestors. Black nationalism seduced us as non-white races to embrace white supremacist discourse which rendered us servile, burdened with hallucinatory whiteness and self-hate, which massa was unable to inflict on our ancestors with the same intensity and potency. In the 21st century behold the collapse of the handiwork of the Caribbean black nationalist independence experiment!

Conclusion

This is a road-map that plots the path of liberation at the level of the idea for non-white people assailed with white supremacist discourse and its worldview at the level of the idea which constitutes a problematised self, plagued with hallucinatory whiteness. The ideational terrain chosen to plot this road-map upon is the conjuncture between white supremacist discourse and Qur'anic discourse, with an emphasis on white supremacist discourse which is part of the North Atlantic discourse of science. This first section exposed the inherent flaws of selected authors who placed themselves in the ambit of the North Atlantic discourse of science, such as Marx, Weber etc. This first section focuses on Foucault and Fanon as the formulators of anti-white supremacist discourse vital to the task of liberation at the level of the idea. Foucault is necessary in order to deconstruct the discourse and order of power of white supremacy in the North Atlantic and its neocolonial empire; whilst, Fanon is vitally necessary to the deconstruction of the discourse and order of power of white supremacy and its impact on the psyche of the non-whites under its hegemony. The oeuvres of Fanon and Foucault focus on different realities of the hegemony of white supremacy, but both oeuvres are compulsory for formulation of the road-map to liberation at the level of the idea for non-whites under the assault of white supremacist discourse and its order of power. The second section presents deconstructions of ideas of non-white actors who insisted that they were engaged with massa in a battle for liberation. What was glaringly revealed is that the definition of non-white liberation depends on whether the discursive agent is in fact liberated from hallucinatory whiteness at the level of the idea. The conclusion is obvious: white supremacist neocolonial domination driven by hallucinatory whiteness is the effective instrument of white power which functionally forestalls any attempt at liberation at the level of the

idea of subjugated non-white peoples. In the Caribbean of the 21st century, the growing embrace of skin bleaching as a means to overcome the perceived limits to mobility imposed by a too black skin, for my skin is my sin, bleach it searching for upward social mobility is but another symptom of the continuation of neocolonial domination.

References

Al- 'Azm, Sadiq Salal (1984): "Orientalism and Orientalism in Reverse" in "Khamsin, an Anthology Forbidden Agendas Intolerance and Defiance in the Middle East" Al Saqi Books England

Allen, Jeffner (1990): "Women who Beget Women must Thwart major Sophisms" from "Feminism/Post-Modernism" edited by Linda J. Nicholson, Methuen/Routledge and Kegan Paul USA

Brown, Dee (1976): "Bury My Heart at Wounded Knee" Bantam Books USA

Castaneda, Carlos (1992): "Tales of Power" Washington Square Press USA

Castaneda, Carlos (1992): "The Power of Silence" Black Swan Books England

Fanon, Frantz (1969): "Towards the African Revolution (Political Essays)" Grove Press Inc USA

Foucault, Michel (1986): "Revolutionary Action Until Now" from "Language, Counter Memory and Practice" edited by Donald F. Bouchard Cornell University Press USA

Foucault, Michel (1982): "I Pierre Riviere having slaughtered my mother, my sister and my brother. A case of parricide in the 19th century" University of Nebraska Press USA

Foucault, Michel (1980): "Power/Knowledge Selected Interviews and Other Writings 1972-1977" Pantheon Books USA

Foucault, Michel (1979): "Discipline and Punish" Peregrine Books Ltd Britain

Foucault, Michel (1978): "The History of Sexuality Volume 1 An Introduction" Pantheon Books USA

Foucault, Michel (1972): "The Archaeology of Knowledge and the Discourse of Language" Pantheon Books USA

Haley, Alex (1976): "The Autobiography of Malcolm X" Penguin Books Britain

Harris, Joseph E. (1972): "Africans and their History" Mentor USA

Jackson, George (1971): "The Prison Letters of George Jackson" Penguin Books USA

Kamenka, Eugene editor (1983): "The Portable Karl Marx" Viking Penguin Inc. USA

McNeil, Maureen (1993): "Dancing with Foucault: feminism and power-knowledge" from "Up Against Foucault" edited by Caroline Ramazanoglu Routledge Britain

Morris, Donald R. (1976): "Washing of the Spears" Sphere Books Ltd Britain

Naipaul, V. S, (1982): "Amongst the Believers: An Islamic Journey" Vintage Books USA

Nesbitt, Nick editor (2008): "Toussaint L'Ouverture The Haitian Revolution" Verso Britain

Ponchaud, Francois (1978): Cambodia Year Zero" Penguin Books Britain

Rushdie, Salman (1991): "Imaginary Homelands" Penguin Books Britain

Rothstein, Richard (2017): "The Color of Law A Forgotten History of how our government segregated America" Liveright Publishing Corp. USA

"The Qur'an" Translated by Yusuf Ali Egypt

Said, Edward W. (1985): "Orientalism Reconsidered" in "Arab Society, continuity and change" edited by Samih K. Farsoun Croom Helm Britain

Said, Edward W, (1979): "Orientalism" Vintage Books USA

Sharabi, Hisham (1988): The Neo-patriarchal Discourse in Contemporary Arab Society" in "Arab Civilization" edited by George N. Atiyeh and Ibrahim Oweiss State University of New York USA

Sharabi, Hisham (1985): "The Dialectics of Patriarchy in Arab Society" from "Arab Society: Continuity and Change" edited by Samih K. Farsoun Croom Helm Britain

Sheridan, Alan (1980): "Michel Foucault, The Will To Truth" Tavistock Publications USA

Van Sertima, Ivan (1976): "They Came Before Columbus" Random House USA

Von Hagen, Victor Wolfgang (1978): "The Ancient Sun Kingdoms of the Americas" Paladin Britain

Walcott, Derek (1976): "Sea grapes" Johnathan Cape Britain

Walcott, Derek (1973): "Another Life" Johnathon Cape Britain

Weber, Max (1989): "Science as a Vocation" edited by P Lassman, I Velody and H Martins Unwin Hyman Britain

Weber, Max (1965): "The Sociology of Religion" Methuen &Co. Ltd. Britain

Weber, Max (1958): "The Religion of India, The sociology of Hinduism and Buddhism" The Free Press Ltd USA

Weber, Max (1951): "The Religion of China, Confucianism and Taoism" The Free Press Ltd

Wolf, Fred Alan (1991): "The Eagles Quest" Mandala Britain

Also by Daurius Figueira

Discourse of Slavery

Massa's White Supremacist Discourse of West Indian Negro Slavery
Deconstructed Volume 1
Massa's White Supremacist Discourse of West Indian Negro Slavery
Deconstructed Volume 2

Frantz Fanon for the 21st Century

Frantz Fanon for the 21st Century Volume 1 Frantz Fanon's Discourse of
Racism and Culture, the Negro and the Arab Deconstructed
Frantz Fanon for the 21st Century Volume 2 Frantz Fanon's Discourse of
Decolonisation and Violence, the Nature of Power and Power Relations of
Neo-colonial African States,
Frantz Fanon for the 21st Century Volume 3 The Algerian Revolution,
Islamic Discourse, the Colonizer and the Discourse of White Supremacy

Standalone

Belize: Human Smuggling, Transnational Organised Crime, Politicians
And Public Servants
Biopower, Racism, State Racism and The Modern/Post Modern North
Atlantic State: Michel Foucault's Genealogy of the Historico-Political
Discourse of Race War Deconstructed

Derek Walcott's Poetry Deconstructed, Its Political and Sociological Discourse Revealed

Transnational Organized Crime and Drug Trafficking in the Second Decade of the 21st Century in the Dominican Republic, Suriname, Venezuela, French Guiana, Martinique and Guadeloupe

The Islamic State and the Muslims of Trinidad and Tobago in the 21st Century

A Deconstruction of Michel Foucault's 1979 Discourse of Neo-Liberalism for the 21st Century

A Deconstruction of Qu'ranic Discourse for the 21st Century

Xi Jinping's Discourse of Socialism with Chinese Characteristics for a New Era (2012-2017), Deconstructed

Exiting a Racist Worldview (Revised): A Journey Through Foucault, Said, Marx to Liberation, The Revolution that Failed

Watch for more at https://www.daurius.com.

About the Author

Daurius Figueira is a researcher, analyst and author located in the anti-Enlightenment and anti-Science discourse/worldview/paradigm specialising in the study of the illicit drug trade, the illicit small arms trade and human smuggling of the Caribbean, Islamic extremism and racism/white supremacy with an emphasis on power relations. You can access his website to experience and download his research papers published online and view his range of books. His website address is: https://www.daurius.com and his blog on the Caribbean is at: https://drugtrade.wordpress.com/

Read more at https://www.daurius.com.